ECONOMIES OF VIOLENCE

ECONOMIES OF VIOLENCE

TRANSNATIONAL FEMINISM, POSTSOCIALISM,
AND THE POLITICS OF SEX TRAFFICKING

Jennifer Suchland

Duke University Press / Durham and London / 2015

Designed by Courtney Leigh Baker
Typeset in Minion Pro by Westchester Book Group

Library of Congress Cataloging-in-Publication Data
Suchland, Jennifer, 1974–
Economies of violence : transnational feminism, postsocialism, and the politics
of sex trafficking / Jennifer Suchland.
pages cm
Includes bibliographical references and index.
ISBN 978-0-8223-5941-8 (hardcover : alk. paper)
ISBN 978-0-8223-5961-6 (pbk. : alk. paper)
ISBN 978-0-8223-7528-9 (e-book)
1. Human trafficking. 2. Feminism. I. Title.
HQ281.S85 2015
305.42—dc23
2015008876

Cover design by Natalie F. Smith

for Shannon

ACKNOWLEDGMENTS

There are many people to thank for their mentorship, camaraderie, and love as I have traveled the long and winding roads of academia. In the late 1990s when I was generating a dissertation topic I consciously chose not to research sex trafficking—what I perceived to be a fetishized topic in post-Soviet studies. Instead, I wrote a fairly anachronistic dissertation on the history of sex crimes in Russian law. The project connected me to scholars and activists in Russia and grounded me in the study of law as cultural artifact. The project also saved me from the epistemological "disciplining" of political science. At the University of Texas, I am grateful to Robert Moser, Gretchen Ritter, and Benjamin Gregg for their encouragement and willingness to let me chart my own course. I thank Gretchen for the wise advice to ground my youthful curiosity in the law. Rob Moser was a generous advisor who gave me creative freedom while at the same time keeping me rigorous. I am grateful to Benjamin Gregg and his political theory seminars for keeping me sane at the University of Texas, Austin. I owe a special intellectual debt to Katie Arens for encouraging my exploration of postsocialism and cultural studies.

In time, the research on sex trafficking became an ethical and intellectual imperative for me. How I returned to human trafficking traces an intellectual path through multiple fieldwork stays in Russia and two academic homes. There were language tutors, friends, and many willing to be interviewed in St. Petersburg, Moscow, Saratov, and Nizhny Novgorod. Thanks to Marianna Muravyeva in St. Petersburg for intellectual comradeship and shared meals. On my first trip in 1999, the St. Petersburg Gender Center was a lifeline. I thank Olga Lipovskaya for her willingness to talk to yet another western academic studying Russian feminism. Also, to Irina Savich for her friendship and help as I learned the ropes of living and working in St. Pete. Thanks to Viktoria for being a kind tutor and for the blini. I am also forever thankful to the many women (and some men) who took time out of their work and busy lives to speak with me about law, women's rights, and Russia. With their insights, I am grateful for the special intimacy that comes from sharing pots of hot tea. I owe thanks to Albina Krymskaya for our ongoing collaborations. Expat comrades in Russia also helped during the uncertain days of fieldwork—thanks to Leontina Hormel, Maria Stalnaker, and Katie Gunter. In addition to the people I met and worked with in Russia, I was nurtured by many scents, tastes, and sounds. Some of those wafted from the kitchen of friend and *khoziaka* Angela Supanova—summer borscht, piles of wild berries, apple tart, Chopin, and the time I tried to make tortillas. Thank you for asking me: "Is there still a woman question in Russia?"

To think of postsocialism within the feminist transnational was a project tentatively begun in the dissertation and only finally conceptualized while a visiting professor at Southwestern University. In a creaky corner office in Mood-Bridwell Hall, I spent three years cutting my teeth as a newly minted PhD. I was familiar with that building in particular, having roamed its halls as an undergraduate student. I am grateful to the many dedicated and talented faculty at Southwestern who ignited an intellectual desire in me as an undergrad and who then later became supportive colleagues. In particular I want to thank Helene Myers for hearing my questioning of where postsocialism is in transnational feminist thinking. There are also a few people who transcended the boundaries of former teacher and colleague to become true lifelong friends. For helping me hear my own voice and then for always being around to listen, I am deeply grateful to Eric Selbin. His commitment and respect for the ideas, the theories, and the living of life have made a profound impact on me as a scholar and person. Thank you for being my most cherished mentor, a dear friend, and a valued comrade. My central Texas fan club has evolved from dissertation cheerleaders to adoring caretakers of LMT: thank you Helen Cordes (a feminist role model in so many ways), Eric Selbin, and Jesse and Zoe Cordes-Selbin for all the love, laughs, and food—and there's been a lot! Kathleen Juhl has been a long and trusted friend. I will be forever grateful for your Feminism and Performance class and the many years of friendship. I also thank Thom and Nancy McClendon for their enduring friendship and for horsing around.

The writing and much of the research for this book began in 2008, when I started my position at Ohio State University. This work was accompanied by the birth of my daughter, Micah Simone, and the leaving of a beloved community in Austin. Both events brought intense emotional highs and lows. Through the ups and downs, I was sustained by the patience and compassion of friends and family. In Austin, I am thankful for the abiding friendships of Kristen Hogan, Milly Gleckler, Alison Kafer, and Dana Newlove. I am calmed by their presence in my life, inspired by their ways of being, and grateful to count them in my blessings. To my oldest friends, I thank Meaghen Murphy and Diane Eckhardt for being there and steadfast. I have long benefited from the cool green waters of Barton Springs, a place that still calls to my inner yearnings. And, to the tastes and sounds of ATX that keep me going: tamales, big john cookies, Lucinda and Patty.

In the journey to find one's voice, to reconcile loss and find feminist joy, I thank bell hooks for her friendship (and thrifting companionship).

I am deeply grateful to friends and colleagues in Columbus who, in the day-to-day trenches of life, supported me through the writing of the book. For their friendship as we all traverse the messiness of life and work, I thank Sandra MacPherson, Luke Wilson, Molly Blackburn, and Mindi Rhoades. I also would like to thank my wonderful colleagues in the Department of Women's, Gender and Sexuality Studies and the Department of Slavic and East European Languages and Cultures. For their solidarity and inspiring scholarship, I thank Theodora Dragostinova, Yana Hashamova, Cricket Keating, Jessie Labov, Mytheli Sreenivas, Guisela LaTorre, Mary Thomas, and Judy Wu. I was truly lucky to have two amazing chairs during this process. Jill Bystydzienski in WGSS and Helena Goscilo in SEELC supported my work and life. I am incredibly grateful for that support and for their modeling of feminist leadership. The possibility for this book was opened up by the intellectual freedom provided by working at Ohio State University. I appreciate that freedom and the institutional resources that helped me produce something with it, including the Assistant Professor Research Fund, the College of Arts and Sciences, and the Coca-Cola Critical Difference Fellowship. I also thank the many Ohio State students who took classes with me and enthusiastically discussed postsocialism, human trafficking, Russian law, and transnational feminism. For their research assistance, I thank Andrea Breau, Debanuj Dasgupta, Ally Day, Sonnet Gabbard, and Deema Kaedbey. For their commitment and passion for feminist antiracist work in the trenches of academia, I am grateful to Andy Cavins, Lynaya Elliott, and Tess Pugsley.

I must also thank the incredible caretakers at North Broadway Children's Center and teachers at Clinton Elementary who nourished, cared, and taught Micah while her moms were both working. To have a creative and productive mind requires a mind at ease, and I was always more at ease knowing that our daughter was in good hands.

Beyond Ohio State, numerous supportive colleagues and scholars made an impact on the evolution of this project. I am grateful to feminist area studies scholars Kristen Ghodsee, Alex Hrycak, Janet Johnson, Nadia Shapkina, Valerie Sperling, and Madina Tlostanova for their encouragement and inspiring work. Nanette Funk and Mary Hawkesworth made important interventions, whether they knew it or not, as the project evolved. I benefited from the AWSS gatherings at the University of Illinois summer workshop, in particular the sage advice from Rochelle Ruthchild, as well as the miniconferences at ASEEES on "socialism and neoliberalism." Although it happened very late in the book process, the Transnational Feminisms Summer Institute was inspiring and energized me at the very end. I thank my coorganizers Laura Briggs, Karen Leong, Katherine Marino, Daniel Rivers, and Judy Wu for modeling feminist collaboration and enriching my sense of radical work.

My immediate and extended family has been a fount of support. My parents, Jay and Margaret Suchland, remain steadfast supporters and enthusiastic cheerleaders at the crucial moments. All through the years of research on human trafficking, my mom sent me everything from news articles to documentary films relating to the topic. Their love and sunny home have been crucial sources of respite from the storms of life and work. Though miles apart, I continue to rely on the love and support of my sister, Mary Suchland Grundy. She is always just a call away. Pat and Ton Winnubst are generous with their love and have enriched my life a great deal. Luck struck when I scored Kimmy Dee Winnubst, Sue Rivers, and Mark Winnubst as a crew of "out-laws." My debts to them for their love and generosity are as big as the state of Texas, but I know they aren't counting. The extended Winnubst clan in Dallas and Zaandam has been great fun as well as supportive over the years.

While some of the concepts for the book slowly evolved, the creative coming together and writing was very intense. For hearing my ideas out and for feedback at crucial moments I thank Kristen Ghodsee, Yana Hashamova, Alex Hrycak, Cricket Keating, Guisela LaTorre, Eric Selbin, Mytheli Sreenevas, and Mary Thomas. I am incredibly grateful to Courtney Burger at Duke University Press for seeing the project's potential and then for helping me hone its strengths. The two anonymous reviewers were outstanding critics and supporters of the project. Their input was crucial to the shaping of the final version. Any remaining flaws are certainly of my own making. For guiding me through dark waters at a critical work and life moment, I cherish Molly Blackburn, bell hooks, Sandra MacPherson, Sadie Michael, Meaghen Murphy, and Mary Suchland Grundy.

The end is actually where it all begins—a journey started many years ago with Shannon Winnubst. As she knows, I do most everything from scratch and without a recipe. This approach can be creative, certainly not always easy, sometimes annoying and often deeply rewarding. Shannon has patiently and lovingly supported me as I've found my way. More than anything, I treasure her wisdom, intellectual passions, still waters, and sense of humor. Happiness is traversing the pleasures, pains, confusions, and routines of life with Shannon. Micah Simone burst into our universe and brought unimaginable joy. I have learned so much about unconditional love from both Shannon and Micah. When I needed it most, Shannon took on the lion's share of domestic labors of love and laundry, sacrificing her own work so that I could write this book. Thank you for the really long ride in the red wagon. With deep gratitude and love, I dedicate this book to you. I cherish our feline companions Phaedrus, Bucco (who is immortalized by his songs and memories), Mozoe, and Sir Walter, for the calm and silliness they bring to our lives. To my beloved family—all the way to the moon, and back.

INTRODUCTION / TRAFFICKING AS ABERRATION / THE MAKING OF GLOBALIZATION'S VICTIMS

At the end of the Cold War, the problem of human trafficking received new-found attention as a violation of human rights. With particular emphasis on the influx of sex trafficking victims from the former Soviet Union and East-ern Bloc, human trafficking became a subject of growing regional and global concern—even as a last aberration and obstacle to the forward march of de-mocracy. Indeed, in the 1990s, the image of the duped and violated "Natasha" victim of sex trafficking seemed to replace the threat of communism as the global specter of abjection.[1] But what has the increase in concern for and ex-pansion of laws on trafficking brought to current approaches to human rights, to practices of governance, to understandings of globalization? Framed as a violation of bodily integrity and problem of criminal behavior, human traf-ficking gained recognition as an aberration of capitalist systems. While impor-tant as framing devices, neither bodily harm nor criminal behavior exposes how trafficking is intertwined in the constitutive operations of economic sys-tems. Despite the immense amount of attention the problem now receives, the politicization of human trafficking has obscured the economies of violence that sustain it.[2]

FIGURE I.1. Antitrafficking poster provided by IOM Moscow and displayed during the 2007 social poster contest "Slavery. XXI Century." The contest was funded by Prevention of Human Trafficking in the Russian Federation, an EU project. The text states: "Looking for work abroad? Learn more about the problem of human trafficking on our site: www.notoslavery.ua."

The recent politicization of sex trafficking in particular has generated greater sensitivity to *seeing* violence. Numerous feature films, documentaries, and public awareness campaigns now expose trafficking around the world. These representations reveal much about how trafficking is understood and combated today. As in the poster shown here (see figure 1.1), trafficking is often represented by the individual victim. The individual is the site of the harm of trafficking, and it is the violence done to that individual that we are supposed to see: a woman stands clutching a chain-link fence; she is a potential victim of trafficking. The poster warns about a possible future of personal hardship and bondage that can come from labor migration. The fence serves as a metaphor for that potential bondage, while the background is faded and disconnected from the threat. The text advises against looking for work abroad. Emphasizing that some work ends in enslavement, red text highlights the root of the term "work," *rab*, which means "slave" in Russian.

Together, the image and text mark trafficking as the result of bad choices that trap individuals in a criminal world beyond the fence. Whatever lies behind the woman makes little difference: the focus is on an outside potentiality and the contemplation we see in her face as she considers her future choices. The image captures the idea that there are looming criminals "out there" who would turn her decision to look for work abroad into a nightmare and make her a modern-day slave. The aim of the campaign is to educate the public that trafficking exists. Specifically, the poster represents the efforts of local advocates in Moscow to generate political and public concern about trafficking—something that the Russian government has been slow if not delinquent in addressing. While that work is very important, the poster also draws on common antitrafficking tropes. The image defines trafficking as a problem centered on the individual—it directs our attention to *the* victim of trafficking. Rather than seeing human trafficking as structural, the poster presents it as something that befalls individuals. And today's antitrafficking apparatus is largely focused on locating, identifying, and categorizing "victims of trafficking." Indeed, human trafficking is only legible when a victim is identified or can claim that she was enslaved by force, fraud, or coercion. Revitalized and reconceived after the Cold War, human trafficking discourse primarily focuses on locating individual rather than structural violence.

The heightened presence of and awareness about human trafficking has intensified the locating and claiming of proper victims. "What can one choose?" "How is one deceived?" "What does one know?" These are the sorts of questions adjudicating the lives of those in detention halls, police cells, temporary shelters, and shipping containers waiting offshore. Masses of people travel through migratory survival circuits, labor in informal or unregulated economies, and experience the violence and precarity of dispossession and immigration regimes, but only some are identified as the proper victims of such processes. The advancement of antitrafficking discourse after the end of the Cold War created a distinction between victims and losers—between those who can make claims or who are legible as victims and those who are not. This distinction between victims and losers, however, is based on particular beliefs about human action and registers of sympathy rooted in racialized and gendered constructs of respectability. It does not necessarily correlate with a fixed distinction between bodies or experiences. Yet human trafficking discourse operates under the assumption that there are distinguishable, proper victims to identify and locate.

Figure 1.1 sketches the contours of the proper victim; figure 1.2 depicts the losers. In this image of the garment factory in Dhaka, Bangladesh, some may view the workers as victims, but their labor is most often deemed to be an unfortunate but necessary aspect of global capitalism.[3] Someone has to work

FIGURE I.2. Dhaka, Bangladesh, March 2010. Image courtesy of Clean Clothes Campaign (www.cleanclothes.org).

the sewing machines that clothe humanity. In contrast to the antitrafficking poster, the photograph of the garment factory invites a critique of structural exploitation. We can see global capitalism and economic inequalities in this photo. The sea of anonymous workers is collectively referred to as a sweatshop. In contrast, representations of trafficking have heightened our sensitivity to violence on an individual level while obscuring the structural. Even while statistical estimates present us with the growing number of people in forced labor conditions, human trafficking is conceived of as something individuals succumb to rather than being a part of. While the circumstances, experiences, and even choices of the people in the two scenarios are intertwined, they are made into distinct categories. By juxtaposing the two images, we can see the discursive bifurcation between the victims and losers of globalization—victims of trafficking are an aberration of the dominant economic order, whereas the losers are not.

While the two visual stories represented by these images may seem unrelated, the distinction between a victim and a loser is not so clear. Ethically, which bodies should be allowed to prosecute wrongs and thus have legitimacy? Experientially, how does someone know whether or when she is a victim or is simply managing a life of bad or limited choices? Such lines of distinction are hazy, but the bodies themselves have one thing in common: they exemplify contemporary global precarious labor. Yet the common contexts that structure the lives and practices of mobile masses recede into the background, while political debate and advocacy work focus on the *distinct* experiences of victims and losers. I use the term "precarious labor" to refer to the formal and informal work that people do in order to make a living. This labor is structured by policies and practices of the formal economy and the state and is shaped by race, ethnicity, nation, gender, and sexuality. I am not just referring to the loss of industrial wage labor due to post-Fordism. While precarious labor has increased as more people work in part-time, un(der)regulated formal labor, as well as informal and unpaid productive and reproductive work, it has always been at the center of capitalist expansion. Despite the importance of this labor for generating wealth in the general economy (gross world product), it remains precarious because people are vulnerable to exploitation, lack rights, and are undervalued.

This book aims to redirect the immense attention that human trafficking has received since the end of the Cold War. It aims to redirect us away from a focus on the individual victim and toward a structural view of violence. To do this, I diverge from the now common focus on searching for, finding, counting, and saving victims of trafficking. There are victims of trafficking, but the global apparatus to combat human trafficking has failed to address the problem as a symptom of complex economic and social dynamics precisely because the focus has been on defining and deciphering the proper individual victim. I value the insightful research done by activists and scholars who interview victims of trafficking and those working in labor contexts intertwined in the antitrafficking apparatus. This book, however, contributes something different. In order to move beyond some of the pitfalls of the current antitrafficking approach, I present a genealogical analysis of how the current system came into being. We do not need a better definition of human trafficking. What we need is a more critical approach to the economic and social dynamics of trafficking as a symptom of—not as distinct from—our political and economic systems. There has been a block to engaging trafficking in this way because of the way it reemerged as a human rights violation during and through the end of the Cold War. This book traces how that happened: it traces how the convergence of the global campaign against "violence against women" and the collapse of socialist projects in the former Soviet Union and Eastern Bloc shaped today's dominant antitrafficking apparatus.[4]

I use the term "antitrafficking apparatus" to refer to government and police agencies, intergovernmental organizations such as the UN, the European

Union, the International Organization for Migration (IOM) and the International Labour Organization (ILO), and nongovernmental organizations engaged in advocacy and the management/monitoring of human trafficking. There is wide variation in the ways organizations and people approach antitrafficking; I do not want to oversimplify a complex field of actors. At the same time, there has been a dominant paradigm at work, which is represented by the UN Optional Protocol to Prevent, Suppress, and Punish Trafficking in Persons, Especially Women and Children and the United States Victims of Trafficking and Violence Protection Act (TVPA). This dominant paradigm is represented by the "3 PS" approach (prevention, prosecution, protection). According to the U.S. Department of State, the 3 PS paradigm continues to serve as "the fundamental international framework used by the United States and the world to combat contemporary forms of slavery."[5] In 2009, Secretary of State Hillary Rodham Clinton announced a "fourth P"—partnerships—to the paradigm. This paradigm shapes the activities of the various actors within the antitrafficking apparatus.

It is common to hear trafficking referred to as modern-day slavery.[6] For example, linking historical African slavery in the United States with human trafficking, U.S. president Barack Obama declared January "National Slavery and Human Trafficking Prevention Month" on the 150th anniversary of the U.S. Emancipation Proclamation.[7] While the reference to slavery suggests a critical understanding of the problem, trafficked labor is often disjointed from the socioeconomic and cultural formations that undergird it. The trans-Atlantic slave trade was not an anomaly but was central to capitalist expansion and settler colonialism in the Americas and was sustained by moral, racial, and political systems (Marable 1999; Rawley 2009; Sweet 1997). Since its declarative abolition in the United States, slavery has been described as an aberration with regard to the democratic ideals of the United States as a nation. The idea of trafficking as "modern-day slavery" references an outrage of slavery in the past. Yet imaging human trafficking as modern-day slavery actually furthers the idea that trafficking is an aberration, rather than symptomatic of political economy.[8] Human trafficking is attributed to pathologies, criminal behaviors, and violence against individuals that circulate beyond the moral boundaries of the proper state. In this understanding, human trafficking is a last vestige of barbarism in the evolution toward democratic capitalism. The discourse of trafficking as modern-day slavery has not spurred public debate about the acceptable limits of precarity or a serious questioning of the strata of violence that serve as the ground for contemporary subjugation. Rather, this discourse spawned a global criminal justice regime narrowly focused on locating proper victims and criminals. In casting human trafficking as an aberration from local and global economies, the juridical definition of the victim of human trafficking sets the limits of acceptable precarity for the losers of globalization as well.

The post–Cold War politicization of human trafficking, I will argue across this book, has exposed the perilous lives of forced laborers *and has simultaneously* obscured the greater sea of exploitation. To interrogate this fraught distinction between globalization's victims and losers, this book focuses on two distinct yet intertwined events: the success of feminist advocacy against what has come to be formally termed "violence against women" in the UN (and beyond) and the prioritization of a prosecutorial response to postsocialist trafficking. I use the term *postsocialist* to refer to the countries that constituted the Soviet Union and Eastern Bloc (communist states of Central and Eastern Europe). I use the term as a (critical) regional designation for a set of unevenly aligned (if altogether unaligned) countries that nonetheless share a common recent history (Stenning and Hörschelmann 2008).[9] But *postsocialist* can also refer to contexts in Latin America, Asia, and Africa where state socialist projects have collapsed or been hybridized (Pitcher and Askew 2006; Zheng 2009). Thus, the term does not describe a singular experience and is not located in one region. At the same time, while the term has different regional resonances, it is not a term that accurately describes the post–Cold War global landscape. The fall of the Berlin Wall and the dissolution of the Soviet Union meant the collapse of only a particular model of socialism. While acknowledging these nuances, I use the word *postsocialist* as a critical geographic term because I want to forefront how the experiences in and imagining of the former USSR and Eastern Bloc was productive in the assemblage of antitrafficking discourse.

From this critical geographic position, I offer a genealogy of the institutional and popular discourses that enable certain forms of violence to operate as rights violations. I craft the genealogy through close analyses of primary documents, a retracing of policy/advocacy dialogues, and interviews from fieldwork.[10] Together, the success of the "violence against women" agenda and the dominance of a prosecutorial response to postsocialist trafficking have dominated the (re)formulation of how trafficking—legally and culturally—is understood, represented, and ultimately combated today.

My approach is informed by theorists who challenge the naturalness of social categories and who excavate the social formations that bring them forth (Foucault 1972; Patton 2002; Riley 1988). A genealogy is a practice that exceeds and even defies the diachronic history of a social category or problem. According to Michel Foucault, a genealogy investigates "the conditions necessary for the appearance of a . . . [social problem], the historical conditions required if one is to 'say something' about it, the conditions necessary if it [the social problem] is to exist in relation to other objects" (Foucault 1972, 44). To grasp these conditions, I analyze key historical artifacts, events, experiences, and policies that converge to create the assumptions and forces that have made human trafficking visible and abhorrent in the contemporary political field. Crafting this genealogy reveals the underpinnings of the contemporary fixation on human trafficking as a human rights violation *and* the policy solutions aimed at addressing it. The articulation, advancement, and professionalization of antitrafficking are part of the emergence of human trafficking as a visible problem. Thus, in order to alter the way we see and address human trafficking, the underlying formations that give voice to the problem and the solution must be scrutinized.

While human trafficking is a global phenomenon, current antitrafficking political commitments were produced by specific opportunities and compromises structured by the Cold War and later by the specific example of post-socialist victims of sex trafficking and the economic transitions of the 1990s. The evolution of global women's rights principles, specifically the institutionalization of the composite category "violence against women," continues to shape how trafficking is understood and debated. The success of feminist organizing around "violence against women" was tied in part to the idea that geographic and cultural differences between women could be bridged by the common experiences of and outrage against gender violence. Certainly, the legitimacy of fighting "violence against women" today is the result of that important political struggle. Yet that legitimacy also means that, as sex trafficking became categorized and politicized as a form of "violence against women," the understanding of human trafficking was restrained by certain feminist commitments and debates.

To understand sex trafficking primarily as a form of "violence against women" is to prioritize (individual) bodily harm and ultimately to focus on the question and issue of woman's agency and her status as a victim.[11] I do not question whether sex trafficking is violence—it is, on many levels. Rather, I detail how the institutionalized "violence against women" framework prioritized individual violation as the core harm of sex trafficking when alternatives were (and continue to be) in circulation (Agustín 2007; Brennan 2004; Kempadoo 2005; Parreñas 2011). For example, in the 1970s and 1980s, feminists critiqued development programs that (re)produced sexualized economies, like sex tourism (Truong 1990). These voices contextualized sex work and violence within national and global political economy as well as racial and patriarchal norms.

However, such critical economic evaluations of sex tourism, sexualized labor, and development were deprioritized as the Cold War came to an end. In addition, U.S. women of color feminist organizations had also linked critiques of imperialism, sexism, and racism (Roth 2003; Springer 2001). Perspectives from organizations such as the Third World Women's Alliance saw the linked nature of oppressive systems. But these more radical voices were muted as a much louder liberal voice gained institutionalization within the UN. Exposing sex trafficking as "violence against women" has been a powerful tool to advocate against forced labor, but it has also helped create a perverse distinction between victims and losers—between individual and structural violence.

This distinction between victims and losers is a racialized one. In particular, the success of the campaign against "violence against women" relied (in part) on the notion that the experience of violence united women across different nations and races. This political strategy emphasized a universal problem of gender violence and thus "violence against women" did not necessarily denote the racial, ethnic, and other equally as important vectors of violence against women. When sex trafficking became an example of violence against women, it lost political connection to antiracist, anticolonial, and critical development perspectives that saw historical racial formations and neoimperialism as key to understanding exploitation and violence. In addition, the entrance of post-Soviet, Central European, and Eastern European women into the global intimate labor economy redirected previous discourses focused on development and sex tourism. The postsocialist victim of trafficking was framed as a victim of criminal behaviors endemic to failed political systems and corrupt political elites. Ironically, the discourse of postsocialist transition helped deracialize what were long-standing racialized dynamics. In this way, the concern for postsocialist trafficking also advanced a "color blind" discourse of human trafficking. If smart, well-educated, and seemingly white women could become victims of trafficking, anyone could. This subtle shift to the racialization of human trafficking discourse contributed to the displacement of critical economic perspectives on the issue—like those coming from the global south and U.S. women of color.

The argument presented here is not a strict historical one, but much of what I detail is situated in and shaped by the Cold War and its aftermath. In many ways, the story of "modern-day slavery" is a postsocialist story. The current focus on human trafficking emerged because of feminist movements against gender violence that took shape during, and were shaped by, the Cold War and achieved doctrinal success at its close. In addition, the specific phenomenon of the trafficking of women from/in the former second world—termed the "fourth wave" of trafficking or the "Natasha trade"—motivated new actors to politicize the issue and ultimately launch a global campaign to combat it. This campaign to combat trafficking prioritized a prosecutorial approach to human rights focused on locating victims and prosecuting criminals in the midst of monumental economic restructuring. In combination, the recognition of trafficking as violence against women and the prosecutorial response to postsocialist trafficking shaped the current norms that now guide the way human trafficking is understood, studied, and combated.

Violence, Neoliberalism, and the "Postsocialist" Condition

> We need to think of neoliberalism not as something invented and imposed by the west, but as a truly global bricolage assembled from various parts of the world.
> —GIL EYAL

> By far the broadest reach of state power is found in its transformation of sexual violence into a social, medical, and legal problem.
> —KRISTIN BUMILLER

The emergence of postsocialist trafficking in the 1990s signaled a global crisis. Despite its prior existence, the presence of new trafficking victims initiated fresh concern for the problem. The victim of the fourth wave of trafficking, or "Natasha," became a symbol of the failures of socialism as well as a new subject of the postsocialist condition. We must, I argue, theorize postsocialism as a critical geographic difference integral to the making of contemporary antitrafficking discourse because of the important role the Natasha trade played in the politicization of the issue. While it is common to hear references to a post–Cold War temporality or a postsocialist condition, such references often lack a theorization of and from the geographic location of the former Eastern Bloc and Soviet Union. Of course, the idea of postsocialism should not be tethered to that location, but in the case of human trafficking it is critical to locate this discourse in those locations. The "Eastern" experience is actually quite vital to grasping the conditions of contemporary understandings of human trafficking.

Nancy Fraser argues that the "postsocialist condition" is one that privileges a politics of recognition over a politics of redistribution (Fraser 1997, 11). Similarly, I argue here that the post–Cold War politicization of trafficking has deprioritized critical economic analyses of violence. The feminist campaign against gender violence gave unprecedented recognition to sex trafficking *as violence* but often at the expense of economic critiques of social hierarchy and historical formations of empire. However, while Fraser's formulation is relevant here, there are important distinctions and clarifications related to postsocialism and feminism that illuminate how and why trafficking ignited a criminal justice agenda.[12]

For one, the success of representational or identity politics at the expense of redistribution is not the common experience in the "actually postsocialist" region (Gille 2010). The dismantling of redistributive economic systems has simultaneously occurred with the *delegitimation* of identity politics. Certain rights categories, such as women's rights and labor rights, lost prestige during late state socialism and remained deactivated during transition. In many countries there is now a resurgence of conservative nationalisms that constrain a politics of representation (Gal and Kligman 2000; Kalb 2009; Ost 2005). The consolidation of Russian neoliberalism is precisely the interlinking of opposition to identity politics (particularly toward women's and gay rights) with an authoritarian managed market.[13] At the same time, the dynamics critiqued in Fraser's postsocialist condition exist in and have influenced antitrafficking politics in the region—and not just as an external influence, but as intersecting and coterminous events.

I situate postsocialism both within and outside of the global. This makes sense in my analysis of human trafficking discourse because the problem of trafficking existed in the postsocialist region and was projected as a global phenomenon to which international institutions and powerful governments needed to respond. My approach addresses the fact that former socialist states played a role in the making of the postsocialist condition. While Fraser is not alone in her thinking, her formulation assumes that the "postsocialist condition" originated and spread from the west (Harvey 2007). This historical and geographic understanding of neoliberalism is quite limited. As Bockman and Eyal reveal, state socialist economists worked alongside western economists during the Cold War to develop key ideas now associated with "western" conservative economic policy (Bockman 2007; Bockman and Eyal 2002).[14] Similarly, it is clear that the "Washington Consensus" that dominated Latin American development policy was orchestrated by elites from within the region and not simply imposed by the United States. These examples further prove Gil Eyal's claim that neoliberalism is a global bricolage. Neoliberalism also is not limited to a western political chronology. For example, Boyer and Yurchak explain that current cultural practices in the United States already existed within state socialism (Boyer and Yurchak 2010). They examine the cultural practice of *stiob*, or irony, that circulated in late socialism and is now ubiquitous in U.S. popular culture and associated with neoliberalism. If neoliberalism is linked to a set of practices incubating across the globe, and prior to the end of the Cold War, then we must evaluate the temporality and locations of this global "postsocialist" condition.

Exposing these blind spots is important. However, my goal here is not just to reinsert the second world, but to think about why it matters to theorize (from) it. I do not advocate a politics of resentment and thus am not asking for a *centering* of the former second world. That turn would problematically maintain a kind of Eurocentrism hidden by Cold War hegemonic thinking.[15] Rather, in the case of human trafficking, dynamics and processes at work in the postsocialist region played a role in the emergence of the problem and influenced the current global policy regime that undercuts critical economic analyses. "Postsocialism" played a role both as a subject and object of human trafficking discourse. As a subject, the politics of postsocialist transitions defused globalization debates and naturalized policies that had come under fire.[16] The transformation of formerly planned economies brought a massive reorganization of the state and the terms of citizenship across the region. Yet the very language of *transition* often delimited the politics of these radical shifts. The discourse of transition circulated as a mandate for the market and its authoritarian entrepreneurs to dictate the outcomes of postsocialist economic transformations. Global processes such as privatization, flexibilization, and informalization were dimensions of transition, but the terms of transition did much to normalize rather than politicize them. This diversion was made possible by political elites both inside and outside the region (Appel 2004; Wedel 2001). Thus, the postsocialist condition in the former USSR and Eastern Bloc does not denote the introduction of neoliberalism after 1989, but the normalization of controversial economic policies amid socioeconomic strife and growing critiques of globalization.

The inevitability of capitalist economic transition undercut serious criticism of specific policies, yet the negative outcomes or failures of those policies were often cast as lingering pathologies of state socialism. This was particularly the case regarding privatization, marketization, and criminal activity. Evaluations of economic transition created a distinction between wild versus civilized capitalism. The fact that Russia was referred to as the "Wild East" during the 1990s illustrates that distinction. Indeed, the news coming from Russia at times seemed unbelievable, with stories of contract killings in broad daylight. Yet there also was a tendency to *not* see the underlying dimensions of globalization (and critiques of it) when evaluating the successes and failures of transition.

The emergence of postsocialist sex trafficking was no different. Postsocialism became an object of analysis that filtered how the fourth wave of trafficking was understood (Suchland 2013). In the end, the "Natasha" trade became a discourse focused on transnational organized crime at the expense of a grasp of the critical economic dimensions of the problem. If Susan Buck-Morss is correct that the Cold War was internal to western hegemony, then postsocialism was instrumental to maintaining that hegemony—even as the abject failure of the former enemy (Buck-Morss 2002).

While criminal behaviors fuel human trafficking, it takes place within existing systems and practices. As such, trafficking also should be situated in the myriad circuits of informal, flexibilized, and nonstandard labor as well as the legacies of imperialist state formations. This kind of labor is most often analyzed in the context of the global south and with regard to north-south migration patterns (Bakker and Gill 2003; Fudge and Owens 2006). Precarious postsocialist labor escaped an analysis like the one associated with the global south. Certainly, those concerned with democratization considered the political costs of economic hardship and the backlash it could cause. But many of the negative effects of transition were normalized as temporary pains for long-term goals, rather than challenged as part of growing discontent toward global capitalism.

Yet it is also important to recognize that transition-related economic practices that are associated with neoliberalism (like informalization) already existed under state socialism. State socialist citizens used various survival skills to get by in an economy of scarcity that became a part of the wider context of a cultural economy of life (Smith 2002). Practices such as using connections to obtain resources or jobs (*blat* in Russian), relying on semilegal or illegal papers for travel, establishing circuits of bartering and an "economy of jars" to supplement personal income were widespread and common (Ledeneva 1998; Pickles and Smith 1998). These informal practices were recycled as survival strategies during and after transition (Caldwell 2004; Seabright 2000). Creative entrepreneurialism flourished at all levels of society, from the babushka selling her jars of ferments at the metro stop to the new political and economic elite scamming the purchase of former state assets at bargain prices. But the presence of such practices and their persistence under capitalism were not linked to common experiences of globalization (or neoliberalism) in the 1990s when antitrafficking policy was being reformulated. Rather, the successes and failures of former state socialist countries—and the political and economic programs advanced within them—were evaluated on the basis of the concept of transition.

An important reason for the disconnect between postsocialist transition and critiques of globalization is because of the powerful "three-worlds" mapping of ideas and regions, or metageography, that was created during the Cold War. A metageography is a "set of spatial structures through which people order their knowledge of the world" (Lewis and Wigen 1997, ix). The three-worlds Cold War metageography was not only a tripartite division of the first, second, and third worlds. It also operated as a twin dyad, setting the directionality of the circuits of two oppositions. The assumption was (is) that one dichotomy was between the first and the third worlds and the other was between the first and the second worlds. The first world/third world dyad was based on the violent encounter with and resistance to western European colonial arrangements. From that, the third world is associated with development and decolonization. The first world/second world dyad was based on the ideological "world-historical" differences propped up by the Cold War. From that, the second world is associated with irrational modernization. This kind of formulation is problematic and easily challenged by the reality of settler colonialism, hybridized power and diasporic subalterns (Chow 2006; Shohat 1992). In the case of Russia, Madina Tlostanova uses the insightful language of subaltern empire to describe its global metageography (Tlostanova 2006). While the twin dyad idea is inaccurate, I suggest that it nonetheless informed the way postsocialist transition was tied to the emergence of human trafficking in the region. When the Cold War ended, many (wrongfully) assumed that the task of transition was a simple rejection of the semiperipheral past that would not require cultural translations. The Cold War metageography concealed underlying similarities to the projects of mass utopia promoted in the USSR and the capitalist west as well as cultural differences not explained by the east/west political axis.[17]

This linking of spaces with certain meanings of difference and opposition to the first world played into how governments evaluated and responded to postsocialist trafficking. The "fourth wave" of trafficking did *not* get linked to problems of development and globalization because it was first projected as the result of incomplete or incompetent transition. In addition to the misreading of postsocialist trafficking by many in the west, local elites refused to take responsibility for the human costs of transition. Thus, the elision of a critical economic response to trafficking also concealed the political consolidation of different postsocialist neoliberal arrangements across the region.[18]

Instead of linking the emergence of postsocialist trafficking to critiques of globalization, a strange bifurcation formed. When thousands rallied at the World Trade Organization meeting in 1999 in protest of globalization's discontents, meetings in Washington and New York were under way to address human trafficking as a form of violence against women and transnational organized crime.[19] The distinct political fields of these actions are not explained by Fraser's "postsocialist" condition, yet they reveal an epistemic divide between the victim and loser of globalization. While Fraser's general description of the displacement of economics fits with what I describe as the framing of trafficking as an aberration, the underlying temporalities, dynamics, and implications she associates with the postsocialist condition fail to fully capture how and why human trafficking operates as a neoliberal discourse. Part of the aim of this book is to make explicit the role of the second world in the making of that discourse.

At the same time, the theorization of postsocialism I present here is situated in feminist discourses circulating beyond the geography of the former east. I connect the deprioritization of an economic approach to rights in the postsocialist region to feminist critiques of neoliberalism and the state. Specifically, in the context of neoliberalism, there is an important connection between a postsocialist critique of "the state" and feminist critiques of a criminal justice response to rights. Connecting these two perspectives is particularly relevant in response to those who favor a "return" to the welfare state as the primary remedy to contemporary neoliberalism (Fraser 2009). The loss of the Fordist welfare state as a result of neoliberal economic practices is lamentable, but it is crucial to recall that not only was it not a panacea of social justice but the state itself was built through violent empire (Byrd 2011; Hall 2008; McRobbie 2011; Smith 2011). The post-1945 industrial economies of the United States, Western Europe, and the USSR were predicated on classed, gendered, and racial imperial projects not easily resolved by redistributing resources. After all, many activists and scholars advanced a variety of critiques of the welfare state because it had failed to challenge or compensate for racial inequality and sexism in society.

Rather than valorize an ideal that never was, I suggest an alternative line of thinking. Neoliberalism has decimated the Fordist welfare state, but the turn away from critical economic analyses of social injustice was also due to the valorization of a liberal-individualist corrective to injustice. In the context of trafficking, this meant that concepts like choice and agency were made the key normative devices to regulate the recognition and rights of victims *and* attempts to redistribute economic opportunity (typically through entrepreneurship programs). As the genealogy I present in this book reveals, it was not just the co-opting of feminism by neoliberalism but also the perceived expediency of a liberal feminist approach that supplanted critical economic approaches.

We should thus also think through what feminists want from the state given that the redistributive welfare state can be an instrument for violence. Consider, for example, feminist critiques of the state as an agent of governmentality in extending benefits to victims of domestic violence (Bhattacharjee 1997; Bumiller 2008; Incite! 2006). As the quote from Bumiller at the start of this section cautions, the successful institutionalization of feminist politics has enlarged the state's power to regulate and control women's lives through state bureaucracies. A return to a redistributive state itself will not remedy the economic dimensions of violence and injustice. Similarly, many in the post-socialist region are not nostalgic for the "rights" granted by the state of the past (Einhorn 2006; Salmenniemi 2008; Slavova 2006). This is not to say that the state plays no role. Rather, as Bumiller suggests, "concerns about rape and domestic violence need to be primarily addressed in the context of communities and in terms of their links to social disadvantage and impoverishment" (Bumiller 2008, 15). Similarly, scholars such as Elizabeth Bernstein and Kamala Kempadoo argue that increased engagement with the state to prosecute sex trafficking has bolstered a carceral response to social injustice (Bernstein 2012; Kempadoo 2005). The rise of "carceral feminism" has further undermined economic critiques of violence and has empowered the state to regulate precarity. These analyses should make us pause as we consider any call to return to the redistributive state.

Economies of Violence: Sex Trafficking as Precarious Labor

Throughout the work of this project I have felt unease about challenging the current framing of trafficking as a form of violence against women and the attendant antitrafficking agenda focused on prosecution. My critique of the discourse of "violence against women" does not mean that I am unsympathetic to the violence of trafficking. To the contrary, I am deeply affected by it. Traveling and working in Russia over the past decade, I witnessed many of the realities of "economic involution" that the market has brought and saw a connection to precarious labor.[20] For me, it was the juxtaposition of fieldwork in Russia with the disturbing representations of trafficking that revealed a contradiction. I came to ask: "Why is the violence of trafficking so visible and the violence of precarious labor not, and why has the affective power of representing trafficking not translated into heightened criticism of the market or economic policy?" Still, at multiple junctures in the project I had to remind myself that I am not discounting the important work that has been done by many committed advocates of women's and human rights. I am not suggesting that trafficking is not a form of violence against women. Yet this book questions what the current discourse of human trafficking enables and forecloses.

The phenomenal amount of attention given to the issue of trafficking since the end of the Cold War suggests that there is a genuine concern for this human rights violation. But if we are to move beyond an antitrafficking strategy that seeks to isolate individual victims and criminals, we must turn to broader strategies that seek to alter dimensions of current global and local socioeconomic orders. Otherwise, the immense attention to trafficking may turn out to be a perverse obsession in the midst of widespread exploitation. Because trafficking does not exist until a victim is produced through the state's juridical process, we fail to see the problem of trafficking outside that legal arrangement. A deeper economic analysis of trafficking may reveal solutions to the problem that do not require a plaintiff.

Without undervaluing the violence and hardship that victims of trafficking endure, we need to now "normalize" trafficking within political economy and precarious labor in particular.[21] To give a sense of what I am speaking to, I sketch some ways that trafficking is tied to political economy. I do not suggest that the problem of trafficking be reduced to an issue of class or economic determinism.[22] For some scholars/activists precarity is a class-based political statement (Standing 2011).[23] While class dynamics are important, my use of the term *precarity* draws on a feminist political economy that critiques classed, gendered, racialized, and social hierarchies that enable and are produced by economic structures. Trafficking is a global phenomenon, but it should be studied and combated at multiple levels, including the local. The examples I give here are meant to give some sense of the broader and specific dynamics at play.

The term *precarity* has come to be specifically associated with the processes of deindustrialization, flexibilization, and informalization that began in the 1970s. These processes and their impact on core economies radically transformed global economic practices. In core industrial economies, there was a shift away from large-scale industrial production toward services and knowledge-based industries. This shift meant a loss of the Fordist-type jobs in core economies as nonindustrialized or recently industrialized countries began to view "(unregulated) labor as their most competitive resource" (Peterson 2003, 50). Deindustrialization transformed previously skilled manufacturing jobs into unskilled labor, and new postindustrial commodities generated growth in the services economy. Both dynamics created precarious labor—the formerly skilled laborer loses secure waged labor, and the new unskilled laborer loses the value of his or her labor and, often, his or her labor rights.

Within the context of deindustrialization, there is a greater reliance on flexibilization and informalization in all sectors of the global economy. Flexibilization "refers to shifts in production processes away from large, integrated worksites, unionized workers, and mass production of standardized consumer goods to spatially dispersed (global) production networks . . . and is the key metaphor for neoliberal restructuring" (Peterson 2003, 59). Business and government policies contribute to flexibilization. Companies "flexibilize" their workforce by altering the terms and structure of labor, for example, favoring part-time, temporary, and subcontracting (outsourcing) arrangements. In conjunction, governments have allowed for the deregulation of production processes in the name of reducing "inefficiencies" in the market. Informalization practices result from and feed into flexibilization. Spike Peterson explains that informal labor includes the nonwaged work of the "social (or domestic) economy" and the "irregular economy," which can be broken down into licit or illicit activities (Peterson 2003). Informal labor in the social and irregular economy has grown as shifts have occurred in the formal economy. More people now rely on this type of labor to supplement and accommodate the loss of wages in the formal economy.[24]

Feminists have analyzed these large-scale processes for some time (Benería 2003; Enloe 1990; Gibson-Graham 1996; Sassen 2003; 2006). In particular, scholars have argued that flexibilization and informalization *depend* on, as well as exacerbate, gendered and racialized hierarchies and histories of domination. Thus, precarious labor is not just the latest category of Marxist critique but is a concept that captures the life struggles of the world's majority. For example, the myth that women's labor only supplements family incomes has promoted the practice of hiring women as flexible labor on a short-term or part-time basis. This myth also has contributed to the undervaluing of feminized labor affecting both men and women in export processing zones. In addition, the nonwaged work that women perform in the home is naturalized and then taken advantage of by "homework" subcontracting (Mohanty 1997). The assumption that women should work at home allows for enterprises to enlist women for waged labor in the home, for example piecework sewing and other fragmented production processes. While flexible labor is desirable for many skilled privileged female workers because it allows them to balance family and work obligations, it also feeds into a system of informal labor practices that takes advantage of gendered and racialized hierarchies. While informal and flexible labor is an economic asset only for the very elite professional/skilled laborer, some argue that precarious labor includes both the highly paid and low-paid workers of the current global economy (Ong 2006; Ross 2009). In addition, the retraction of the welfare state has only increased the need for informal labor, particularly in the realm of intimate labor, including home health care, elder care, and child care (Boris and Klein 2012; Kofman and Roghuram 2012; Parreñas 2000).

While human trafficking is not a new phenomenon, it can be contextualized within these processes of flexibilization and informalization. The labor that is done by those who are trafficked exists in formal and informal economies. Trafficking follows already existing systems—it is a means, not an end (Kopp 2012). For example, it makes sense to think about trafficking as embedded in intimate labor, which includes services provided by maids, nannies, and other domestics and sex workers (Boris and Salazar Parreñas 2010). These jobs are often the tasks women are traditionally expected to do because of gender and racial norms. Yet, as some women seek (or are required to find) waged labor in the formal economy, unskilled laborers are hired to pick up the necessary labor in the domestic sphere. The work is precarious because the laborer can be without a contract and possibly even a legal right to negotiate with her employer. The work certainly is vital to the survival of the family and the productivity of the broader labor force, but its value is not integrated into standard economic analyses. Racialized and geopolitical hierarchies also structure care work. As Peterson states, "who hires and who serves may reflect colonial histories (black maids of white madams in South Africa) or new geopolitical hierarchies of international debt and employment opportunities (Filipino maids in Saudi Arabia)" (Peterson 2003, 104). Thus, cultural and racial stereotypes are important to and are reinforced by patterns of international intimate labor practices (Agathangelou 2004).

Human trafficking is not isolated from care work, including tourism industries, where a whole host of formal and informal domestic laborers fulfill "care work," from hostesses and chambermaids to tour guides to entertainment venues, bars, and cafés. On the contrary, the victims and losers of precarious labor tread the same migration routes, share similar socioeconomic practices, and coexist in industries. As a result, it is rather difficult to disentangle the web of people and practices that exist in precarity. The blurriness between formal and informal labor is illustrated in Amalia Cabezas's research on women's care work in the tourism industry in Cuba and the Dominican Republic. Cabezas finds that women create affective relationships with foreigners that generate a range of financial and personal benefits. These women most often do not identify as sex workers despite the fact that sex is a part of their work (Cabezas 2009). The affective relationships are informal and are facilitated by formal labor in the tourism industry. Thus, as Cabezas argues, sexual-affective services are interwoven into the reproduction and accumulation of capital in the tourism industry. Transnational tourism industries structure those relations, while informal labor "subsidizes transnational capital" (13).

Leyla Keough draws similar conclusions from her ethnographic work on Moldovan migrant women involved in care work in Turkey. Relying on legal and illegal means, migrants live temporarily in Turkey and send remittances back home. As with the women in Cuba and the Dominican Republic, the Moldovan women's material exchanges are conflated with their affective ones as they build and rely on personal relationships in Turkey (Keough 2003, 75). Keough found that migrants are not easily separated into discrete categories in terms of the type of work they perform. Contrary to antitrafficking discourse that typecasts migrants into specific vulnerable categories, Keough reveals a much more complex landscape. This scholarship challenges the assumptions that sex work is an unintended by-product of tourism or that it exists independent of the attendant industries that make up care work. In fact, sex work and affective labor are structured into those industries. Cabezas's and Keough's research reveal the erotic underpinnings of transnational tourism and the informalization of hospitality services as the context in which this (trafficked) labor exists.

Sexual labor is also a commercial trade that has undergone significant postindustrial reorganization (Altman 2001; Bernstein 2007; Zheng 2009). Once only associated with street prostitution, commercial sex is now more geographically dispersed, privatized, even normalized. In her study of San Francisco, Elizabeth Bernstein details how since the 1990s commercial sexual encounters were relocated to interior venues, such as "men's clubs," massage parlors, and private residential areas, marked by class- and race-segregated customers (Bernstein 2007, 6). In an effort to "eliminate the visible manifestations of poverty and deviance from urban spaces," politically diverse policies aimed at regulating street prostitution have in fact further marginalized the most vulnerable women while remaining largely complacent in the face of the proliferation of privatized commercial sex venues. Bernstein provocatively argues that in order to address the burgeoning economy in commercial sexual services, which includes circumstances of exploitation, "a sober analysis of the global inequalities (of sex, of class, of race, and of nation) that drive women into sexual labor, and of the ways that these inequalities are themselves created through specific practices and policies" is needed (185). And it is this analysis of the broader political economy of precarious labor that is missing from most approaches to antitrafficking.

Post–Cold War trafficking has yet to be fully theorized as an object of global political economy. Certainly, there are scholars working to fill that gap (Bloch 2013; Humphrey 2002; Keough 2006; Morokvasic 2004; Salazar Parreñas 2011). Future analyses of trafficking must grasp the particularity of former state socialist economies in connection with wider global dynamics. Until recently, much of the research on precarious labor and globalization has focused on core/periphery relations that are based on orientalist constructs of power (Mackie 2001). The idea of "scattered hegemonies" is better suited for grasping the nuances of human trafficking and precarious labor (Grewal and Kaplan 2004). Anna Agathangelou's research on the gendered and racialized migration patterns between Turkey, Greece, Russia, and Romania is particularly insightful in this way (Agathangelou 2004). Her work reminds us that considerations of wealth and poverty alone are not sufficient for grasping the political economy of precarious labor.

Outline of the Book

This book is a genealogy of human trafficking discourse. At the center of that genealogy is a mapping of two discrete yet intertwined processes: on the one hand the development of sex trafficking as a feminist subject of analysis dominated by specific imaginings of violence and on the other hand the politics of postsocialism as a particular location and a metageographically imagined space. I analyze these processes in multiple ways. In the first two chapters (part I), I take a global approach and analyze the language used in the UN to articulate and then advocate against sex trafficking. I closely examine UN documents, conference proceedings, and other primary texts, looking closely at the UN Decade for Women (1975–1985) and the period leading up to the 1993 UN World Conference on Human Rights and subsequent Declaration on the Elimination of Violence Against Women. In that analysis, I identify competing feminist investments in politicizing women's rights and argue that in the case of trafficking, the success of the "violence against women" frame demobilized critical economic responses to violence. Importantly, chapter 1 reveals how politicizing violence has clarified but also problematically limited feminist claims.

With the emergence of the fourth wave of trafficking, antitrafficking discourse in the United States and the UN coalesced around the twin problems of violence against women and transnational crime. The connection between violence against women and trafficking prioritized a carceral response and fed into the emphasis on postsocialist criminal behavior. In chapter 2, I provide an analysis of UN proceedings and U.S. government debates to show that while transnational crime is a mechanism that fuels trafficking, it was not inevitable that a convention on transnational organized crime would be the basis on which a new post–Cold War antitrafficking norm would be built.

The intertwined dynamics that I trace in chapters 1 and 2 are approached anew in chapters 3 and 4 (part II). The development of a coherent global discourse on violence against women has a specific relevance when thought through postsocialist locations and temporalities. In chapter 3, I consider the evolution of women's rights discourse at the UN, looking at how the second world was situated during the UN Decade for Women, when global women's rights discourse was gaining coherence and power. The positioning of "second world" perspectives at the UN during the Cold War set up dynamics that later stymied the inclusion of newly independent voices. The displacement of such voices from the former second world exacerbated the deprioritization of feminist economic responses to violence, including trafficking. While this displacement is not universal across the postsocialist region or necessarily ongoing, it was an important dynamic in the early 1990s (Ghodsee 2003; Hemment 2007). The obscuring of a feminist economic frame for trafficking was particularly perverse in the case of those countries undergoing postsocialist transition. Looking specifically at the Russian experience, I illustrate how the language of violence against women both enabled and circumvented the mobilization of feminist discourse in the context of democratization and economic transition.

I also situate the evolution of the global criminal justice response to post–Cold War trafficking within postsocialism. In chapter 4 I analyze how the discourse of *transition* became a platform for neoliberal economic policies that local and foreign elites used to undermine alternatives to market Bolshevism. The flattening out of the political meaning of transition depoliticized the everyday forms of violence that postsocialist citizens encountered. By normalizing the violence of "real existing transition," sex trafficking was then viewed as an aberration of violence and crime. This, I argue, is critical to the social formations that politicized human trafficking so intensely after the Cold War. At the same time, the global "violence against women" framework for sex trafficking helped politicize the issue of trafficking in Russia and the wider postsocialist region. The validity and resources that the global campaign against gender violence lent to local organizations were vital to exposing the problem. However, the language of "violence against women" ultimately weakened economic critiques of transition because individual, rather than structural, violence became the focus. As a result, antiviolence activism continues to be connected to the depoliticization of economic discrimination and systemic violence.

We are over two decades past the political events that created the current global antitrafficking regime. There is now more attention to trafficking as a market and as a highly profitable industry. In fact, much of the language surrounding trafficking relies on an economic vernacular. However, the incorporation of economic terms into antitrafficking policy discussions actually reflects a deep carceral logic at work. For those invested in the future of antitrafficking, we must turn to political economy and not just economic rhetoric to alter the direction of the current global antitrafficking regime. In chapter 5 (part III) I detail how a carceral response to trafficking that focuses on individual victims and perpetrators shapes economic analyses of trafficking. Through this carceral framework, the individual—*homo economicus*—becomes the rational economic actor making bad decisions or maximizing profits. As with the liberal underpinnings of the "violence against women" category, concepts of choice and agency organize how trafficking is grasped as an economic activity. This is illustrated in the tendency to see and measure trafficking as a separate market such that everyday economic practices are bracketed from the field of trafficking.

The tendency to see trafficking as a separate and measurable market sets it off as an aberration from "regular" economic practices. In this way, the problem of human trafficking is viewed as exceptional to neoliberalism rather than as a symptom of it. A neoliberal economism that privileges rational market choices dominates current economic approaches to trafficking. Ironically, two of the most prominent activist positions today, neoabolitionist and pro–sex workers' rights, promote *choice* within the market as an economic solution to human trafficking. The moral choice of consumers to not purchase sexual services or products made by exploitative labor ("demand reduction") is presented in the same terms of rationality as is sex workers' choice to pursue their profession. This economism-in-trafficking discourse has further displaced critical economic analyses that more deeply contextualize human trafficking in everyday economic practices and conditions of precarious labor.

Finally, one does not write a close analysis of human trafficking discourse without becoming deeply invested in policy and advocacy. At least, that is my experience. In an effort to be generative as well as critical, this book ends with some preliminary ideas for future action and a discussion of positive changes to consider.

Part I. Global

The success of feminist organizing against gender violence is considered one of the most significant for global women's rights. To expose violence against women is to expose a basic and common experience of female subjugation. Indeed, who is not against gender violence? But the recognition of violence is not neutral; it carries specific understandings of why violence happens and even meanings of what violence is. The robust feminist discussion on issues such as female genital cutting, war rape, and domestic violence demonstrate the contested meanings of personhood, community/nation, and gender that are part of and enable the naming of violence (Bhattacharjee 1997; Crenshaw 1991; Davis 2000; Gunning 1998; Incite! 2006; Sudbury 2006). When diverse feminist groups converged around the problem of gender violence, the category of "violence against women" was legitimated and ultimately enshrined in UN doctrine as well as in national legislation. This success also meant a prioritization of certain meanings and policies regarding violence.

Rather than take the violence of sex trafficking as self-evident, I trace why sex trafficking came to be categorized as a form of violence against women within UN women's rights documents *and* what that categorization has meant for understanding the violence of trafficking. For years, sex trafficking was presented as a distinct problem albeit understood as a women's rights issue. With the dominance of the "violence against women" paradigm, sex trafficking came to be seen as a form of gender violence and ultimately grouped with other forms of gender violence such as rape, domestic violence, female genital cutting, and *sati*. The key to including sex trafficking in the composite category of "violence against women" was the view that sex trafficking primarily entails forced prostitution.

The (ongoing) emphasis on establishing sex trafficking as forced prostitution has defined how sex trafficking is understood and combated. Namely, forced prostitution defines sex trafficking as a violation of individual bodily (sexual) integrity. In this way, as a form of violence against women, forced prostitution/sex trafficking is different from but fundamentally similar to rape and domestic violence. As a result, the exploitation of trafficking is confined to the bodily experience of the victim—that is, sex trafficking is conceptualized through the individual victim. Certainly violence against an individual *is* part of sex trafficking. Yet the framing of sex trafficking in this way means that the tension between advocates against prostitution and advocates for sex workers' rights continues to dictate policy/advocacy work (Doezma 2010). These opposed viewpoints dominate policy discussions and have become the naturalized political axis along which sex trafficking is debated. As a result, feminists and antitrafficking advocates spend a lot of time emphasizing questions of consent and agency in *identifying* trafficking victims. Other viewpoints—such as those that see how trafficking is linked to structural inequalities and precarious labor—remain secondary or even silenced. As part of this book's effort to move beyond the focus on the individual, chapter 1 traces how this focus came to be in the first place.

Feminists generated conceptual clarity about sex trafficking as a form of violence against women, but the issue did not garner the high level of political attention it currently has until the mid-1990s. The dismantling of state socialism in the former Soviet Union and Eastern Bloc and the emergence of the "Natasha trade" catapulted the issue to the global political forefront. By the year 2000, new international norms were crafted at the UN, in the United States, and in Europe, thus setting the post–Cold War antitrafficking agenda. Chapter 2 analyzes how the emergence of postsocialist trafficking cases influenced the creation of new antitrafficking approaches. The "Natasha trade" discourse generated concern about a perceived explosion in sexual exploitation and a new international threat of transnational crime. The example of the Slavic woman (i.e., the "Natasha"), viewed as the innocent victim of criminal groups and faulty postsocialist states, facilitated a carceral response to trafficking.[1]

The language of "violence against women" helped interpret postsocialist sex trafficking as a specific crime of sexual violence that downplayed the radical "unmaking" of life that was precipitated by the dismantling of state socialism (Humphrey 2002). Compounding this particular feminist interpretation was an emphasis on mafia criminality that politicized only some practices of violence amid widespread and state-sanctioned violence.

1 / SEX TRAFFICKING AND THE MAKING
OF A FEMINIST SUBJECT OF ANALYSIS

Sex Trafficking: Before "Violence Against Women"

Before sex trafficking, there was the "traffic in women." Understood as a problem
of fallen women in prostitution, the issue was first politicized in the nineteenth
century and defined in the 1949 UN Convention on the Traffic in Persons and
the Exploitation of the Prostitution of Others. Of major concern was the presence of foreign women in domestic brothels in Europe (Bernstein 1995; Bristow 1982). While moral panic and sensational accounts brought the language of
"the traffic in women" into common usage, after 1949 the issue had a minimal
profile within the UN (Grjebine 1986). The 1949 Convention was regularly catalogued as a statement for women's rights in the UN, but it lay dormant until
feminists repoliticized prostitution and gender violence beginning in the 1970s.

Two major centers of feminist thought were instrumental in repoliticizing
prostitution—one focused on "female sexual slavery" and the other on critiques
of development. These interventions are not homogenous positions, but they
have served as distinct voices in the politicization of prostitution during the
Cold War and in its aftermath. Both feminist interventions had varying de-
grees of influence in the evolution of women's rights norms in the UN as well.

The term "sex trafficking" was not widely used in the 1970s or 1980s, but feminists raised concerns about prostitution, forced prostitution, sexual violence, and sex tourism. It is first important to recall here the myriad feminist claims against "sex trafficking" before it was officially redefined in international law.

FEMALE SEXUAL SLAVERY

Before the language of "violence against women" gained political currency, there was "female sexual slavery." While not the only feminist concerned with violence against women, Kathleen Barry's published work and activism had immense influence on the evolution of the feminist antiviolence discourse. Barry coined the concept of sexual slavery in her 1979 book *Female Sexual Slavery*. The terminology of sexual slavery was used when she (with Charlotte Bunch and Shirley Castley) organized a session at the 1980 NGO forum at the UN Conference on Women and again for an international workshop in 1983.[1] For Barry, prostitution is the central harm of sex trafficking. This view of sex trafficking is tied to the emergence of radical feminist voices in the United States in the 1970s and was essential to the feminist reclaiming of sex trafficking as an important issue. In doing so, Barry advanced a feminist analysis of the root causes of sex trafficking. While prostitution had already been the focus of the "traffic in women," Barry identified male sexual domination as the cause of prostitution and sexual slavery.

For Barry, "sexual slavery" is not confined to the international traffic in women but encompasses various forms of the restriction and abuse of women's sexuality. Sex trafficking is the outcome of an ideology of cultural sadism that views sexual exploitation and violence against women as normal. As she states, sexual domination is the first cause of sexual power (Barry 1979, 8–9). Cultural sadism biases society to not see forced prostitution as a form of slavery. Throughout her book she extends the boundaries of sexual slavery beyond forced prostitution to include domestic violence, female genital cutting, pornography, and polygamy. According to Barry, to combat the traffic in women, society must address this deep ideology of cultural sadism and female sexual domination.

There are two fundamental beliefs in Barry's conceptualization of sex trafficking as female sexual slavery that are important to delineate here because they continue to be important views within contemporary debates about sex trafficking. First, a decontextualized patriarchy is the central cause of sexual slavery. Any local institution of prostitution is produced by the same ideology of cultural sadism. Thus, the "trafficked" aspect of sex trafficking is understood as the exchange of women's bodies within patriarchal systems of sexual domination. As such, local patriarchal norms nor the political and economic relationship between nation-states are important to understanding or defining sex trafficking. This transcultural claim about sexual slavery is illustrated in her chapter "Sex Colonization," in which she discusses how different practices (polygamy, domestic violence, and female genital mutilation) around the world are united in a core belief system incorporating female sexual submission. She makes an argument against viewing culture as specifically relevant for analyzing women's oppression and instead envisions a universal claim for all women across the globe. She states, "There is nothing unique across cultures in the practices of the enslavement of women except perhaps the diversity in the strategies men employ to carry them out" (Barry 1979, 140).

Barry's emphasis on a critique of patriarchy drew on but clearly diverged from Marxist understandings of female subjugation. Ironically, the language she uses is quite reminiscent of the Marxist terminology used by socialist thinkers such as Alexandra Kollontai. In the classic Marxist formulation, prostitution is a distinctly female symptom of capitalist exploitation. In their writings, both Friedrich Engels and Kollontai argued that socialism would alleviate the problem of prostitution.[2] Barry takes the architecture of the Marxist model of exploitation but sees patriarchy rather than capitalism as the driving force. Sex colonization (rather than economic colonization) is the primary form of power in the world. Barry uses the term "colonization" in order to give lower priority to the inequality between nation-states than to the inequality between men and women. For example, in the provocatively entitled Fourth World Manifesto, she and others declared that "women, set apart by physical differences between them and men, were the first colonized group. And this territory colonized was and remains our women's bodies" (Barry 1979, 165).

The prioritization of sexual colonization keeps Barry from analyzing sexual slavery and sex trafficking as produced through the relationships between states and economies and within the global arena. Thus, sexual slavery is never looked at as a transnational economic phenomenon. For Barry, the importance of immigration laws, neocolonial economic arrangements, and military engagements is truncated by the core engine of sexual domination. For example, she describes the growth of prostitution due to the demands of military and business tourism, but she never analyzes the political and economic dimensions of those demands. For Barry, sex trafficking is rooted in a culturally universal patriarchy. Economic dynamics only serve as a distraction from the primary, essential oppression of sexual slavery.

The lack of any geopolitically informed economic analysis of sex trafficking is tied to a second core dimension of Barry's understanding of sex trafficking. That is, the harm of sex trafficking is the sexual domination of women. This belief is in many respects the linchpin for why and how opposition to prostitution and opposition to trafficking are linked. Women's participation in prostitution remains the central focus of the sexual slavery approach (termed neoabolitionist today) to antitrafficking. Though Barry recognizes that not all women are forced into prostitution, she is suspicious of whether women can be empowered within prostitution because of the exchange of money for women's bodies. Barry disagrees with competing claims about women's choice to participate in prostitution. She claims that "economic analysis has often functioned to undermine the feminist critique of sexual domination that has gone on since the beginning of the women's movement. Undoubtedly economic exploitation is an important factor in the oppression of women, but here we must be concerned with whether or not economic analysis reveals the more fundamental sexual domination of women" (Barry 1979, 8).

Barry's work on female sexual slavery was an important part of the feminist activism that reinvigorated interest in sex trafficking in the 1970s and 1980s. The importance of her work is that it pushed an emphasis on antiprostitution from a specifically feminist concern for women's sexual freedom. This was a new approach to thinking about sex trafficking and a departure from the more socially conservative campaigns against "vice" in the late nineteenth and early twentieth centuries. Of course, Barry's activism did not take place in isolation from other emerging voices. She was part of a growing field of activists interested in different facets of the issue. For example, religiously oriented organizations as well as sex workers' rights organizations attended the conference "Female Sexual Slavery" that Barry helped to organize in 1983.[3] Over the course of the 1980s and 1990s, the space for networking between those advocating against female sexual slavery and those advocating for sex workers' rights dissipated. This turn of events was foreshadowed somewhat in Barry's comments at the 1983 workshop: "In examining the relationship between the feminist movement with prostitute organizations we face the serious question of how to support the work with individual women in prostitution without supporting the institution, something that will place us in opposition to the prostitute organizations" (Barry, Bunch, and Castley 1984, 29).

Advocates against sexual slavery specifically started to politicize the issue of sex trafficking in the late 1980s. Organizations such as the Coalition Against Trafficking in Women (CATW) were founded on Barry's principle that prostitution is not labor but is inherently degrading to women. In addition to Kathleen

Barry, Dorchen Leidholdt was one of the founding members of CATW and was present at the First Global Conference Against Trafficking in Women in 1988, when CATW was launched. She had been active in antipornography campaigns (as a member of Women Against Pornography) and in advocating on behalf of victims of domestic violence and rape. This work, and her philosophical view on gender violence, influenced the strategic link CATW made between sex tourism, sex trafficking, prostitution, and violence against women.[4] In a 2004 speech, Leidholdt recalled the history of CATW and how their work was distinguishable from other feminist antitrafficking organizations.[5] She explained how prostitution and sex trafficking essentially are the same issue, as follows:

> Prostitution and sex trafficking are the same human rights catastrophe, whether in local or global guise. Both are part of a system of gender-based domination that makes violence against women and girls profitable to a mind-boggling extreme. Both prey on women and girls made vulnerable by poverty, discrimination, and violence and leave them traumatized, sick, and impoverished. Both reward predators sexually and financially, strengthening both the demand and criminal operations that ensure the supply. The concerted effort by some NGOs and governments to disconnect trafficking from prostitution—to treat them as distinct and unrelated phenomena—is nothing less than a deliberate political strategy aimed at legitimizing the sex industry and protecting its growth and profitability. (Leidholt 2004)

Leidholdt's position, like Barry's, is that prostitution cannot be legitimate labor. Furthermore, the fundamental harm of prostitution is the source of the rights violation of both sex trafficking and sex tourism. There is no economic critique of sex trafficking.[6]

The CATW position on prostitution and trafficking held sway in the late 1980s and early 1990s in political discussions at the UN. There was already a connection between prostitution and sex trafficking in the 1949 UN Convention for the Suppression of the Traffic in Persons and of the Exploitation of the Prostitution of Others. The 1949 Convention sought to challenge "prostitution and the accompanying evil of the traffic in persons for the purposes of prostitution" (UN 1949, Preamble). Indeed, sex workers' rights advocacy groups were opposed to the 1949 Convention because of the connection it made between prostitution and trafficking (Pheterson 1989). However, as a result of the work of CATW, an antiprostitution approach to trafficking continued to dominate discussions at the UN in the 1980s.

Kathleen Barry, for example, who was executive director of CATW, played an important role as an expert to the UNESCO meetings of 1986 and 1991. By the time of the 1991 UNESCO expert meeting on trafficking, the antiprostitution campaign successfully ensured their preferred language in UN discourse. That language depicted any form of prostitution as a violation of women's rights. A document prepared for the meeting proclaimed, "Free prostitution does not exist, whatever the means of exercising it. Thus, starting from this new approach and after 1986, it appeared necessary to the Group of Experts to undertake a more thorough review of the Convention of 1949 and to revise it so that it can be applied at the international normative level" (*International Meeting of Experts on Sexual Exploitation, Violence, and Prostitution* 1992, i). This strong antiprostitution language, however, ultimately was *not* institutionalized in post–Cold War antitrafficking norms. As I will continue to explain in greater detail, the "violence against women" agenda dampened the strength of the sexual slavery language. At the World Conference on Women in 1995, when the Beijing Platform for Action was presented, key voices of the sexual slavery paradigm argued that the platform was a defeat for their cause (Raymond 1998; Sullivan 2003).

THE POLITICAL ECONOMY OF SEX TOURISM

Amid the growing attention to female sexual slavery, feminist economic critiques of sex tourism industries also appeared. According to Kamala Kempadoo, the topic of sex tourism reemerged in public discourse in the 1970s because of feminists' concern with the social impacts of the reconstruction and development of the Southeast Asian region after the Vietnam War and the stationing of U.S. military troops there (Kempadoo 2005, xi). Beginning in the 1970s, feminist perspectives involving NGOs, researchers, and intergovernmental bureaucrats focused on development issues. In time, some of those perspectives included a critique of sex tourism as a problematic outcome of development programs. The Women in Development (WID) agenda opened a window for feminist economic critiques. At first, the WID agenda primarily was concerned with incorporating women into development strategies (Benería 2003, 48). Scholars emphasized that women were an undervalued economic agent, ready to be tapped for the advancement of their families and societies. Esther Boserup's 1970 book on women in economic development is often noted as playing a vital role in advancing the WID agenda that emerged in conjunction with the UN Decade on Women. As a result of the work of scholars, activists, and bureaucrats, new agencies within the UN and development organizations were pushed to recognize the importance of women in development. Margaret Snyder, chief of one of those new agencies, the UN Development Fund for Women, positively declared at the end of the UN Decade for Women that "the fate of women is a critical determinant of the fate of whole societies" (Helmore 1985).[7]

The issue of sex tourism and sex trafficking were not prominent topics in those early discussions. The more critical feminist positions on economic policies promoted by development agencies had not infiltrated policy discussions at the start of the UN Decade for Women. Rather, "the implicit assumption behind many of these programs was that women's main problem in the Third World was insufficient participation in otherwise benevolent process of growth and development" (DAWN 1987, 15). With the materialization of problematic tourism-driven development regimes, along with other failed development programs such as "structural adjustment programs," feminists increasingly pushed for the recognition that it was not sufficient just to recognize women's role in development. They argued for a need to closely analyze how women, gender, and race operated within development strategies and for an assessment of women's economic empowerment (DAWN 1987). A critical feminist intervention into political economy thus emerged.

The focus of much of that intervention was in the development strategies promoted in the global south. For example, starting in the 1970s, with the encouragement of developed countries, some countries in South and Southeast Asia adopted policies that promoted domestic cheap labor for national and international capital to produce manufactured goods for the world market (Phongpaichit 1982). Rather than invest in the technology needed to industrialize their economies, countries such as Thailand and the Philippines sought to gain comparative advantage by selling the cheap labor of their citizens. This strategy put incredible pressure on the primary agricultural sector and led to the mass migration of peasants to the urban core. Both men and women migrated for work to the urban core; however, women were seen as ideal employees because of their presumed docility and moral obligation to family (Mies 1986, 116–17).

In addition, developing economies in Southeast Asia adopted tourism-driven development in order to draw western and Japanese businesses, businessmen, and wealthy tourists to spend money in their countries. As Thanh-Dam Truong explains, western countries promoted tourist-driven development. The idea emerged from a growing perspective that travel could be used as a strategy for "education and fostering international understanding" in the United States in the late 1950s. Such thinly veiled foreign security strategies were coupled with U.S. corporate interests, particularly the civilian aviation sector (Truong

1990, 116). According to Truong, Checchi and Company, a U.S.-based private firm specializing in tourism and regional development, conducted a reconnaissance study on tourism in the less developed countries. The report they produced supported the idea of international tourism as a desirable development strategy. The UN, development agencies, and investment banks embraced this perspective. In her assessment of this strategy, Truong is emphatic: "To recapitulate, the motor behind the formulation of tourism policy as an alternative development strategy may be located in the interests of large financial institutions involved in aircraft production as well as the travel and tourism conglomerates which sought new pastures for the expansion of their business" (Truong 1990, 121–22). This strategy fit with the dominant beliefs in the 1980s in "trickle-down" theories and a focus on commercialization for strategic economic development.

In Thailand, for example, services related to foreign travelers emerged as the government promoted tourism to boost the economy. Hotels, bars, cafes, massage parlors, and the like catered to foreign male tourists and often served as a front for sexual services. Prostitution was officially banned but was allowed to flourish in the guise of "tourist packages" and hospitality services. Using the "R&R" model of the U.S. military, western and Japanese corporations encouraged their male employees to enjoy the sexual pleasures of foreign travel (Enloe 1990, 36; Truong 1990, 99). Thus, sex work was generated as an important component of economic development. It was not an unintended consequence of that development strategy. Sex tourism is "not an anomaly" (Enloe 1990, 36). Truong argues that "the upsurge of tourism and its interconnection with prostitution in Southeast Asia are outcomes of policies skewed toward investment in personal services which contribute to the maintenance of the working capacity of U.S. military, and of a newly emerged international working class and managerial class" (Truong 1990, 100).

Yet, while tourism-related industries contributed to growing proportions of domestic growth in Thailand in the 1970s and 1980s, ultimately neither the domestic economy nor the citizens garnered the most benefit.[8] Because the tourist industry was largely financed by external investment, foreign currency expenditures circled back into privileged pockets (Truong 1990, 163–67). The informal sex sector was instrumental for supplementing women's insufficient factory incomes as well as providing a necessary backup in the case of layoffs. According to Aihwa Ong, the 1974–75 market recession led to thousands of layoffs of women workers by electronic firms in Malaysia, Singapore, and the Philippines. "Women who lose their jobs fall back upon the so-called 'informal sector,' this shadow economy for all kinds of people displaced by rural development projects" (Ong 1985, 17). It was then clear that the sex industry was integrated into formal and informal sectors of tourist-driven economies. Moreover, undemocratic regimes oversaw these development programs in some countries. This ensured that GDP growth did not benefit the throngs of citizens toiling in the tourism industry. In effect, some argued that the disregard for human rights by authoritarian regimes encouraged the idea that women are sexual commodities "to be utilized for furthering the national economic good" (Ryan and Hall 2001, 142).[9]

Feminist responses to economic development and its relationship to women's rights came from a variety of corners. Of major importance was the formation of the feminist collective Development Alternatives with Women for a New Era (DAWN) in 1984, born out of frustrations and concerns for women in the global south. The collective's founders were focused on grassroots initiatives at the community level that could be linked to a macro-level perspective (DAWN 1987, 9). That macro-level perspective was a comprehensive critique of diverse development strategies in the global south that had similarly resulted in multiple oppressions. The collective was spurred too by the UN Decade for Women, in particular the need to give voice to women's experiences and perspectives from the global south. In preparation for the final UN Decade conference, DAWN participants met to organize their presence at the NGO Forum in Nairobi. Part of that preparation was the creation of, through "extensive debate and discussion with researchers, activists, and policymakers," a platform document that would articulate the current aspirations and struggles "for a future free of the multiple oppressions of gender, class, race" (DAWN 1987, 10).

Implicitly, the DAWN platform was also an evolutionary step beyond the WID agenda that had come to dominate official UN discourse during the Decade for Women. For example, Devaki Jain, one of the founding members of DAWN, explains that the questionnaire sent to countries in preparation for the Nairobi conference was based on the "ladders approach" promoted by the WID group (Jain 2005, 96).[10] She recalls how, at that first meeting of the DAWN collective, "the Bangalore group struggled to fit their issues within the framework for Nairobi, finally rejecting the entire questionnaire outright" (96). The inadequacy of the dominant WID model compelled the DAWN collective to craft an alternative platform, which was published as *Development, Crises, and Alternative Visions* (DAWN 1987). Jain states that "DAWN's new framework initiated a shift in development analysis characterized by the central location of poor women in development planning, the merging of 'women's issues' with macroeconomic structures and global crises, and the linkage of local organizing efforts with global themes and networks" (97). Of key importance in Jain's statement is her point that "women's issues" are connected to macroeconomic structures and global crises. This is important because it speaks to how a discrete issue like sex tourism, prostitution, or violence against women is approached from a broader recognition of the economic, social, and global forces at play. The DAWN platform does not speak specifically to sex tourism, but it does emphasize the impact of export-based industries and informal economies (among others) on women.

The general approach promoted by the DAWN platform characterizes the way many feminists from the global south understand women's rights. That is, women's rights are inseparable from national, class, ethnic, and global dynamics. Women's rights cannot be achieved in isolation from challenges to national and global economic inequalities. One example of this approach is found in the work of the Asian Women's Human Rights Council, which organized six tribunals in the early 1990s. The tribunals were used to give voice to women's rights in Asia. Issues such as sex trafficking and violence against women were presented as intertwined with development issues. Nelia Sancho-Liao, a member of the Asian Women's Human Rights Council, explained: "Advocacy of human rights for Asian women should mean, working for their total liberation from all the forces that oppress them and ensuring their development and empowerment. It should mean opposing the domination and exploitation of poor nations by the few rich and powerful ones and promoting a new world economic order and the genuine development of Third World countries" (Sancho-Liao 1993, 36). The Christian-based Third World Movement Against the Exploitation of Women also incorporates a critique of development that it says is vital for understanding the prevalence of sex tourism (Perpiñan 1986).

Scholarship on sex tourism by Cynthia Enloe, Maria Mies, and Thanh-Dam Truong are examples of feminists promoting a critical economic approach to "women's issues." From NGOS and scholars, the increasingly emphatic message emerging in the late 1980s was that there are important links between development policies, former colonial arrangements, local class and gender stratifications, and women's empowerment. This seemed to be the message at the close of the UN Decade for Women in 1985—"although the Decade that proclaimed so bravely 'Development, Equality, Peace' has given so little of these to the majority of the people, what we have learned in its course has already empowered us for the long haul ahead" (DAWN 1987, 96).

Unlike the sexual slavery agenda, however, this critical feminist economic perspective did not hold sway in the UN during the Decade for Women in terms of how sex tourism and sex trafficking were addressed. Although WID practitioners gained acceptance in UN bureaucracies, particularly in the newly established departments of the UN Development Fund for Women, they did not present a critical assessment of sex tourism or sex trafficking. One reason for this may be the brief gap between the emergence of the WID agenda inside the UN and the appearance of sex tourism industries. A general indication of this gap is that Ester Boserup's influential book *Women's Role in Development* was published in 1970, which was in close proximity to the institutionalization of tourism-driven development. For example, the World Bank established a special department in 1970, the Tourism Projects Department, to be in charge of the financing of tourism projects (Truong 1990, 122). Some credence should be give to this time lag. However, it is also the case that the WID agenda grew out of a fairly traditional neoclassical economic approach (Benería and Sen 1981). This traditionalism may be a better indication for why feminist macro-economic critiques of trafficking were less influential in UN discourse in the 1980s.

Irene Tinker explains that "the original concept of WID was based on the adverse impact of inappropriate economic development programs that undercut women's economic activities by treating them only as mothers" (Tinker 1990, 39). The goal of the WID interjection was to focus on efficiency and thus convince the development community that their projects would be more successful if they took women's work into consideration (39). This strategy did not challenge the fundamental approach of development policy, only women's placement within them. This meant that "WID advocates and practitioners, because their objective is to influence the development community, tend not to raise basic theoretical issues but rather seek to adjust current development practices to include and benefit women" (48). There were limitations to that type of analysis, although it was an important interjection to the masculinist field of economics.

The tacit acceptance of modernization theory silenced the advancement of a feminist critique of economic theory (Benería 2003, 48). For example, feminists critiqued the common reliance on female labor force participation as an indication of women's economic empowerment. Feminists argued that such a measure misses the uneven, and at times problematic, impact of women's participation in new industrial economies. The sex tourism industries that were built up as a result of tourism-driven development are an excellent example of this. However, a critical feminist economic lens on violence, and sex trafficking in particular, did not prevail through the UN women's rights process. By the end of the UN Decade for the Advancement of Women there was a new appreciation for women's role in development. There was also no united feminist economic perspective inside the UN. The emergence of DAWN marks the burgeoning of feminist networking outside the UN, but DAWN's perspective did not have influence on how sex trafficking evolved within UN bureaucracies.

Sex Trafficking as a Women's Rights Issue—The UN Decade for Women (1975–1985)

I have detailed two different feminist perspectives on "sex trafficking" that were present in the 1970s and 1980s. These perspectives existed outside and to some extent also circulated inside the official channels of the UN. However, the discursive trajectory of the problem of sex trafficking in the UN has its own particularities to detail. The issue of sex trafficking started out as a discrete women's rights issue during the UN Decade for the Advancement of Women (1975–1985). What I mean by discrete is that it was categorized on its own in UN documents. While thought of as a women's rights issue, with women being the primary victims, it stood alone. There were many discrete women's issues floating around the UN until feminists pushed for the advancement of women's rights concerns by collecting and organizing those rights. The strategy was to see women's rights as a coherent collective claim. A turning point in that process was the passage of the Convention on the Elimination of All Forms of Discrimination Against Women in 1979.[11] The success of the campaign against gender violence mobilized governments and activists in unprecedented ways. To this day, VAW is a broad and dominant category within the UN that dominates women's rights discourse.

PRIOR TO THE DECLARATION on the Elimination of All Forms of Discrimination against Women (1967), there was no comprehensive document to represent a coherent vision of women's rights. The 1949 Convention on the Suppression of the Traffic in Persons was always included in the listing of UN women's rights doctrine, but it was not sutured with other pieces of doctrine into a single vision. The Declaration on the Elimination of All Forms of Discrimination against Women changed that. It was the first document of the Commission on the Status of Women (CSW) to establish a coherent approach to women's human rights.[12] Until that point, it was believed that women's rights were best protected and promoted by the general human rights treaties. But many were not satisfied with this and pushed for greater recognition of the patterns of discrimination against women and maintained that the concept of "human rights" was ineffective when used to combat gendered rights violations. Women's human rights gained greater recognition as a necessary component of human rights (Keck and Sikkink 1998).

The Declaration was only a statement of political intent, however, and had no binding force. A decade later the CSW prepared the Convention on the Elimination of All Forms of Discrimination Against Women, which was the first comprehensive and internationally binding UN instrument for women's rights. The Convention was passed by the General Assembly in 1979. In the Declaration and the Convention, sex trafficking is situated as a discrete form of discrimination. Borrowing directly from the 1949 Convention, article 6 of the 1979 Convention says that "state's parties shall take appropriate measures, including legislation, to suppress all forms of traffic in women and exploitation of prostitution of women." Sex trafficking is not tied to other issues but holds a discrete location within the general framework of discrimination. The status of sex trafficking as a discrete issue changed over the course of the UN Decade for Women.

A significant indication of the distinct nature of the issue of sex trafficking during the UN Decade for Women is that it was never taken up as a priority within the troika theme "Equality, Development and Peace." No serious interventions within the UN regarding sex trafficking occurred until the 1985 Forward Looking Strategies document. Until that point, the language used in the 1949 UN Convention was simply inserted into the emerging women's rights agenda. The first document of the UN Decade was the 1975 World Plan of Action. In it, the language of the 1949 UN Convention was used to highlight "prostitution and the illicit traffic in women" as one of the "other social questions" addressed by the World Plan (World Plan of Action 1975). The controversial Declaration of Mexico, presented as a kind of preface to the World Plan, articulates thirty principles to advance. The twenty-eighth declares, "Women all over the world should unite to eliminate violations of human rights committed against women and girls such as: rape, prostitution, physical assault, mental cruelty, child marriage, forced marriage and marriage as a commercial transaction."

In addition, a set of resolutions and agreements were made at the 1975 conference. One of the resolutions was on the prevention of prostitution and the exploitation of women and girls.[13] As these documents and resolutions illustrate, at the beginning of the UN Decade for Women, sex trafficking was not distinguished from the associated critique of prostitution. Mirroring the sexual slavery discourse and the formal language of the UN 1949 Convention,

TABLE 1.1. Categorization of Sex Trafficking in Key Documents, 1949–present

	Key documents and events	How sex trafficking is categorized
1949	UN Convention on the Traffic in Persons and the Exploitation of the Prostitution of Others	Discrete issue—focused on the social vice of prostitution
1975–1985	UN Decade for Women: Mexico City (1975); Copenhagen (1980); Nairobi (1985)	Discrete issue—multiple problems identified including female sexual slavery and problematic development projects
1983	International Workshop on Female Sexual Slavery	Grouped—trafficking is a form of sexual domination
1993	UN World Conference on Human Rights and subsequent Declaration on the Elimination of Violence Against Women	Grouped—sex Trafficking is a form of "violence against women"
1995	UN World Conference on Women and accompanying Beijing Declaration and Platform for Action	Grouped—sex Trafficking is a form of "violence against women"
2000	UN Protocol to Prevent, Suppress and Punish Trafficking in Persons, Especially Women and Children	Grouped—sex trafficking is a distinct form of human trafficking which is tied to transnational crime and corruption
2000	U.S. Victims of Trafficking and Violence Protection Act	Grouped—presents sex trafficking as a distinct form of human trafficking and is tied to the reauthorization of certain federal programs to prevent violence against women

prostitution was viewed as a violation of women's rights as "one of the most grievous offences against the dignity of women" (World Plan of Action, resolution 7).

Prior to the 1975 Mexico City International Women's Year conference, very little attention was paid within the UN to sex trafficking. In 1974, the Sub-Commission on the Prevention of Discrimination and Protection of Minorities established the Working Group on Slavery, which was under the UN Economic and Social Council's Commission on Human Rights. At the International Women's Year conference in Mexico City, the Working Group on Slavery unsuccessfully lobbied to have a country reporting mechanism on forced prostitution (Barry 1979, 54; UNESCO 1976). The lack of attention to the issue inside the UN was symbolic, for some, of the inadequacy of the institution to address women's issues head on (Barry 1981). It also indicated a lack of clarity regarding the jurisdiction of women's rights. At this time both the Sub-commission of the Commission on Human Rights and the CSW were invested in addressing women's issues.

By the time of the next UN World Conference on Women in 1980, there was growing attention to sex trafficking as an issue of sexual slavery and economic development. Yet, even with that growing attention, the status of sex trafficking did not change in the conference's Program for Action. Listed under the Resolutions and Decisions of the conference (number 43), the "exploitation of the prostitution of others and traffic in persons" is included with a bevy of other issues not falling into the broad Program for Action. At the parallel NGO Forum, there was debate about what constituted sexual slavery and what was at stake. In her reflection on the 1980 NGO Forum, Kathleen Barry argued that a "left antifeminist" contingent had promoted a platform that normalized prostitution and tried to co-opt the message of prostitution rights groups such as COYOTE (Call Off Your Old Tired Ethics) and PUMA (Prostitutes Union of Massachusetts) (1981, 47). She states that the group Wages reduced "prostitution to a merely economic problem" and "participated in the phallacy [sic] that prostitutes need pimps as protectors and that prostitution is a form of work like any other" (45). Barry's account suggests that a debate about how to frame sex trafficking and what to focus on had already begun at the 1980 NGO Forum discussions—specifically one that pitted sex workers' rights against prostitution.

The final conference of the UN Decade for Women, in Nairobi (1985), introduced new language to global women's rights doctrine on sex trafficking. As at the previous two UN world conference documents, sex trafficking was separated from the main themes of equality, peace, and development, which were articulated in the main body of the Forward Looking Strategies. Appended to the Forward Looking Strategies was a set of decisions and resolutions. In section 4, "Areas of Special Concern," sex trafficking was raised as a problem of prostitution. Paragraph 290 states: "Forced prostitution is a form of slavery imposed on women by procurers. It is a result of economic degradation that alienates women's labour through processes of rapid urbanization and migration resulting in underdevelopment and unemployment. Sex tourism, forced prostitution and pornography reduce women to mere sex objects and marketable commodities" (UN 1985). This statement is a milestone in the evolution of feminist language on sex trafficking within the UN. Two new perspectives are added for the first time.

First, the language of *forced* prostitution is an important (and controversial) qualification that suggests that prostitution itself does not qualify as "slavery" but the forcing or lack of choice is what makes participation in prostitution a form of slavery. This point of qualification is still a contentious one. In the development of global norms on antitrafficking, the tension between those who promote an antiprostitution (or abolitionist) perspective and those who promote a sex workers' rights perspective has been prominent. At the time of the 1985 UN conference there was a mingling of these contentious views. So, while sexual slavery is defined as "forced prostitution," there is also recognition of the radical feminist (abolitionist) perspective with the mentioning of pornography and women as sex objects.

Second, the mingling of these contentious views is further illustrated in the sections that raise the economic aspect of sex trafficking. For the first time, the economy and not just patriarchy is presented as the cause of forced prostitution. The statement that forced prostitution was the result of economic degradation, underemployment, and unemployment was a watershed. No previous UN statements had made the link between economic and sexual rights. The inclusion of sex tourism as a feminist concern was the reason for this connection. While a development perspective was percolating within (and pushing from outside) the CSW, sex trafficking was isolated from discussions of economics. Critiques of sex tourism changed that and made the link between women's sexual oppression and economic oppression more apparent. In the Nairobi statement, sex tourism is listed as a vector of sexual slavery, with forced prostitution and pornography. In paragraph 291, solutions are provided, including prevention of prostitution (abolitionist perspective) as well as assistance to prostitutes. There is real attention to the need to provide assistance to prostitutes as workers, including economic opportunities and protections from violence.

By the end of the UN Decade for Women, there was greater attention to women's issues within the UN and a stronger commitment to addressing the economic concerns of women in the global south. The issue of sex trafficking had discursively evolved from how it was represented in the 1949 Convention on the Traffic in Persons and the Exploitation of the Prostitution of Others. While the sexual slavery perspective remained, it was joined by voices who promoted the rights of sex workers and those who saw economics and postcolonial arrangements as important causes of prostitution. These three components—sexual slavery, sex tourism, and sex workers' rights—were intertwined, at times conflicting with and at times supporting the other.

Claiming Sex Trafficking as "Violence Against Women"

Before the concept of "violence against women" was institutionalized in UN terminology, there was recognition of domestic violence and rape in the family. Feminists inside and outside the UN were able to establish the private sphere as a legitimate area of concern for the UN. No doubt, grassroots organizing in the 1980s played a role in establishing that justification (Schuler 1992). In the 1980 UN Copenhagen Programme for Action, a resolution was passed on battered women and violence in the family. Later, in 1985, UN Resolution 40/36 recognized violence in the home and set the stage for the 1986 UN meeting on violence in the family. Over the course of the decade, leading up to the fourth world conference in Beijing in 1995, different forms of gender-specific violence gained greater recognition as a coherent collection of violations. By the time of the writing of the Beijing Platform for Action, the concept of "violence against women" had evolved from wife battery to a composite category that encompassed expressions of violence such as trafficking in women, sexual harassment, and rape. Within ten years, thinking within the UN had shifted to recognize "violence against women" as a broad and distinctive issue.

The paradigm of "violence against women" was institutionalized after the UN Decade for Women and was a new claim for women's human rights. Due to feminist networking and organizing, in 1993 "violence against women" was recognized as a human rights issue in the Vienna Declaration and the UN Declaration on the Elimination of Violence Against Women. In addition, a special rapporteur on violence against women was appointed in 1994 to conduct fact-finding projects to deepen an understanding of the forms and breadth of gender violence, including forced prostitution and trafficking. These official recognitions of violence against women were due in part to the hard work and dedication of activists outside the UN. For example, a major force in global political advocacy against violence against women was (and is) the work done by the Center for Women's Global Leadership. In particular, the 16 Days campaign, which was started in 1991, was very influential. The campaign annually marks the sixteen days between November 25, International Day Against Violence Against Women, and December 10, International Human Rights Day. The first 16 Days campaign was a petition drive directed at influencing the UN World Conference on Human Rights that was held in Vienna in 1992. Ultimately, that campaign and the strategic advocacy of the anti–"violence against women" feminist network at the conference succeeded in institutionalizing a "violence against women" agenda within the UN and advancing the language of women's human rights.

Leading up to the UN World Conference on Human Rights, many feminists were frustrated with the overly politicized decision-making process within the UN that had weakened a unified women's rights agenda. The three worlds schism of the Cold War divided UN delegates into competing camps, emphasizing equality or development or peace. Conflict over some politicized issues seemed to stonewall the overall process and frustrated many inside and outside the UN. Clearly a conceptual alternative was needed in order to move women's rights beyond the politics of the Cold War.

In response to the fissures created by the Cold War, increased mobilization took place on behalf of "violence against women," and this mobilization was presented as a unique opportunity for transnational networking (Basu 2000; Keck and Sikkink 1998; Weldon 2002). The "violence against women" discourse emerged out of a global context where gendered forms of violence and discrimination were not recognized within the human rights framework of the UN. There was a need to articulate the difference of gender within the human rights framework of the UN because development and human rights agencies had *not* taken up the issue of gendered forms of violence and discrimination. The composite category "violence against women" became that difference.

National and regional organizations across the globe initiated efforts to combat and publicize different forms of violence against women. Some early examples include the holding of the International Tribunal on Crimes Against Women in 1976, the first Latin American Feminist *Encuentro* in 1981, which addressed violence and discrimination, and in 1982 the "No More Violence Against Women" march in Puerto Rico.[14] A march in South Africa in 1991 was organized in the name of "People Opposed to Woman Abuse." Feminist and other organizations in the United States also gained momentum in their ef-

forts to combat rape and domestic violence (Heise and Chapman 1992; Mc-
Guire 2010). Due to these pressures growing from outside the UN, there was
a shift in awareness about forms of discrimination and violence that women
experience in the privacy of their own homes, in their communities, and at the
hands of governments and militaries.

The first sign of official recognition of "violence against women" as a new
global agenda item within the UN was UN Resolution 40/36 in 1985, which
recognized violence in the home. The Resolution was followed by a conference in 1986 on violence in the family. This was a crucial shift because the UN
had largely focused on the violence perpetrated by the state or agents of the
state in the public sphere, such as torture. But even in these instances gendered forms of state violence were not recognized. The language of "violence
against women" evolved from a general statement that referred to violence in
the domestic sphere to a composite category strategically used to promote a
set of women's human rights. From the mid-1980s to the early 1990s, the term
"violence against women" transformed into a composite category for women's
human rights and no longer referred merely to discrete instances of rights
violation.

The transformation of "violence against women" into a composite category
began with the issuing of General Recommendation 19 by the Committee
on the Elimination of Discrimination Against Women, the committee that
oversees the Convention on the Elimination of All Forms of Discrimination
Against Women.[15] In General Recommendation 19, gender-based violence is
recognized as a form of discrimination, whereas in the Convention document
it is not mentioned. General Recommendation 19 was proposed in preparation for the 1993 UN Conference on Human Rights in Vienna. In addition, a
separate but connected UN agency, the Commission on the Status of Women
(CSW), met in September 1992 to start drafting a declaration on violence
against women. In combination, the advocacy work at the 1993 UN Conference
on Human Rights and the passage of the UN Declaration on the Elimination of
Violence Against Women that same year crystallized the language of violence
against women into the powerful category of "violence against women." By
the early 1990s, the discourse of "Equality, Development and Peace" that had
animated the UN Decade for Women was eclipsed by the issue of "violence
against women."

With that shift, sex trafficking was claimed as a central issue for women's
human rights and framed as a form of "violence against women." The sexual
slavery perspective had always conceived of prostitution as violence, so there
is some inevitability to the fact that sex trafficking would be incorporated into

the "violence against women" agenda. In many respects, the category "violence against women" is the heir to sexual slavery—and this legacy is certainly important for understanding why such a range of issues (wife battery, trafficking, rape, prostitution, and pornography) became subjects of one composite category "violence against women." The politicization, and thus emphasis, on individual/bodily violence was promoted early on by those criticizing female sexual slavery. Representing sex trafficking as sexual violence was central to the sexual slavery agenda that was so integral to reclaiming sex trafficking as a feminist issue in the late 1980s. Indeed, it is the violation of women's sexual inviolability that distinguishes sex trafficking as a violation of women's human rights.

Playing a significant role in the evolution of global advocacy against "violence against women," Charlotte Bunch continued her work with the Center for Women's Global Leadership. Under her leadership, the Center launched the Global Campaign for Women's Human Rights, a coalition of 950 women's organizations from around the world. The Global Campaign was a major engine behind the recognition of women's human rights at the 1993 Vienna Declaration. In an interview with me, Bunch explained that her commitment to staking the claim for women's human rights was solidified in part because of Kathleen Barry's work on sexual slavery and their discussions at the 1983 Global Feminist Workshop on the Traffic in Women (Barry, Bunch, and Castley 1984).[16] For Bunch, it was the issue of sex trafficking presented *as* an example of violence against women that highlighted the need to stake out women's human rights. As she said, there was never any question that sex trafficking would be used as a case in the tribunals for the Vienna Conference.[17] And by the mid-1990s, the link between sexual violence and sex trafficking was solidified as the feminist strategy for politicizing and thus "reclaiming" sex trafficking.

If the conceptual link between sexual violence and sex trafficking was made prior to the 1993 Vienna Conference, it was rhetorically solidified by the close of the conference. In the Vienna Declaration on Human Rights, women's human rights are mentioned several times. The recognition of gender violence was critical for advancing the argument that women's rights are human rights. It was the development of the category "violence against women" that illustrated that women had human rights. It was also the claim against the category of violations now termed "violence against women" that successfully bypassed the cultural, political, and religious divides that had stymied consensus-building and networking during the UN Decade for Women (Basu 2000). The "violence against women" agenda presented an opportunity to extend women's rights activism in a way that united efforts rather than dividing them along the multiple differences that existed among the world's women. It was an effective and powerful strategy.

The 1993 Vienna Declaration is the first global document to situate sex trafficking within the context of "violence against women." As I detailed already, prior to 1993, sex trafficking was treated as an isolated issue within UN norms. In Point 18 of the Declaration, sex trafficking is clearly positioned as a form of gender violence: "Gender-based violence and all forms of sexual harassment and exploitation, including those resulting from cultural prejudice and international trafficking, are incompatible with the dignity and worth of the human person, and must be eliminated. This can be achieved by legal measures and through national action and international cooperation in such fields as economic and social development, education, safe maternity and health care, and social support." Later that year, in December, the UN General Assembly passed the Declaration on the Elimination of Violence Against Women. Article 2 lays out the different forms of "violence against women"—in the home, in the community, and perpetrated by the state. Sex trafficking is located in article 2 in the section on violence occurring in the general community. In addition to sex trafficking, rape, sexual abuse, sexual harassment, and intimidation at work and in educational institutions are mentioned.

The impact of the "violence against women" framing of sex trafficking in the Vienna Declaration and in the Declaration on the Elimination of Violence Against Women also had an impact on the 1995 Beijing Platform for Action. The culmination of years of preparatory meetings and feminist networking, the 1995 Beijing Conference and NGO Forum are recognized as a major milestone in the evolution of global women's rights activism. The Beijing Declaration and Platform for Action remain the reference point for global women's rights norms today.[18] Sex trafficking and forced prostitution is mentioned several times in the document but most predominantly is situated in section D, which covers "violence against women."[19] In addition to adopting the three arenas of gender-based violence that are used in the Declaration on the Elimination of Violence Against Women, a lengthier statement is made about combating sex trafficking and forced prostitution, including a call for the implementation and strengthening of the 1949 UN Convention on the Suppression of the Traffic in Persons. Further on in the section a "strategic objective" is presented: eliminating "trafficking in women and assist[ing] victims due to prostitution and trafficking" (UN 1995). States are requested to "take appropriate measures to address the root factors, including external factors, that encourage trafficking in women and girls for prostitution and other forms of commercialized sex, forced marriages and forced labour in order to eliminate trafficking in women" (UN 1995).

By positioning "sex trafficking and forced prostitution" as part of a broader concern for "violence against women," there is some indication that the rights violation of sex trafficking thus constitutes force, whether through physical, psychological, or other means. In that respect, the phrase "sex trafficking and forced prostitution," used throughout the document, is somewhat redundant. The redundancy reveals that the different feminist approaches to prostitution were not reconciled in the Beijing document. Rather, there is a lingering contentiousness around how to frame sex trafficking.

Feminist Investments and Compromises— Sex Trafficking as "Violence Against Women"

The evolution of the global women's rights agenda through the Cold War and to the 1995 Beijing conference reflects the dedication and perseverance of feminist activists and scholars across the globe. There was no inevitability to the ultimate achievements of that agenda—from the push to include women in development programing to gender mainstreaming and to the recognition of rape as a punishable war crime, all achievements were fought and won. The evolution of UN women's rights norms on sex trafficking has been no different. Feminists from differing political and institutional positions reclaimed this crucial human rights issue. My accounting of that evolution emphasizes the uncertain and contested fate of the framing of sex trafficking as a global woman's rights issue.

The Cold War three worlds division animated the UN Decade for Women. These differences were rhetorically, and strategically, reconciled (in part) by crafting a political agenda for women's human rights, and specifically in terms of the category "violence against women." This strategy coincided with the collapse of socialist projects in the USSR and Eastern Bloc and the emergence of a new global order that emphasized the principle of "TINA" ("There Is No Alternative"). More than a mere political coincidence, the end of the Cold War and the advancement of neoliberal economic doctrine contributed to the success of a liberal feminist approach to women's rights. This is reflected in the fact that sex trafficking came to be categorized in UN women's rights documents in terms of sexual violence, a violation largely neutralized in terms of macroeconomics and its connection to racialized imperial projects.

Although "violence against women" is recognized as a development issue, it does not operate as an economic critique of development or sex trafficking. The "violence against women" agenda crystallized an approach to women's rights that emphasizes choice/agency and women's bodily integrity. This has unintentionally deprioritized feminist economic analyses. Insofar as "violence against women" is used strategically to address women's rights worldwide, the register operates in conjunction with, rather than as a critique of, neoliberal governance. Advocacy against "violence against women" emerged as a discourse to critique the lack of a structural analysis of gender inequality beyond political rights. Women's political rights were a well-established concern at the UN and, increasingly, women were being included in development programs. Yet little attention was paid to the gendered impacts of development or women's empowerment beyond the voting booth (Pickup, Williams, and Sweetman 2001). Advocates of the WID agenda had made inroads in expanding the narrow political agenda of the women's rights platform of the UN. However, by the mid-1980s, "the initial euphoria about the beneficial effects of 'incorporating women into development' became tempered by the recognition that despite high rates of participation, women's potential would continue to be thwarted by their subordinate status and low social value" (Schuler 1992, 3).

The deprioritization of feminist economic analyses is evident in how development gets taken up as an issue of "violence against women." With the growing rhetorical power of the "violence against women" discourse, there was an attempt to cast violence against women as a development issue (Bunch and Carrillo 1991). But the logic of agency dominates that engagement as well.[20] The link between "violence against women" and development was articulated in two ways. First, domestic violence and other forms of gender violence were recognized as unintended outcomes of development programs. For example, when women gained greater economic autonomy in their families and communities, there was the possibility of violent retaliation for the shifts to the gender order that such empowerment brought. Second, "violence against women" also was viewed as an impediment to women achieving greater economic participation in development programs. This too is an example of women's agency. While important issues to highlight, both of these examples reveal a fairly shallow understanding of the relationship between violence against women and development.

The "violence against women" paradigm exposed important issues within development programs but it did not instigate a critical assessment of development or neocolonialism. While "violence against women" is recognized as a possible unintended consequence of development programs, it is not viewed as an economic issue beyond the recognition of women as economic actors. This limited view of the relationship between sexual violence and economic justice has also placed restrictions on how sex trafficking is understood. Once sex trafficking was incorporated into the composite category "violence against women," there was a weakening of the macroeconomic analyses that had been prominent in the feminist critiques of sex tourism and development. While there were and are important advantages for promoting a comprehensive vision against violence against women, the institutionalization of the "violence against women" agenda has coincided with a weakening of critical feminist economic interventions since the end of the Cold War.

2 / THE NATASHA TRADE AND THE POST–COLD WAR
REFRAMING OF PRECARITY

Organized crime is the new communism, the new monolithic threat.
—**SENATOR JOHN KERRY**, "Global Mafia" (1993)

The prioritization of a carceral response to trafficking is evident in the placing of the UN's antitrafficking norm (the Optional Protocol to Prevent, Suppress and Punish Trafficking in Persons, Especially Women and Children of 2000) within the UN Convention against Transnational Organized Crime. The focus on crime and punishment is also evident in the 2000 U.S. TVPA. While (transnational) organized crime is a factor that contributes to trafficking, it was not inevitable that a convention on transnational organized crime would be the normative apparatus to frame post–Cold War antitrafficking norms. Given what I detail in this chapter, it is conceivable that the earlier UN 1949 Convention on the Traffic in Persons and the Exploitation of the Prostitution of Others could have been revised and used in conjunction with the Declaration on the Elimination of Violence Against Women or the Beijing Platform for Action. It is also conceivable that the 1949 Convention could have been revised and/or incorporated into existing conventions on human rights and forced labor.[1] The fact that there continues to be a confused and politicized distinction between trafficking, smuggling, and forced labor is a reminder that transnational organized crime was not the only option for framing trafficking after the Cold War.[2]

How was it that trafficking was picked up by those concerned with transnational crime and corruption? One important impetus came from the feminist antiviolence agenda that had recently gained credence within the UN.[3] The promotion of victims' rights was a new agenda that was making a wider impact on UN decision-making. In my investigations, it is unclear whether sex trafficking would have garnered an elevated status in the Commission on Crime Prevention and Criminal Justice, the UN body that negotiated the 2000 Convention, if it had not been for the introduction of "victims' rights" language into the workings of that Commission. The recognition of female victims of sexual violence opened the door for the Commission to undertake the burgeoning problem of sex trafficking. This discursive opportunity also took place in the United States. In the aftermath of the 1995 Beijing conference, President Bill Clinton established the Interagency Council on Women and soon after a working group on trafficking. A concern for "violence against women" was paramount to developing both operations (Bevacqua 2000; Weldon 2002). In the United States, the close conceptual connection between human trafficking and "violence against women" is evident in the fact that the TVPA is reauthorized as part of the Violence Against Women Act, which was first passed in 1994.[4]

In addition to the heightened attention to violence against women, there was a growing concern for global criminal activities coming from the post-socialist region. Weak and corrupt governments, social chaos, and economic vulnerabilities created the perfect breeding ground for the "red mafia" (Friedman 2002; Serio 2008). The link between "violence against women" and post-socialist criminality was made in response to the emergence of the Natasha trade. Ultimately, the focus on sex trafficking as a symptom of transnational organized crime allowed for a prioritization of concerns and approaches to antitrafficking efforts that emphasized the role of criminal behavior. In this new post–Cold War context, trafficking was cast as an aberration from the global democratic capitalist order. Some even declared the collapse of the USSR the "End of History" and in doing so marked the injustices of transition and even democratic systems as aberrations from, rather than systemic problems of, those systems.[5]

But why would we not criminalize human trafficking? Was there any doubt that a prosecutorial response was inevitable? The point here is not that criminalization was not necessary but that as a result of framing trafficking as primarily a problem of criminal activity, other approaches (including human rights and development) were truncated and even rationalized through a prosecutorial approach. Let me provide a few examples. The criminal justice response to trafficking positions both the criminals and victims of trafficking as *legal subjects* that the state regulates in the antitrafficking apparatus. For example, the widely used language of the "3 PS" (prevention, protection, prosecution) constructs an antitrafficking agenda that hinges on prosecution. Prevention is concerned with targeting vulnerable populations and educating them about trafficking. Prevention strategies thus are largely about how to avoid victimization, not eliminating it. Furthermore, prevention is considered a positive outcome of increased prosecution. In fact, prosecution rates are used as the index for ranking countries in the annual U.S. Trafficking in Persons (TIP) reports. A privileging of prosecution also is evident in how protection is understood. Protection is concerned with granting victims of trafficking services. Yet, victims of trafficking only receive those services once they become potential plaintiffs in a legal case.

Furthermore, the governmental focus on prosecution has constructed an antitrafficking apparatus that includes a whole host of private actors, including international organizations, police, NGOs, private businesses, and others who are empowered as antitrafficking agents. Each of these actors possesses unique agency in the antitrafficking apparatus that is structured by a focus on prosecution. The devolution of power from a central decision-making government to courts, NGOs, police officers, informed citizens, and the like has created what Cornelius Friesendorf calls "security governance" (Friesendorf 2007). Security governance is a state strategy to include a range of actors in antitrafficking but it effectively displaces critiques of the role of the state and its responsibility in challenging exploitation. Thus a government can show that it works to combat trafficking, but its own culpability in trafficking and its responsibility to its citizens can be obscured. A prosecutorial antitrafficking apparatus has developed, enlisting a whole host of actors, and yet the state is rarely the object of critique. As a result, approaches that are concerned with the role of macroeconomics in preventing trafficking or other areas of "human security" (Lobasz 2009) are necessarily off the table.[6]

Another consequence of a prosecution focused antitrafficking agenda is that there is now tension between victims' rights and prosecution. For example, scholars and advocates have exposed the reality that an emphasis on prosecution can perpetuate victimization and violence against migrant laborers and others (Davidson 2006; Global Alliance Against Traffic in Women 2007; Goodey 2004). From police raids to the "reflection periods" granted to possible victims, the state is positioned as the arbiter of rights and their violation.

As a result, a tension between human rights protections and state interests in prosecution is a primary focus of current political engagements with trafficking (Berman 2010; Gallagher 2001; Gallagher and Pearson 2010). Over the past decade demands have increased for the protection of victims of trafficking in the process of prosecution, including special visa regimes, safe houses, and possible protection in repatriation. These and other concerns are highlighted in the 2002 UN Principles on Human Rights and Human Trafficking, which is a new standard for human rights protections in antitrafficking norms. These examples illustrate the importance of advocating for human rights within the antitrafficking prosecutorial system. Yet the tension between human rights and prosecution has narrowed the terrain for a broader approach to antitrafficking advocacy. The insertion of a human rights perspective has ameliorated the harsh prosecutorial system but has not dethroned prosecution as the focus of state concern regarding trafficking.

The collapse of socialist projects in the USSR and Eastern Bloc did not precipitate a global discourse on the connection between economic policies, precarious labor, and human rights regarding human trafficking. Ironically, the antiglobalization activism of the 1990s did not intersect with the political momentum behind reforming antitrafficking norms at the UN. Activism against human trafficking, especially in the 1990s, did not address the possible role of governments and intergovernmental agencies in creating the conditions for human trafficking. Rather, the shockingly little attention to the economic determinants of trafficking has coincided with the obfuscation of the roles of the state and political economy as actors in the perpetuation of some of the very mechanisms of trafficking. This chapter tracks how governments and key international agencies interpreted the emergence of postsocialist trafficking. The year 2000 marks a key moment in redefining the problem of trafficking. Before the 1990s, the issue was part of a broad and diverse political vernacular within the UN and Europe. With the introduction of the Natasha trade, governments gradually came to emphasize criminal behavior as the cause of this new global epidemic. This refocusing on trafficking as a criminal aberration ultimately decoupled questions of development and violence. To this day, economic analyses of trafficking are a significant area of prevention that is undertheorized (Friesendorf 2007).

Before human trafficking became a political category of heightened urgency after the Cold War, it was part of discussions on prostitution, social welfare, slavery, and political economy. The 1949 UN Convention on the Traffic in Persons and the Exploitation of the Prostitution of Others is a compilation of previous agreements on "the white slave trade."[7] The issue of trafficking, or "white slavery" as it was known at that time, concerned the presence of foreign women in domestic prostitution markets. According to Anthony Bristow, the concern for white slavery served an important function in domestic debates about the regulation of vice. At that time, brothel prostitution was sanctioned, though regulated, in most of Europe, with the exception of the United Kingdom, where prostitution was not sanctioned but regulated by the Contagious Diseases Act of 1864–1886. The ineffectiveness of brothel regulation in diminishing contagious diseases or the "protection of social decency" motivated reformers to push for the abolition of regulated prostitution (Bristow 1983). The issue of white slavery was used to curry social support for reforming government policies toward prostitution. Stories of female abduction and ruination were used as powerful rhetoric in order to shape social beliefs about commercial vice (Bernstein 1995; Bristow 1983).

The white slave trade discourse focused primarily on European women trafficked within Europe and its dominions. The first connotations of the sex trade, even if inaccurate, were of "proper" white women who had fallen into misfortune. As Bristow states, "at a political and social level the white-slavery movement coincided with widespread fears about the quality of the racial stock" (Bristow 1983, 41). Thus, while "white slavery" was used as a gendered rather than racial distinction, it also played out in racialized ways. For example, Jewish women and Jewish "traders" were often the focus of concern in Europe and the United States. At the same time, the public feared that innocent white girls could be caught in this "Jewish trade."

The 1949 Convention provided strong language against prostitution and focused on prostitution as the central violation of the traffic in persons. All participation in prostitution was treated as problematic (article 16). Trafficking required special attention because foreign "victims of prostitution" did not automatically receive the benevolence of the state (article 17). In contrast to later antitrafficking doctrine, consent was not an issue. Trafficking occurred when a person "procures, entices or leads away, for purposes of prostitution, another person, even with the consent of that person" or who "exploits the prostitution of another person, even with the consent of that person" "to gratify the passions of another" (article 1). In an effort to suppress the traffic in persons and the exploitation of the prostitution of others, the parties to the Convention agree to punish any person who "keeps or manages, or knowingly finances or takes part in the financing of a brothel" or who "knowingly lets or rents a building or other place or any part thereof for the purpose of the prostitution of others" (article 2).

The 1949 Convention was not widely adopted by UN countries, yet it remained the reference point for international discourse on sex trafficking for the next fifty years. The jurisdiction of the 1949 Convention was in the Economic and Social Council of the UN. Parties to the Convention were required to submit reports on their laws, regulations, and prosecutions regarding the terms of the Convention. In addition, with a Council decision in 1951, a biennial report based on information gleaned from questionnaires directed to UN member states was due to the secretary-general. However, neither the questionnaires nor the Convention were given much regard.[8] Eight years passed before new communications on the issue surfaced, when at the request of the Social Commission a report on the traffic in persons and prostitution was prepared by the Secretariat in 1959. The report provided an assessment of the traffic in persons and suggested measures for advancing the goals of the 1949 Convention. The report was intended as an assessment of the Convention and did not initiate new policies (UN 1959, 3). The report's author claims that while the traffic in persons still exists, the problem has declined and that "prostitutes are generally recruited among the nationals of the country concerned" (5). At the conclusion of the report, the Economic and Social Council adopted a resolution that applauded the Convention and encouraged additional countries to ratify or accede to it. After that point, the report collected dust on the shelves of the UN library until the 1970s.

In 1974, the Sub-Commission on the Prevention of Discrimination and Protection of Minorities of the Commission on Human Rights set up a Working Group on Slavery. The Working Group included the traffic in women and children as a form of slavery in its work (Fernand-Laurent 1985, 6). The Interpol report reprinted in Kathleen Barry's book was forwarded to the Sub-Commission in 1974 and supported the focus on the traffic in women within the activities of the Working Group. Previously, a report on slavery had been made by the Sub-Commission in 1966 and had included information on the exploitation of the prostitution of others. But it was not until the efforts of the Working Group on Slavery and the CSW that renewed interest and resources were directed to the trafficking issue. At the 1980 Copenhagen UN Decade for Women conference, the CSW requested that the secretary-general prepare a report on prostitution. As a result, in 1982 the Economic and Social Council passed a resolution for a request for a special rapporteur to "make a synthesis of the surveys and studies on the traffic in persons and the exploitation of the prostitution of others" (5). Jean Fernand-Laurent was appointed special rapporteur in October 1982 and submitted his report in January 1983.

Part of the mandate for the special rapporteur was to catalogue all actions in regard to trafficking since 1949. An evaluation of his catalogue shows the varied UN competencies that had some jurisdiction regarding the issue of trafficking. At that time, the Centre for Human Rights was the secretariat for the Commission on Human Rights and for its Sub-Commission on Prevention of Discrimination and Protection of Minorities. The Working Group on Slavery was a subgroup of the Sub-Commission and facilitated its work on trafficking. The special rapporteur's report discusses the work of the Centre as the primary entity responsible for the 1949 Convention (Fernand-Laurent 1985). For example, the Centre administered the questionnaire previously mentioned while the Working Group prepared the summaries. Fernand-Laurent reveals the paucity of resources and comprehensive research done on the topic.[9] The questionnaires had not generated substantial information on trafficking or prostitution. Overall he suggests that greater resources and time need to be invested in the Sub-Commission in order to gather more and better evaluations of trafficking. In addition to the Centre for Human Rights, the report lists other UN entities whose work is tied to the issue of trafficking.[10] Importantly, the CSW is recognized as playing a "key role in prompting action against this problem" (27).

The Fernand-Laurent report is instructive because it reveals that the issue of trafficking had stalled out in the UN. Not until the late 1970s did disparate corners of the UN bureaucracy pick the issue up again. The Working Group on Slavery was clearly the center for UN activities on trafficking in the 1980s. The link to the Commission on Human Rights tracks back to when the UN adopted the 1949 Convention, which was regarded as one of the earliest human rights treaties (Clark 1994, 12). The "social defense" or criminal justice unit also had early jurisdiction; however, it did not pay much attention to the subject. In 1983, the Centre for Human Rights (the secretariat for the Commission on Human Rights) was designated "a focal point of this endeavor" (13).[11] Yet it was the Committee on Crime Prevention and Criminal Justice, the successor to the early "social defense" branch, that became the bureaucratic center for revising UN trafficking doctrine. Clearly, there were other locations within the UN to house the work of revising antitrafficking doctrine in the late 1990s.

The Fernand-Laurent report also shows that trafficking was approached largely as a problem of prostitution, per the normative frame of the 1949

Convention.[12] The brief indication that women might choose to sell sex is over-shadowed by the report's claim that "even when prostitution seems to have been chosen freely, it is actually the result of coercion" (Fernand-Laurent 1985, 10). However, the report also reflects new language about the link between trafficking and women's social status, in particular with the adoption of the language of "sexual slavery," which is clearly tied to Kathleen Barry's publication (Barry 1979). The similarity between the normative frame of the 1949 Convention and the repoliticization of trafficking from the "sexual slavery" perspective is evident in this report. Both present a critique of prostitution as the central harm of trafficking. The link between sexual slavery and trafficking fits too with the framing of trafficking as a form of slavery, which was the thinking of the Working Group on Slavery. One new interjection in the report is a reference to "developing countries" and "foreign troops" as feeding the demand for prostitution (Fernand-Laurent 1985, 10–11). In terms of developing countries, Fernand-Laurent briefly discusses the "exodus" of women from rural to urban settings where they become vulnerable to prostitution.

Outside the UN, there were other signs of renewed interest in the issue of trafficking in the late 1980s. Importantly, the Dutch government requested that the Council of Europe commission a report on the traffic in women and forced prostitution.[13] The report introduces new perspectives on the issue, building on the normative frame of the 1949 Convention and adding an economic dimension as well. In particular, women from developing countries working in Europe are of special interest. The author of the report, Licia Brussa, contextualizes European prostitution in terms of ideological shifts in the treatment of prostitution and shifts in the sex industry. Notably, Brussa explains that major changes in prostitution in the 1970s were brought on by the commercialization of sexuality and the growth in leisure industries. The rise of leisure industries created "sex industry multinationals" (Brussa 1991, 32). Using a political economy frame, Brussa details how the migration and trafficking of third world women into European prostitution markets broadened prostitution as an industry, expanding sexual services beyond the brothel or street corner to bars, saunas, hotels, and nightclubs. As such, "procuring has become property-based, and now tends to hide its activities behind the façade of legality, with companies operating on several different levels" (32).

The expansion of sex services (my term, not Brussa's) was made possible by the internationalization of prostitution as well. "Sex industry multinationals" set up commercial activities in "poorer" countries and in Western Europe. "The principal features of the international sex industry are therefore its search for new markets and activities and its capital investments both in certain third world countries and in prosperous countries" (Brussa 1991, 37). This search for new markets and the migration patterns that followed began to be referred to as waves. In the 1970s, most of the foreign women in the European prostitution market came from Asia (wave one). In the early 1980s, Latin American women began to appear and then African women (wave two and three). Finally in the early 1990s, women from the former Eastern Bloc are found in Western European markets—the fourth wave.[14] Brussa's report shows how the presence of foreign women in European prostitution markets is tied to structural changes in the sex market, immigration policies, and the socioeconomic consequences of development programs. The report is notable for its economic analysis of sex trafficking and reflects the kind of language that feminists critical of development programs introduced during the UN Decade for Women. Brussa's report is a critical assessment of the intersection of economic, social, and criminal dynamics that feed into sex labor industries and thus the internationalization of prostitution and its attendant phenomenon, sex trafficking.[15]

The report also picks up on the beginnings of postsocialist trafficking. It is important to note that the entrance of East European women into the dynamics of the internationalization of prostitution is not viewed as exceptional by Brussa. Rather, Brussa places the movement of Eastern European women into Western European markets in the same context as the previous movements of women from the developing world. This provides some evidence that postsocialist trafficking could have been read in a different way. Another example of work that viewed postsocialist trafficking in the context of migration from the global south is in Belgian journalist Chris De Stoop's book *Ze zijn zo lief, meneer* (1992), translated into English in 1994 as *They Are So Sweet, Sir* (1994). While his report is not as analytical as Brussa's, De Stoop reveals numerous stories of women from the third world trafficked into Dutch, Belgian, and German prostitution markets. De Stoop describes how "waves" of women from different regions of the world entered into European prostitution markets. He states that "zero immigration" policies in Europe that required obligatory visas precipitated the first wave of women from Asian countries such as Thailand and the Philippines (De Stoop 1994, 103). De Stoop's fourth wave consists of women from Eastern Europe. Like Brussa, he does not distinguish the fourth wave as qualitatively or quantitatively different from previous waves.

The Brussa and De Stoop studies are examples of how the problem of sex trafficking was approached in political and journalistic discourse in the late 1980s and early 1990s. The studies are different from each other in terms of the style and scope of their projects, but they both regard the fourth wave of trafficking as a continuation of previous social, criminal, and economic dynamics as well as migratory patterns of formal and informal laborers. Thus, they do not treat the fourth wave as a qualitative break in the patterns of global north and global south trafficking. Both publications also indicate a growing European discussion on trafficking.[16] Clearly, individual countries like the Netherlands and Belgium took up the issue of foreign prostitution in domestic markets prior to 1989.

The Natasha Trade

In subtle and important ways, as the decade progressed, popular and political rhetoric began to emphasize the difference that the influx of postsocialist trafficking was making. The descriptive wave metaphor morphs into qualifications about the explosion of trafficking in women with the capitalist transformation of the formerly planned economies. The so-called fourth wave in trafficking was like a tsunami of women's bodies into the illicit market of forced prostitution. While there was a numeric increase in the number of women involved in irregular migration as a result of the opened borders of the former Eastern Bloc and USSR, I suggest that the changing quantitative character of sex trafficking implicitly supported heightened rhetoric about trafficking as primarily caused by criminal activities. Though the discourse links this explosion to the economic instability of the region, it is the rise of postsocialist criminals and corruption that is blamed for the onslaught of trafficking. With the categorization of a new wave in sex trafficking, rhetoric about trafficking shifts.

The beginnings of this shift are present in a 1995 IOM report on trafficking from Central and Eastern Europe.[17] This report was one of the first analyses of trafficking specifically in the former state socialist region and was referenced in key political documents that came after it.[18] For example, the IOM report was used by the UN special rapporteur on violence against women in her 1996 report on sex trafficking and forced prostitution (Coomeraswamy 1996). As before, the IOM report uses the wave metaphor to contextualize East-West trafficking (IOM 1995, 8). However, the wave metaphor has two different meanings in the report. At times the metaphor denotes the fact that Eastern European women have started to replace women from the developing world in European sex markets. But the wave metaphor also connotes a numeric understanding of trafficking, and thus a qualitatively different approach to antitrafficking emerges.

The report begins by claiming that "the trafficking of women from East to West is increasing rapidly. This form of exploitation and abuse of human rights is no longer confined to women from developing countries" (IOM 1995, 3). The increase in women from the East is said to be about the presence of new ethnicities in European markets. The report explains that "trafficking in women from East to West is increasing because it is easier and cheaper for traffickers to bring women from Central and Eastern Europe than to recruit women from developing countries" (4). The change in residency permits and the close proximity of Eastern Europe are given as reasons why recruitment for sex trafficking shifted from the third to the second world. The data used in the report are based on 155 cases of women trafficked to the Netherlands in 1994. In contrast to the past, two-thirds of these women were from Central and Eastern Europe and only one-third from developing countries (3).

The report suggests that east-west trafficking is occurring at a disturbing albeit unknown rate: "trafficking in women from Central and Eastern European countries to Western Europe is increasing at an alarming rate" (IOM 1995, 3). However, the basis of this claim is the proportion of women from Central and Eastern Europe among the women serviced at the Foundation Against Trafficking in Women, a Dutch antitrafficking NGO. No additional data are provided to suggest that the Foundation was providing services to an overall number of women that had increased from previous years. While the limitations of the data are openly disclosed in the report, the report was nevertheless used and referenced later in governmental and intergovernmental studies of trafficking to suggest a quantitative crisis.[19] The uncertainty surrounding the actual numbers of trafficking victims did not inhibit the ensuing focus on magnitude as a qualitative dimension of postsocialist trafficking. In fact, the IOM report and most of the proceeding policy documents rely heavily on unreliable numeric accounts of trafficking.[20] As I described in the previous section, states did not comply with the 1949 UN Convention on the Traffic in Persons and the Exploitation of the Prostitution of Others by submitting annual reports. In the early 1990s most countries were still not collecting data on trafficking, so early estimates on the prevalence of trafficking was dependent on self-reporting, as with the data obtained from the Foundation Against Trafficking in Women.[21]

Data collection on rates of trafficking can only serve as an estimate of an economy that is circumscribed by the definition of trafficking used and the ability to collect a meaningful accounting of it. For example, criticism of the inconsistency and confusion over trafficking data led to a UNESCO project to compare the methods and findings of trafficking estimates (UNESCO 2004). The comparison sheet looked at how the United States, the ILO, UNICEF, the UN Development Fund for Women, the UN High Commissioner for Refugees, and the IOM collected data. Remarkably, the range of estimates for global trafficking was between 500,000 (the lowest estimate provided by the UN Development Fund for Women) and 2.5 million (the highest estimate provided by the UN High Commissioner for Refugees). Even as late as 2008, significant imprecision remained in the estimates of the extent of trafficking. And yet the prefaces of many studies and reports on trafficking begin with a claim about the extent of the problem—as if the quantitative measurement of the issue is an indication of the extent of society's ethical obligation to combat it. While a quantitative understanding of trafficking is an important pursuit for policy-making and social advocacy efforts, the tendency to rhetorically wield a quantitative image of trafficking after the collapse of the USSR has played into certain understandings of the problem of trafficking and thus influenced responses to it.

Importantly, the tendency to assume the magnitude of trafficking fed into the overemphasizing of the criminal dimension of trafficking.[22] The IOM report notes that the economic transition to market economies in Central and Eastern Europe created job losses and an increase in poverty. With strict limits on legal migration, "many women are forced to accept the services of traffickers if they wish to migrate" (IOM 1995, 10). However, the contextualization of prostitution as part of the global economy that was evident in the 1991 Brussa report is largely absent. Instead, there is a new emphasis on the role of criminal groups from Eastern Europe who are "highly organized, extremely violent, and often involved in other criminal activities, such as drug smuggling" (10). The report further states that Western European brothel keepers "find themselves under increasing pressure from organized gangs in CEEC [Central and Eastern European Countries] to hire Eastern European women" (10–11). Problematically, the report does not contextualize these new criminals within the broader political or economic context of transition. Nor is there reference to the "sex industry multinationals" described in the Brussa report.[23] The IOM document, rather, invokes the term "traffickers" to identify the myriad agents who procure, transfer, pimp, and employ women. The more economic rhetoric of "sex industry multinationals" is replaced with the term "traffickers," which operates as a prosecutorial category.

The context of confusion and hyperbole about the magnitude of trafficking existed alongside sensationalized media representations of sex trafficking that generated a kind of hysteria over the trafficking of post-Soviet women (Pickup 1998; Radulescu 2004). In particular, news reports picked up on the violent and dramatic aspects of a complicated political and economic situation developing after 1989. The centerpiece of that drama was the postsocialist female victim. The "Natasha" victim was presented as innocent and duped by traffickers. Newspaper titles such as "Ex-Soviets Fall Prey to Sex Trade," "East European Women Tricked into Sex Trade in West," "East Europeans Duped into West's Sex Trade," and "Traffickers' New Cargo: Naïve Slavic Women" illustrate an emphasis on a particular trafficking scenario. "Natasha" is a sexually innocent victim of failed governments that cannot adequately protect their citizens: Natashas are the "lost girls" of failed democratization.[24]

This image of "Natasha" fit in with preexisting western characterizations of the Soviet Union. Soviet state socialism was presented in American Cold War culture as repressed and ignorant of life on the other side of the Wall. Ultimately, this cultural envisioning of the USSR would provide an explanation of why women were vulnerable to trafficking once the Wall came down. For example, in a 1990 ABC News *Nightline* report "Sex in the Soviet Union," the supposed ignorance and excess of late Soviet sexual practices are showcased.[25] We see a Soviet woman so oblivious to her sexuality that she does not know about her newest pregnancy until the baby starts to kick in her womb. We also see women burdened by "newfound" sexual freedoms that they are unable to manage. The planned economy has ensured that "wholesome sex, like so many other commodities, is in short supply in the Soviet Union" (Goodman 1990). Soviet women are ignorant of even "wholesome sex," and this has made them the perfect prey for traffickers.

The image of sexuality in the Soviet system in these news pieces presented a gendered and racialized view of "Slavic" women through which sex trafficking was understood.[26] The Russian female prostitute was made culturally unique because she challenged the (problematic) assumption that a lack of education is the cause of women's participation in sexual labor. Unlike the negative racialization of women in the global south who work in brothel prostitution or sex tourism, Russia (and Eastern European) women were positively racialized as educated. Thus, postsocialist women who engaged in prostitution were distinguished by their beauty and smarts (despite being sexually naïve) and not marked as "uncivilized." In contrast to the image of women in the global south, the image of "Eastern girls" did not incite the kinds of racial fears often associated with first/third world racial politics (Penttinen 2008).[27] However, the perceived whiteness or racially unthreatening category of Eastern European women also carried an "othering" based on criminality. The wave of Eastern European women into the West signaled the infiltration of chaos and criminality.

Take for example a U.S. news article from the 1990s that explained: "Many of the young women haunting hotel bars today have attended college and speak English. But the Soviet system doesn't pay doctors and university professors enough to live on" (Hamilton 1991). By this depiction and the interviews in the article, Russian women are elevated above the typically classed stereotypes of sex workers. It is the miserable Russian state and criminal traffickers that are at fault for subjecting even doctors and university professors to "the only thing they have for which there is always a steady demand" (Hamilton 1991). Ironically, there is no recognition that it was the Soviet model of gender equality that educated women in such fields as medicine and science—something the West is still struggling with. Rather, the women are represented as victims and given no credit for the way they are negotiating their gendered and economic conditions.

This envisioning of Russian women was also produced in an intersecting and parallel discourse on mail-order brides in the 1990s (Johnson 2007; Taraban 2007). According to Erika Johnson, foreign women searching for romance online are often presented in a pejorative way as victims or gold diggers. Her ethnographic work aims to counter those representations to give the quite heterogeneous group of women who are labeled "Russian mail-order brides" agency in their own activities. This is not to say that hardship and even possible violence are not happening within this industry. Rather, the blanket envisioning of "Slavic" women as beautiful, smart, and tragic flattens out the complex terrain in which they exist. This lack of nuance is evident in how news reporting on trafficking often conflates categories of women, grouping the mail-order bride, sex worker, and trafficking victim together (Hughes and Denisova 2002; Osipovich 2004; Taraban 2007). This conflation perpetuates an emphasis on victimization and violence against women at the expense of understanding the complex, precarious economic conditions these women are negotiating and even succeeding in.[28]

The romanticized view of the Russian prostitute, and consequently victim of trafficking, is repeated throughout the U.S. congressional hearings on trafficking that I discuss later in this chapter. It is this image of the trafficking victim that facilitates a simplified distinction between victims of trafficking and other victims of the exploitation that attends illegal migration. But it was not just the reception of the women that shaped the image of the Natasha victim of trafficking. The female victims were coupled with their male perpetrators (Williams 2011). Here, criminality was highlighted as endemic to post-Soviet Russian culture. Representations of Eastern European mafia and innocent female victims were popularized in the 1990s and persisted over time, as in the films *Eastern Promises* (2007) and *Lilja 4-Ever* (2002) as well as in nonfiction, for example Victor Malarek's book *The Natashas* (2004). These accounts mirrored the tendency in documentary works to emphasize the criminal and most extreme cases (Suchland 2013).

For example, one of the first documentaries on sex trafficking from the former Eastern Bloc was researched and produced by the Global Survival Network. In many ways, the production, *Bought and Sold* (1997), is commendable for revealing the troubling dynamics of east-west trafficking. For example, the documentary shows how in the postsocialist context of business entrepreneurship, a range of false agencies operated as the conveyer belt for women seeking work and experiences outside their homelands. It also presents the commodification of women and sexualized femininity in postsocialist capitalism. At the same time, this documentary emphasizes the innocence of women who end up in forced sex work abroad. This is not to say that women were not tricked but that an emphasis on this example (and dimension) has oversimplified the general picture of trafficking. The documentary does not reflect on the fact that many women were taking advantage of a new entrepreneurial spirit or even a desire to travel across formerly closed borders. Such dimensions are no less important to analyze because women's strategies and migration practices are part of the globalizing of state socialist economies and not just about criminal behavior (Keough 2006).

This emphasis on unequivocal force and sexual bondage veils the underlying economic dimensions as well as the fluidity that exists between consent and force in human trafficking and exploitative labor. The Global Survival Network's representation of egregious cases of sex trafficking may be more helpful in currying popular and political concern, but there are negative consequences to this strategy. Namely, an overemphasis on the extreme skews an accurate understanding of the problem and sets an extremely high bar for claiming "victim" status.[29] The focus on unambiguous cases of forced prostitution remains a part of the contemporary media discourse on trafficking today.[30]

Representations of extreme cases of trafficking often rely on the criminal dimension of trafficking over the precarious labor strategies women engage in order to negotiate their economic conditions (Sassen 2000). This linking of the extreme with the criminal—and thus marking trafficking as an aberration— is illustrated in the case of the highly publicized murders that took place in a Frankfurt brothel in 1994. Tragically, four sex workers and two owners of an elite brothel in Frankfurt were found murdered, strangled with hair dryer cables. Police suggested that the killings were mafia related and potentially the result of unwanted competition, though that was never proven (Crawshaw 1994).[31] This case was indeed tragic, but it also illustrated the common way that trafficking was understood in the popular press and within policy circles in the 1990s. The chaos that ensued across the former Eastern Bloc and Soviet

Union after 1989–1991 was profound. But the criminal behaviors and seeming lawlessness were decontextualized from their historical and cultural contexts.

I provide some of that contextualization in chapter 4, but it is helpful here to highlight the specific problem of singularly focusing on mafia criminality amid what was culturally understood as *bespredel*—a Russian word that means lawlessness and people acting beyond the limits of acceptability. The profound transformations that followed post-Soviet capitalization took place without a basic "social contract" in place or blueprint for transition (Oushakine 2009, 20; see also Burawoy 2002; Andor and Summers 1998; and Lovell 2006). As Olga Shevchenko elegantly explains, the multiple shifts, uncertainties, and hardships that Russian citizens experienced invoked an overall sense of *bespredel*, *krizis* (crisis), or *katastrofa* (catastrophe) (Shevchenko 2009).[32] The "violent entrepreneurs" and private security services that emerged in the 1990s were both a part of and produced by state-led lawlessness as well as "shock therapy" privatization (Volkov 2002). Thus, to see the Russian mafia as a distinct (singular) problem of/in postsocialist transition ignores the sanctioned policies of the Yeltsin government.[33] Trafficking victims were not just managed by the mafia but by the devastating neoliberal policies of transition.

Another important dimension of this history is the long-standing role of the informal economy and informal practices that had been commonplace under state socialism. The informal economy was particularly relevant in an economy of scarcity, as friends, neighbors, coworkers, and even strangers exchanged goods and services under the table. In Russian, the term *na leva* (on the left) is a euphemism for such informal exchange of what is known as *blat* (favors). *Blat* was a vibrant economy of favors and continues to thrive in the post-Soviet context, albeit transformed by the introduction of capital (Oushakine 2009; Ledeneva 2006; Verdery 1996). Most of this widespread "cheating" was viewed in a positive light and was associated with being clever and even ethical. The idea that someone would use a contact to find a job or to obtain travel papers or to trade services to get ahead was entirely the norm in the USSR. The fact that informal practices were, in many ways, the norm challenges the idea that Natashas were always innocent victims who got caught in a separate criminal world. The women who sought employment abroad or sideways methods for migration were part of a sizable population of "dispossessed" who were shuttling and migrating for economic opportunities (Humphrey 2002).[34] While traffickers are indeed criminal, the prioritization of an unambiguous criminalizing language to frame postsocialist trafficking discounted the adaptive strategies people used during and after state socialism. The varied survival strategies they had used during the state socialist period were deployed as survival strategies during economic transition. In many cases (as it was in Russia) a proper legal apparatus to mediate the capitalist economy was absent. Thus, illegal behavior and practices of survival intersected in complex ways.

For instance, in some cases the existence of bandits (*bandity*) as well as other informal practices are due to a lack of proper official protection (Ledeneva 2006). The common Russian business practice of requiring/finding a "roof" (*krysha*) emerged because there was no one else to "cover" local sellers or businesses from illegal competitive practices and cheating (Reis 2002). As I have mentioned, there was practically no regulatory system in place when privatization was undertaken. In that vacuum, entrepreneurs filled the space with private security services. Rather than being in competition with or hiding from the police, they often work in plain sight. This dynamic is detailed by an informant in an interview with anthropologist Nancy Reis. The bandit explains: "The police know us. They know all the *bandiugi* [affectionate diminutive of *bandity*] in town, who works for whom, whom we protect. They know everything. And they rely on us to provide order which they themselves can't; they don't have the resources. There would just be chaos if not for us, because the businessmen are incapable of running their affairs in an orderly way" (Reis 2002, 281). In this depiction, it is clear that the mafia or bandits are part of a complex social context. Thus, an emphasis on the mafia as a deviation from a legal norm is highly problematic when taking Soviet history and transition into consideration. In addition, the blanket category of *mafia* is simply too general for the quite diverse group of individuals who are often labeled by it, such as new capitalists, private security services, and (trans)national gangs (see Castells 2000).

Yet the chaos that ensued in Russia after 1991 was attributed to criminal behaviors understood as a deviation from an expected legal norm. Certainly the failure of Boris Yeltsin's leadership contributed to the lawlessness of privatization (as well as a botched war in Chechnya). The near complete lack of a legal apparatus to justly divest state assets has had a long-standing impact on the economic and political scene in Russia in particular (Sakwa 2014). But there was little attempt to interpret the complexity of the context, let alone to see the culpability of western advisors for that chaos (Wedel 2001). A continued Cold War suspicion (and western triumphalism) depicted the Russian mafia as vicious and operating with "chess master" brilliance, two abused tropes of Slavic culture.[35] These judgments, held by politicians and represented in popular media, produced the "myth of the Russian mafia that fits with a longstanding demonic image of Russia itself" (Finckenauer 2001, 166; see Rutland and Kogan 1998).

This image of the Russian mafia was then presented as a looming threat for global law and order. As the John Kerry quote that opens this chapter illustrates, the end of the Cold War ushered in a new global threat—not communism but transnational crime. This view represented the opinions of many American foreign policy experts, like Senator Kerry, until the terrorist attacks of September 11, 2001. The American political concern for postsocialist criminal behavior more than the social tragedy of transition was especially perverse in the context of the 1998 economic crisis. Congressional hearings on U.S. policy toward Russia reveal this bias (Williams 2011). In Kimberly Williams's analysis of congressional hearings between 1994 and 1999, she finds that politicians presented the United States as an innocent bystander to the shortcomings of Russia's economic transition. After a 1999 scandal in which the U.S. news media exposed that Russian government officials had illegally diverted foreign aid through the Bank of New York for personal use, "congressional hearings focused explicitly on crime and corruption in Russia and how the United States should move forward in the wake of its apparently failed Russia policy" (7). The so-called failure of U.S. policy consolidated the belief that Russian crime and corruption was culturally endemic.[36]

Ultimately this overemphasis on Russian mafia criminality shaped how trafficking was understood.[37] Given the kind of discourse on postsocialist crime and corruption in the congressional hearings, there was no alternative lens for interpreting the "fourth wave" of trafficking.[38] Examples of random violence and illicit activities became the focus of how trafficking was understood, despite the reality that economic transition had precipitated the everyday violence of loss of income, employment, and social security.

Reforming Antitrafficking Law after the Cold War—The U.S. Scene

The production of the Natasha discourse that linked trafficking to the menace of transnational organized crime, especially the "red mafia," spurred high-level negotiations on developing a post–Cold War antitrafficking standard and evolved through them. In the United States, the perceived explosion in postsocialist sex trafficking propelled a political response that prioritized a concern for combating criminal activities. This section analyzes how the specter of postsocialist sex trafficking informed the creation of U.S. antitrafficking law. The U.S. TVPA was passed in 2000. In addition to generating a domestic antitrafficking industry (including NGOs and government bureaucracy), the TVPA shaped the UN Optional Protocol to Prevent, Suppress and Punish Trafficking in Persons, Especially Women and Children (2000). While the economic transitions in former state socialist countries were often referenced as part of a generic context for sex trafficking, those transitions and their relationship to globalization were not part of the politically contentious evolution of antitrafficking norms. In the consolidation of post–Cold War priorities, sex trafficking was not linked to problematic economic policies, a connection that some had argued for with respect to sex tourism in Southeast Asia. Ironically, at the very moment when an economic analysis was desperately warranted, there was a turn to valorizing national security and the criminalization of trafficking. This was achieved through the politicization of trafficking by U.S. and European policy-makers and supported by a feminist discourse of "violence against women."

The 1993 Declaration on the Elimination of Violence Against Women and the 1995 Beijing Platform for Action called for greater attention to sex trafficking as forced prostitution and thus an example of violence against women. In response to these documents and the efforts of those who promoted them, governments and intergovernmental agencies gradually took on the issue of trafficking as central to their work. In the wake of the Beijing conference, U.S. president Bill Clinton established the Interagency Council on Women in 1995. Led by Theresa Loar, the Council included a working group on trafficking that was led by Anita Botti. With NGOs including the Global Survivor Network and the Russian group Syostri (Sisters), Botti was part of the 1997 Moscow Conference on Trafficking. Botti also was a key witness in June 1999 at the U.S. congressional hearing on sex trafficking. Beyond the Interagency Council on Women, President Clinton assigned Stephan Warnath to the position of special counsel and senior advisor on trafficking. Among his many activities, Warnath presented comments at the U.S.-EU Transatlantic Seminar to Prevent Trafficking in Women that was held in Ukraine in July 1998. These efforts indicate the growth in official U.S. government engagement with the issue of sex trafficking in the late 1990s.

President Clinton presented strong language about the role of the U.S. government in fighting trafficking. In his 1996 speech on Human Rights Day, President Clinton indicated a need to "strengthen our commitment to stop the trafficking of women and children for prostitution and child labor" (Clinton 1996). Then, in a memorandum titled "Steps to Combat Violence Against Women and Trafficking in Women and Girls," in 1998 President Clinton presented his most comprehensive vision for stepping up U.S. efforts against trafficking (Clinton 1998). He asked the Interagency Council on Women and the U.S. attorney general to enact various steps to improve the prevention of trafficking, the protection of victims of trafficking, and the prosecution of traffickers. Thus the 3 PS were born. This memorandum marks the beginning of the U.S. government's involvement in crafting post–Cold War antitrafficking norms. As the title of his memorandum states, the link between "violence against women" and trafficking was instrumental to how political responses evolved.

Within the U.S. Congress there was growing political discussion of sex trafficking as well. Just prior to President Clinton's memorandum, and marking International Women's Day, senators Paul Wellstone and Dianne Feinstein submitted Concurrent Resolution 82, "Related to a Violation of Fundamental Human Rights," on March 10, 1998 (Congressional Record S1702). The political context of this resolution was the growing exposure of trafficking cases in the United States. One in particular, the Cadena case, involved two teenaged Mexican girls who aided the FBI in a raid of brothels where immigrants worked in debt bondage. Additional horrifying examples of debt bondage and human smuggling gained greater representation in the media (DeStefano 2008, 4–5). Then, in 1997, there was the exposure of enslaved Russian and Ukrainian women working in massage parlors a stone's throw from the halls of Congress. The raid on the massage parlor revealed the fact that the United States was a part of post-Soviet trafficking. It also exposed how victims of trafficking were cruelly treated when the women were simply deported after the raid. It was this case of post-Soviet women trafficked into the United States that motivated Senator Paul Wellstone to act (DeStefano 2008).

Wellstone's resolution was commendable for advancing the antitrafficking cause in the U.S. Congress. At the same time, his speech relied on a particular experience of trafficking that ultimately limited a critical economic analysis. Given the growing exposure of different forms of trafficking in the 1990s in the United States, it is important to note that the text of the resolution overwhelmingly responds to the trafficking of women from the former Soviet Union.[39] And it is this type of victim that facilitates a particular imagining of what trafficking entails. The Natasha is a morally unambiguous victim of trafficking who is caught by the tentacles of organized criminal groups. This image of the trafficking victim fuels the rhetorical power of Wellstone's passionate Senate speech and his request for greater government antitrafficking efforts. Wellstone declares: "This resolution will effectively put Congress on record as opposing trafficking for forced prostitution and domestic servitude, and acting to check it before the lives of more women and girls are shattered" (Congressional Record S1702). He begins his remarks by noting that sex trafficking is "one of the fastest growing international trafficking businesses" and that "every year, the trafficking of human beings for the sex trade affects hundreds of thousands of women throughout the world." He references the IOM claim that as many as 500,000 women are annually trafficked into Western Europe. The victims of trafficking are "women and girls seeking a better life, a good marriage, or a lucrative job abroad. Most of these women never imagined that they would enter such a hellish world, having traveled abroad to find better jobs or to see the world. Many in their naiveté, believed that nothing bad could happen to them in the rich and comfortable countries" (Congressional Record S1702).

The post-Soviet woman is presented as an entrepreneur of happiness, in search of a better life. She is naïve and hopeful. Thus, women who are trafficked have made ill-informed choices. While their intensions are pure, "to seek a better life, a good marriage, or a lucrative job," their naiveté entraps them in a sinister world.

The emphasis on innocent and ill-informed victims informs the core strategy of trafficking "prevention." This strategy relies on a calculus for identifying potential victims and then targeting them for public awareness campaigns. By targeting potential victims rather than structures, labor is decontextualized. When prevention programs target individual actors there is an assumption that their choices produce the problem. The conditions of formal and informal labor dissolve into the background. This was certainly the case with regard to women from the former Eastern Bloc (see chapter 4). The irony of western involvement in the postsocialist world in the early post–Cold War period is startling. Simultaneously, one set of western experts advised transitioning economies in structural adjustment programs while another set elevated the violence of those programs in the (economically) depoliticized language of sex trafficking.

The depoliticized dimension was illustrated in the June 1999 congressional hearing leading up to the passage of the TVPA. In particular, trafficking was made distinct from illegal immigration. Representative Christopher Smith, then chair of the Commission on Security and Cooperation in Europe, oversaw the hearing. The discussions of that day presented a variety of views about trafficking. Botti, from the president's Interagency Council on Women, presented testimony along with Steven Galster from Global Survival Network, Louise Shelley, director of the Center for the Study of Transnational Crime and Corruption, Laura Lederer, director of the Protection Project, and Wendy Young from the Women's Commission for Refugee Women and Children. The hearing is important because it was one of the first major U.S. government conversations on the issue of trafficking. While there is no single message to take from the hearing, there are themes that illustrate how trafficking was understood and what priorities were created as a result of that understanding.

Throughout the hearing there is confusion over the use of the terms "human trafficking," "sexual exploitation," "smuggling," and "slavery" by the different speakers. Representative Smith's usage was the least precise, as he did not distinguish between human and sex trafficking and forced labor. In his opening comments he states, "Trafficking in human beings is a form of modern-day slavery. When a woman or child is trafficked or sexually exploited by force, fraud, or coercion for commercial gain, she is denied the most basic human rights to liberty and security of person" (*The Sex Trade* 1999, 1). In the remainder of his introductory remarks, no other examples besides "sexual exploitation" or the "sex trade" are given for human trafficking. This suggests that human trafficking really only refers to sex trafficking, which indexes a specific victim.

Unlike an illegal immigrant, who knowingly tries to deceive by his or her passage over the border, a trafficking victim unknowingly enters a criminal world in her pursuit of legitimate work through legitimate channels. For example, Smith compares trafficked women with "illegal immigrants" when he laments that victims of trafficking are "deported as illegal immigrants, while their perpetrators rarely suffer repercussions for their actions" (*The Sex Trade* 1999, 1). In this comment and during discussions with Botti, Smith's language suggests that there is an important, although imprecisely articulated, distinction between innocent labor migrants who are trafficked and (culpable) "illegal migrants" who require deportation. The importance of this distinction is later revealed when Representative James Greenwood asks Botti about the legal status of the women trafficked into the United States. Greenwood inquires: "Well, for those 50,000 women and children who, according to your testimony, are brought into the United States, can you talk a little bit about what you know about how they arrive, to the extent that they are illegally brought across the border? Is that the predominance of it, or do they come in through Customs and Immigration using legitimate student visas or whatnot to come through?" Botti replies to Greenwood that "my understanding is that a majority do come in illegally" (*The Sex Trade* 1999, 11).

Her answer seems to ruffle Representative Smith, as he interrupts her statement to pursue this point: "This is new to me so I'm just trying to understand it. What we're talking about, I assume, is women conveyed in trucks or however across the border, believing that they are smuggling themselves in with the help of someone to the United States for some purpose and then find that, in fact, when they get here they are indentured in some way or trafficked?" This statement reflects the ongoing confusion about the difference between smuggling and trafficking. Botti attempts to clarify the confusion: "And I would like to qualify that most often they're not—they themselves are not seen as being smuggled. I think most of these women and children, or at least in the cases of women coming in, believe they're coming in to fulfill career opportunities, that they think they're coming in for bona fide jobs" (*The Sex Trade* 1999, 11).

At the end of the exchange between Botti, Greenwood, and Smith, there is no clear sense of what the difference between smuggling and trafficking is, given that no one has clarified the implicit statement that trafficking is based on legal entry. What we do see is a distinction in the type of work being done by different immigrants, with trafficking relating to so-called career employment (dancers, waitresses, nannies, teachers) such that trafficking victims are perceived to have never intended to deceive immigration by going "over the border." Implicitly, Botti then compares illegal immigrants to those who are trafficked: "This includes people who are clearly, in some cases, quite educated. So because of high unemployment, they are looking to find jobs" (*The Sex Trade* 1999, 11). This exchange about the legal status of trafficking victims illustrates how a certain racial understanding of trafficking informed the politicization of the issue in official discussions. Like the stories used in Representative Wellstone's speech, in the congressional hearing there is an emphasis on an innocent victim, someone who would have never deceived immigration regulations and who had respectable desires to earn a living. The seemingly white Slavic or Eastern European woman facilitates that distinction.

There is also an emphasis on forced prostitution as the primary outcome of trafficking. Throughout the testimonies and discussion there is a return to the example of sexual slavery or forced prostitution. Some participants pushed that trafficking included other forms of forced labor. For example, in Steven Galster's testimony he stated very clearly that "our investigations revealed that the victims of sexual trafficking, sweatshop labor, domestic servitude, and other forms of forced labor are all victims of the same kind of labor and human rights abuses" (*The Sex Trade* 1999, 13). He ends his testimony with six recommendations; one is to "recognize forced prostitution as a form of forced labor instead of treating it in a separate category" (*The Sex Trade* 1999, 16). Galster also challenged the idea that there was an unambiguous innocent victim of trafficking. Rather, he described four types of women and girls who are trafficked into the sex trade who range from fully aware to totally unaware of their destination. Importantly, Galster argues that all are victims of trafficking. However, Galster's more nuanced description of trafficking is not carried throughout the hearing. The overemphasis on the example of forced prostitution as the core issue of trafficking is reflected in the very title of the hearing, "The Sex Trade: Trafficking of Women and Children in Europe and the United States."

The hearing also reflects an emphasis on the post-Soviet trafficking victim. Part of that emphasis feeds into the marking of the trafficking victim as innocent. Her innocence is established by her status as "well educated," which is also a qualification that is racially distinguishable from that of "third world" women as economically disadvantaged. As with the exchange about the difference between illegal immigration and trafficking, the "well educated" trafficking victim is someone who is taken advantage of or duped. The emphasis on trafficking from the former state socialist region thus introduces an emphasis on the role of criminal groups in trafficking women into the sex trade.

On this point, Louise Shelley, considered an expert on transnational organized crime, testified in the hearing. Shelley explains that the presence of organized crime groups in the former Soviet Union makes it difficult to fight trafficking. This is because corrupt governments do not have an interest in fighting trafficking. She explained, "Law enforcement is not particularly motivated to address the problem of trafficking in women" (*The Sex Trade* 1999, 19). Shelley's voice was echoed by other researchers not at the hearing who emphasized the link between trafficking and crime, especially those concerned with an abolitionist or "violence against women" agenda (Hughes 2000 and Stoecker 2000, respectively).

Shelley provides an image of trafficking as endemic to the region and fueled by expansive criminal groups and corrupt governments. This image of trafficking as the result of criminal activities fits in with representations of the Russian mafia, which was the subject of separate congressional hearings in the 1990s.[40] The idea that trafficking is essentially a problem of organized crime produces an emphasis on law enforcement and prosecution as a response to trafficking. It also makes the failures of the former state socialist state the subtext of the discourse. Shelley provides credence to this subtext in her testimony.[41] The failure of the Russian government is made explicit in an earlier exchange between Representative Smith and Botti. In that discussion, Smith asks Botti to speak about a country that is "conspicuously absent" from multilateral and bilateral initiatives between the European Union, Ukraine, Finland, and the United States. That country is Russia.

The specific example/experience of trafficked women from the former Soviet Union shaped how other experiences of trafficking are understood. For example, in 2000 another hearing on "International Trafficking in Women and Children" was held before the U.S. Subcommittee on Near Eastern and South Asian Affairs (*International Trafficking in Women and Children* 2000). The scope of the two-day hearing was broader than that of 1999. Testimonies drew on examples of trafficking from around the world and not just the former Soviet region. There was also greater attention to the fact that forced prostitution was not the only form of trafficking or forced labor and that U.S. law should reflect that. At the same time, there was a common focus on forced prostitution and reference to combating prostitution as a separate and particularly egregious form of trafficking.

In particular the concept of trafficking was used to frame older practices such as sex tourism. Given the politicization of sex tourism in Southeast Asia in the 1980s, it would not be surprising to see the language from that discourse introduced to the trafficking language. Instead, the concept of trafficking is used to describe what previously was discussed as sex tourism or international sex industries. For example, Representative Frank Loy describes trafficking in Southeast Asia in this way: "It is reported that in some villages in parts of Southeast Asia there are few young women and girls left. Where have they gone? The answer is that agents for traffickers descend upon villages and harvest these children like a profitable crop to take to market—sometimes abducting them, and often luring and enticing them with tragically false promises, sometimes buying them from desperate parents—to sell into brothels or to force them to perform a wide range of labor and forms of servitude" (*International Trafficking in Women and Children* 2000, 10).

This statement mirrors the descriptions given of postsocialist victims of trafficking. The scenario relies on the portrayal of a criminal presence in underprivileged communities that traps innocent women and girls. The economic dimension of sex trafficking that was once a more prominent part of discussions of sex tourism and international sex trade is absent throughout the two-day hearing. Instead, there is common reference to poverty or economic duress as a general characteristic of where the women and girls are coming from. There is reference to terms such as "economic desperation," "economic distress," and "poverty" at the hearing, but there is no real contextualization of trafficking as a practice that is part of broad global trends or specific economic policies.

For U.S. law, the TVPA represented a clear advancement for combating trafficking and protecting the victims of trafficking. Specifically, trafficking victims are legally identified and provided special accommodations, such as extended stay in the United States with a T-visa. Traffickers are given harsher penalties, and the meaning of involuntary servitude is expanded to include servitude "induced by threat of serious harm or physical restraint; or abuse of the legal process."[42] The TVPA also illustrates some of the limitations of how trafficking is understood. As the congressional hearings reveal, there was an emphasis on exceptional cases of trafficking, and it was this emphasis that helped propel the legislative process. This language of exceptionalism is carried through in the TVPA as well.[43] While trafficking is recognized as a broad category, the TVPA is defined by specific concerns for "women and children" and for those trafficked into the "international sex trade." The category "women and children" is a subject the TVPA often refers to, stating that they predominantly are the victims of trafficking. This language of exceptionalism is further illustrated by the fact that the scope of the TVPA is limited to what are called "severe forms of trafficking in persons," which applies to sex trafficking and involuntary servitude for labor or services.[44] Each form requires that "force, fraud, or coercion" has been used against the victim, except when a minor has been forced to perform sex acts.[45] The language of "severe forms of trafficking" privileges specific concerns, which then define the meaning of trafficking writ large. That meaning is tied to an understanding of trafficking as an aberration.

The marking of trafficking as an aberration is also produced in the juxtaposition of trafficking with smuggling. By forcing a clear distinction between smuggling and trafficking there is a decoupling of development/macroeconomics from human trafficking. There is also a subtle racialization at play, wherein trafficking victims are "well educated" (i.e., white) victims of criminal activities, while those who are smuggled are legally suspect and marked as "illegal" (i.e., nonwhite). While this racialization plays out in different national contexts, in the U.S. the rise of "Eastern girls" facilitated the political (and at times racialized) distinction between trafficking and smuggling. This distinction also became solidified in the UN Convention against Organized Crime.

Reforming Antitrafficking Law after the Cold War—The UN Scene

While U.S. and UN decision-making on antitrafficking law occurred concurrently, the 2000 U.S. TVPA influenced the rewriting of antitrafficking doctrine at the UN. But the U.S. law was not the only influence on the UN decision-making process. There is an important internal history to the UN process as well. As in the case of President Clinton's initiatives on behalf of "violence against women," the evolution of UN antitrafficking doctrine was initially instigated by a concern for violence against women. By the early 1990s there was widespread talk of the need to revise the 1949 UN Convention for the Suppression of the Traffic in Persons and of the Exploitation of the Prostitution of Others. The process of crafting a post–Cold War antitrafficking convention was not self-evident, though. Women's rights advocates in the UN had already established trafficking as a form of "violence against women" in the 1993 Declaration on the Elimination of Violence Against Women. A revised or new antitrafficking convention would need to be orchestrated through one of the units of the UN. The CSW was not that unit, but it played an important role in why the Commission on Crime Prevention and Criminal Justice (CCPCJ) finally took it up.

The CCPCJ was established in 1992 to replace the Committee on Crime Prevention and Control in order to strengthen the program's operational capacity and advisory services ("New UN Crime Commission Meets in Vienna" 1992). The wider context for the creation of the CCPCJ was an increased concern for national and transnational crime. The first priority of the CCPCJ was to consult member states on the desirability of a convention on crime prevention and criminal justice. At that time, no single document contained international agreements on preventing and combating international crime. It is important to note that the issue of trafficking was not mentioned at the beginning of the negotiations that ultimately produced the 2000 UN Convention Against Transnational Organized Crime.

The inclusion of trafficking within the jurisdiction of the CCPCJ discussions was not initiated from within.[46] In the first framework for greater intergovernmental cooperation in the arena of transnational organized crime, the 1994 Naples Political Declaration and Global Action Plan against Transnational Organized Crime, there was no mention of trafficking or the 1949 UN Convention. Then in 1996 a resolution in the Economic and Social Council was passed that requested that the issue of "violence against women" be inserted into the workings of the CCPCJ. The resolution also requested a summary report for the sixth session of the CCPCJ in 1997. At this point, there was a lack of consensus about whether to move forward with a convention, particularly given that the Naples Declaration created little cohesion across the pertinent issue areas. The CCPCJ report for the 1997 session shows that lack of consensus to move forward on a convention (UN 1997).

The report also reflects how trafficking emerges in the discussions when the issue of "violence against women" is inserted. Per the request of the Economic and Social Council resolution, a draft document, "Practical Measures, Strategies, and Activities in the Field of Crime Prevention and Criminal Justice for the Elimination of Violence Against Women," was created in preparation for the 1997 CCPCJ session. In that draft document, trafficking was discussed because it had already been categorized as a form of "violence against women" in the Beijing Platform for Action. A particular focus was the protection of the needs and rights of victims of violence and the implementation of "gender mainstreaming" in the operations of the CCPCJ. It was noted in the UN secretary general's report on the CCPCJ session that some believed the draft document had not emphasized the issue of trafficking enough.[47]

By the time of the seventh session (1998) of the CCPCJ a "broad consensus on the desirability of a convention" had emerged (UN 1998). This turn of events is fairly remarkable given what seemed to be real resistance in previous meetings. The weight of particular countries, including Poland, Italy, and the United States, advanced negotiations toward a convention. Poland had submitted the first draft convention in 1996, which was the working draft used for the 2000 Convention Against Transnational Organized Crime. At the 1998 session it was decided also that there would be optional protocols linked to the convention—a strategy used in order to build consensus for the main convention. An ad hoc committee was created to decide the details for drafting an "international instrument addressing the traffic in women" (UN General Assembly Resolution No. 53/111, Traffic in Women and Girls, 1999).

I want to emphasize the fact that situating trafficking within transnational organized crime was not inevitable. At least within the UN, there had been other bureaucratic centers that had taken up the issue prior to 2000 and even before 1989. Concerns for development, forced labor, and macroeconomics all had conceptual ties to the issue prior to the Cold War. Yet the UN emphasizes the primacy of criminality and the legal and political significance of coercion in identifying victims. The Optional Protocol to Prevent, Suppress and Punish Trafficking in Persons, Especially Women and Children and the second optional Protocol against the Smuggling of Migrants by Land, Sea and Air are "supplements" to the UN Convention against Transnational Organized Crime. As such, their function is to further elaborate on practices of transnational organized crime. In both documents, the scope of the application of the protocol is limited to those offenses that are transnational in nature and involve an organized criminal group.[48] Furthermore, the Optional Protocols only bind states to adopt legislation that criminalizes trafficking and migrant smuggling. The language on protecting victims is very weak. As I mentioned earlier, the primacy of prosecution in antitrafficking laws has placed intense focus on the tension between a prosecutorial state and advocates for human rights. The creation of the 2002 UN Principles and Guidelines on Human Rights and Human Trafficking is a response to that tension. In addition, subsequent laws such as the 2005 Council of Europe Convention on Action against Trafficking in Human Beings and the 2011 EU Directive "on combating trafficking in human beings and protecting its victims" have responded to the weaknesses of the UN Optional Protocol to Prevent, Suppress and Punish Trafficking in Persons, Especially Women and Children and include greater provisions for victims of trafficking and broader definitions of trafficking that include domestic trafficking (Gallagher 2006).[49]

The UN Optional Protocol to Prevent, Suppress and Punish Trafficking in Persons, Especially Women and Children set a minimum standard on which newer legislation has been built. The advancements in victims' rights and the broadening of the definition of trafficking certainly are important. But the primacy of the criminal approach to antitrafficking remains. The UN Convention against Transnational Organized Crime and its optional protocols also established a problematic distinction between smuggling and trafficking that remains highly politicized today. The distinction between trafficking and smuggling was sharply made by creating two separate protocols (Gallagher 2001). The idea of consent is at the heart of the analytical distinction between trafficking and smuggling. Specifically, the Optional Protocol on trafficking defines the means of trafficking as the "threat or use of force or other forms of coercion, abduction, fraud, deception, abuse of power or position of vulnerability, giving or receiving payments of benefits to achieve the consent of a person, for the purpose of exploitation" (article 3[a]). The crime of trafficking produces a victim of trafficking. The crime of smuggling does *not* produce a victim of smuggling because the status of the subject of smuggling is assumed to be illegal. The Protocol against the Smuggling of Migrants by Land, Sea and Air is focused on the actors who smuggle migrants by "illegal entry." Article 5 states that "migrants shall not become liable to criminal prosecution under the Protocol." However, illegal entry by migrants already is articulated in national immigration laws. While the Protocol against the Smuggling of Migrants does not criminalize migrants for being smuggled, their illegal status (i.e., their consent to be smuggled) is the implicit subtext of the protocol.

In practice, the distinction between trafficking and smuggling is often unclear. The primacy of the criminal approach to antitrafficking continues to maintain this distinction despite the fact that the intersection of trafficking and smuggling may be more productive to embrace. For example, an underlying fear of getting caught as an illegal migrant compels some to not come forward as victims of trafficking. A more critical revisiting of the economic dimensions of migration (legal and otherwise) as well as a greater sensitivity to labor exploitation might have a positive impact on identifying victims of trafficking. Furthermore, the economic conditions of trafficking are intertwined with and

TABLE 2.1. Key Antitrafficking Documents and Post–Cold War Events

	Key Documents		*Key Events*
		1989	Fall of Berlin Wall
1991	Council of Europe Seminar on action against traffic in women and forced prostitution as violations of human rights and human dignity; Dutch NGO Foundation against Trafficking in Women (STV) initiates European network La Strada	1991	End of the USSR Yugoslav civil war begins
		1992	Treaty on European Union (Maastricht Treaty) signed
		1994	First former state socialist country (Poland) submits application for EU membership
1995	First International Organization for Migration report on trafficking in Eastern Europe (IOM 1995)	1995	Schengen Agreement creates Europe's borderless Schengen Area
1996	*Report of the Special Rapporteur on Violence Against Women, Its Causes and Consequences* (Coomeraswamy 1996)		
1997	International Conference "Trafficking of NIS [Newly Independent States] Women Abroad" held in Moscow; U.S.-EU Campaign to combat trafficking in women		
1998	Memorandum "Steps to Combat Violence Against Women and Trafficking in Women and Girls" issued by U.S. President Clinton	1998	Russian financial crisis
1999	U.S. Congressional meetings on trafficking		

Key Documents		Key Events
2000	U.S. Victims of Trafficking and Violence Protections Act; UN Optional Protocol to Prevent, Suppress, and Punish Trafficking in Persons, Especially Women and Children (goes into effect 2003)	2001 September 11 terrorist attacks in U.S.
2002	UN Principles and Guidelines on Human Rights and Human Trafficking; EU Framework Decision on combating trafficking in human beings	
2003	Organization for Security and Cooperation in Europe OSCE Action Plan to Combat Trafficking in Human Beings	
2005	Council of Europe Convention on Action against Trafficking in Human Beings	
2010	European Commission appoints an EU antitrafficking coordinator	
2011	EU Directive on preventing and combating trafficking in human beings and protecting its victims	

at times indistinguishable from those of smuggling. In some cases, one person has the experience of both smuggling and trafficking.

In addition to the primacy of an anticrime approach, the decision-making process for the UN Trafficking Protocol displayed the conceptual narrowing of antitrafficking advocacy. As in the debates leading up to the U.S. TVPA, sex trafficking is portrayed as an exceptional case. In the UN Trafficking Protocol sex trafficking is distinguished from human trafficking, with "women and children" receiving particular rhetorical attention. The obvious assumption is that sex trafficking is female trafficking, though there is nothing that precludes women from being identified as victims of labor trafficking. This exceptionalism is present in the full title of the protocol: Protocol to Prevent, Suppress and Punish Trafficking in Persons, Especially Women and Children. The source of this language conceptually links back to the politicization of "violence against women." When trafficking became framed by "violence against women" the issue of consent remained central to identifying victims and shaped how feminists engaged the issue. In particular, competing feminist positions rallied their forces during the process of drafting the UN Trafficking Protocol. These positions coalesced into groups that recognized consent as possible in prostitution and those that did not (Chew 2005; Ditmore 2005; Warren 2012). Thus, the prostitution debate remained central to the evolution of antitrafficking legislation and circumscribed alternative feminist approaches.

Abolitionist groups pushed for strong antiprostitution language, while opposing groups pushed for language that would protect the right to sex work. The pressures from these two groups maintained an emphasis on the prosecutorial framework for trafficking, each emphasizing its claim to the legal apparatus. Even for those who might have had a more critical economic voice to lend, the terms of the debate were circumscribed by the intense focus on the status of sexual consent within a prosecutorial vision of the state's response to trafficking.[50] In fixating on the politics of consent, the issue of the agency of individual (potential) victims overshadowed any possible questioning of the broader social and economic context of migrant labor, sexual labor, or exploitative labor. While the emergence of the Natasha discourse linked trafficking to criminal behavior, feminists had reclaimed the issue of trafficking on nearly the same terms.

Part II. Postsocialist

In the first two chapters I traced the convergence of the movements against gender violence and the politicization of postsocialist trafficking—two forces that have made sex trafficking visible as a social problem. I looked in particular at processes occurring in the UN, Europe, and the United States. In chapters 3 and 4, I expand the genealogy to include an examination of the experiences and locations of postsocialism in the production of the concept of trafficking as a carceral problem and aberration. My central claim remains the same— that there has been a turn away from an economic approach to violence. Yet this shift was not orchestrated by and then imposed by the West. The reemergence of human trafficking as a global aberration was made possible by a bricolage of sociopolitical forces. Specifically, I am concerned with how social forces and shifts in the former second world contributed to the making of human trafficking discourse. I certainly cannot adequately render the diverse range of experiences within the region, and I am aware of the danger of overgeneralization (particularly from the example of Russia). At the same time, it is necessary to take up postsocialism as an actor in, and not just receiver of, global forces. To do so, I consider the role of metageography—or the mapping of concepts and temporalities onto geographic spaces (Harrington 2011; Martin and Wigen 1997). While the Cold War was transnational—ideas, commodities, and people crossed the ideological borders rhetorically referred to as the Iron Curtain—metageography played a role in the development of political discourse and foreign policy and continues to inform them well after the Cold War.

To undertake an investigation of metageography, I articulate second world experiences through two registers important to the genealogy of human trafficking discourse: global women's rights (chapter 3) and postsocialist transition (chapter 4). In chapter 3 I reevaluate the dominant periodization for global women's rights that is tied to the UN to reveal an ongoing allochronism at work. That is, the UN periodization sets up a normative temporality for women's rights, not unlike the western/American feminist waves metaphor (Hewitt 2010; Thompson 2002). The dominant temporality for global women's rights—as it is associated with the United Nations—conspicuously displaces the second world despite its presence in "the global" (Roman 2006; Suchland 2011). This displacement was most visible in the early postsocialist period, when criticisms emerged claiming that Eastern European women were "backward, apolitical, full of apathy" (Slavova 2006, 248). Such evaluations assumed that global women's rights were evolving in what Benedict Anderson refers to, in reference to nationalism, as "homogenous empty time"—time that is simultaneously shared if not fully comprehended by all involved (Anderson 1991). Thus, the assumed temporality of global women's rights can carry assumptions about women's activism and feminism under state socialism and expectations about what postsocialist feminism should look like. We can see this allochronism in critiques of women's activism and feminism in the former Socialist bloc for being "slow to emerge," "absent," or "not in sync" (see Einhorn 2006; Holmgren 1995; and Regulska and Grabowska 2012 for analyses of this tendency).

The presumption of this feminist homogenous empty time creates two types of problems. First, experiences that do not line up with the dominant periodization of how women's rights have evolved seem to suffer from a temporal lag—always referred to in terms of a "neutral" periodization rather than evaluated from within the contexts and genealogies where they exist. The blind spot here is not seeing those contexts and genealogies for their own importance and privileging a metabarometer instead. For example, are there no other ways to interpret the Russian feminist punk group Pussy Riot or the Ukrainian collective Femen than to simply claim them as (finally!) "third wave" feminists? Part of the work of this chapter is to conceptualize an alternative genealogy for Russian feminism (as an example of a postsocialist positionality), not as a hermetically sealed experience, but as one that may operate with alternative temporal markers. This genealogy is important for understanding the unique opportunities and constraints opened up by postsocialism for feminists, as well as the ironies presented by the politicization of sex trafficking in post-Soviet Russia and the wider postsocialist region.

There is a second flaw in feminist homogenous empty time, which is only now visible in the current post–Cold War period. That is, we often do not see how women's rights norms at the UN evolved *because* of particular tensions and investments that stemmed from the three-worlds architecture of the Cold War. The productiveness of the east/west divide gets displaced by the idea of a competitive and ultimately triumphalist narrative of liberal democracy's victory over state socialism. There is, thus, a tendency to not see the role and achievements of state socialism in the evolution of global women's rights (de Haan 2010; Ghodsee 2012; Rothchild 2012). This displacement has distanced contemporary postsocialist feminists from the metanarrative of how global women's rights evolved, particularly in the 1990s. The positioning of state socialism within the periodization of women's rights at the UN presented a particular challenge for Russian and other postsocialist women's groups once the Cold War ended. For example, at the 1995 Beijing conference—the historical high point in global women's rights temporality—many postsocialist representatives felt left out and declared that the second world was treated as a "nonregion" at the meeting (Nowicka 1995).

The "nonregion" statement illustrates the complicated terrain of post–Cold War feminist advocacy. This terrain both enabled and circumscribed the evolution of women's rights discourse within the region. We can see this clearly in the context of politicizing violence against women. In the early 1990s, as I have shown, the global women's rights concept of "violence against women" enabled the recognition of sex trafficking and politicized a range of women's issues. While advocacy work against gender violence in the postsocialist region emerged from indigenous concerns for challenging pernicious cultural/gender norms, there was also at times a tension between the global advocacy category of "violence against women" that carried legitimacy and funding opportunities and the burgeoning postsocialist feminist formulations of violence against women within their contexts (Fábián 2014; Hemment 2004; Johnson 2009). Challenging violence against women is an important project in the postsocialist region. It is also important to reflect on the fact that the discursive shift toward the language of "violence against women" occurred prior to and simultaneously with the end of state socialism. Representatives from state socialist countries took part in the Cold War–era UN process, but that engagement did not reflect what was to become the postsocialist condition.[1]

Rather than a "nonregion," the (former) second world played a globally vital role in the advancement of neoliberalism. In chapter 4, I explore how capitalist transition aided in that process. The discourse of transition resuscitated the ethos of development without conveying the controversial and long-politicized debates circulating in the global south. The maintenance of development in the name of transition depoliticized neoliberalism at a crucial time and place—at the ideological death of the Soviet alternative to western capitalism. The dismantling of socialist systems in the USSR and Eastern Bloc was presented as a short-term project, a simple discarding of an apparatus assumed to be disdained by all. What is less known is how the concept of transition predated 1989. It was a term that referred to refining a hybrid economic model combining the planned and market economic models. The possibility for hybrid models, for comparative economics, was squelched in the 1990s as the term "transition" came to only define the adoption of some version of neoliberal capitalism. In this context of transition, the fourth wave of trafficking crashed onto the shores of Western Europe. But this wave was not viewed as more evidence of precarious labor, problematic migration laws, and decimated social welfare programs. It was viewed as a pathology of postsocialism.

3 / SECOND WORLD/SECOND SEX / ALTERNATIVE GENEALOGIES IN FEMINIST HOMOGENOUS EMPTY TIME

By the time of the UN Decade for Women, state socialist countries presented women's equality as always already there.[1] Indeed, state socialist feminist organizations were instrumental in initiating global discourse on women's rights during the Cold War. For example, the Women's International Democratic Federation is credited with spearheading International Women's Year, which was the launching site for the Decade for Women (de Haan 2010, 548).[2] Kristen Ghodsee also shows that the Bulgarian state socialist feminist organization was an important force during the UN Decade for Women (Ghodsee 2012). Yet, by the end of the Cold War, there was little if any critique of "really existing socialism" at the level of the UN, a situation that in turn produced an important silence within dominant UN discourses as well as within many state socialist states.[3]

The sequencing of the end of the Cold War and the triumph of the global women's rights agenda in the early 1990s meant that UN doctrine would need to pause/adjust in order to encapsulate all of the realities faced by women in former state socialist countries. This unfortunate sequencing was indeed a fluke of history; women's rights doctrine built during the UN Decade for Women was created with the assumption that state socialist states would be represented. But in fact those regimes fell, and a more complex picture of both state socialist gender equality and postsocialist neotraditionalism emerged. Having experienced state socialism (and many of the benefits of it) as well as a nascent market system, the perspectives coming out of the former second world in the early and mid-1990s could not have been possible during the UN Decade for Women.

The tension I want to highlight is that there seemed to be no time or discursive space to allow for the insertion of those newly emerging positions. The 1995 Beijing conference was viewed as the culmination of decades of work and not as the first post–Cold War meeting in which *new* perspectives would alter the momentum that had been generated during the Cold War. The assumption that there were no new voices to integrate/translate into global women's rights discourse stems in part from how metageography worked to categorize regions. For example, there was the common proclamation that the former East was simply joining the West—a return to Europe. There was sufficient rhetoric coming from some leaders in Central and Eastern Europe to support the idea that the end of state socialism meant the return of the lost members of "western civilization." The powerful "end of history" idea also presumed that former Soviet citizens would be happy participants in the dismantling of their political and economic systems—their experiences in transition would speak to the technique of making democratic capitalism rather than presenting unique socioeconomic ideological subject positions.

In addition to the role of metageography, there was an uneven if disjointed connection between socialist women's state-structured connection to the UN system and the newly emerging independent groups who had no experience with the UN process. The state socialist apparatus had supported women's participation in the UN system as representatives, but when those regimes ceased to exist in 1989–1991 that platform was dismantled by processes of democratization. Whether and how the "old" feminist actors would be a part of the new democratic system was an open question. Furthermore, new actors, including autonomous women's groups, had virtually no experience with the UN system. On a practical and symbolic level, state socialist mass women's groups did not seamlessly segue into postsocialist feminist action at the local or global level. Thus, there was a significant learning curve between the two historical periods of the state socialist women's emancipation project/institutions and the post–state socialist democracy/capitalist project.

In addition to this logistical problem, in the post–Cold War era the participation of women from the former second world was circumscribed by agendas that had *already* been solidified, most likely without their involvement. There was no going back in time to alter that fact. For many in former state social-ist countries, the 1995 Beijing conference was the first major opportunity to engage the UN women's rights apparatus. In particular, with regard to human trafficking, by the time of the Beijing conference, the composite category "vio-lence against women" already was the dominant register for the naming of sex trafficking as a women's rights issue. In the case of Russia, the framework of "violence against women" has been useful for politicizing the issue of domestic violence and other forms of violence against women (Johnson 2009; Zaba-dykina 2000). There clearly are important advantages to using the "violence against women" agenda within the Russian context and certainly more broadly across the region. Violence against women was a significant blind spot of state socialist gender quality policy.

But there are also limitations to the success of the language of violence against women. Most important, the "violence against women" agenda has contributed to the depoliticization of the economic dimensions of sex traffick-ing and sexual harassment in Russia. This depoliticization is linked to global processes of neoliberalism and is bitterly ironic given that Marxist critiques of women's oppression once dominated the political landscape. In many re-spects, antitrafficking efforts would have been impossible without the strategic use of the "violence against women" agenda. Yet the "violence against women" framework contributed to the depoliticization of the economic dimensions of trafficking. Linked to and shaped by the "violence against women" agenda, antitrafficking efforts have necessarily focused on victim services *post*trafficking. In addition, trafficking prevention is focused on educating women to make informed choices, as when navigating formal and informal migration networks. These efforts are important, but I argue that they have circumscribed an analy-sis of trafficking as a symptom of economic policies that were promulgated by political elites and their international advisors.

This contradictory outcome of the "violence against women" agenda is also seen in the case of sexual harassment policy. The effectiveness of the "violence against women" agenda in Russia has meant that sexual harassment has not been primarily understood as a symptom of women's economic discrimina-tion. Referred to as "violence against women at work," sexual harassment often is represented as a form of violence, despite the fact that the transition to capi-talism has ushered in a context where women's livelihoods are deleteriously impacted by workplace discrimination. The failure of sexual harassment as a feminist advocacy issue is ironic because popular culture showcases sexual-ized images of femininity (Azhgikhina 1995; Borenstein 2008). Furthermore, on a practical level, because sexual harassment is categorized within the larger category of "violence against women," it is particularly difficult to legally challenge because it does not offer physical proof.

The fact that violence against women is the organizing principle for articulating trafficking and sexual harassment as problems within the Russian context is a product of both the success of the global campaign against violence against women (and its resonance/translation in Russia) *and* the disjointed timing of that global discourse with the emergence of the post–Cold War second world difference. The sequencing of the consolidation of global women's rights norms in the early 1990s and the end of state socialism was significant for challenging trafficking in the region from an economic perspective. The specific example of Russia should not be generalized across the region, but it is an important experience that illustrates many of the tensions that existed in countries undergoing neoliberal transitions. Thus, rather than seeing the former second world as lagging behind global feminist homogenous time, I explore the erasures, disjunctures, and opportunities presented by the expansion of the violence against women platform.

Feminist Homogenous Empty Time in Global Women's Rights

Most accounts of the evolution of global women's rights rely on a periodization that reflects major UN institutional turning points. While accounts can vary, four general phases are commonly identified: phase 1 (1945–1962) is the period when a women's rights agenda focused on political equality was first emerging in the UN; phase 2 (1963–1975) is the period of growing feminist influence with a new focus on development; phase 3 (1976–1985) coincides with the UN Decade for Women and is characterized as a time of growing international momentum also marked by key disagreement on feminist goals; and phase 4 (1986–present) is marked by the 1995 UN Beijing conference (and parallel NGO Forum in Huairou) and the Beijing Declaration and Platform for Action, the global gold standard for women's rights. After 1995, time is catalogued in relationship to Beijing (i.e., Beijing plus years lapsed). Thus, the Beijing conference continues to be an important symbolic point of reference.

This periodization reflects the institutionalization and validation of women's rights issues within the UN. The CSW was established in 1946 and was technically at first only a subcommission of the UN Secretariat Division on Human Rights. The four phases described above relate to the legitimation and growing influence of the CSW as well as the proliferation of associated UN bodies devoted to women's issues. In addition to the institutionalization of women's rights within the UN apparatus, the periodization reflects thematic and normative undercurrents in that process. Importantly, the periodization is based on geopolitical developments and tensions that emerged after World War II and were then reflected in the internationalizing of women's rights. I revisit this periodization to mark an implicit distinction between cultural versus political differences that operated during the Cold War. The distinction between political and cultural differences presumably was reduced to just cultural difference after the delegitimation of the socialist alternative in 1989 and the entrenchment of "TINA" ("There Is No Alternative"). This shift allowed for the displacement and misreading of the former second world—there was no need to translate because there was no cultural difference, and the political difference was now gone.

The three worlds architecture created by the Cold War divided geopolitical approaches to women's rights. This is most evident in the tripartite agenda "Equality, Development, and Peace" established during the International Decade for Women (1975–1985). The focus on equality (which referred to political equality) came from the "first world," the focus on development came from the "third world," and the focus on peace came from the "second world." Rather than seeing each position as distinct, I suggest that they operated as two sets of binaries: between the first and second worlds and between the first and third worlds. The first world/second world dichotomy was presented as a *political* divide based on the competing ideologies of capitalism and socialism. The first world/third world dichotomy was presented as a *cultural* divide rooted in ethnocentric and colonialist assumptions of civilized/uncivilized or modern/developing societies. While both dichotomies were racialized, the first world/third world division was based on overt racialized categories, whereas the political difference of communist difference was more subtly racialized.[4]

These tensions proved to be very important in the evolution of global women's rights at the UN and globally. For example, the socialist bloc had generated momentum for the International Women's Year at the UN that then grew into the International Decade for Women (Chen 1995; Ghodsee 2012; Popa 2009). The organizing power of socialist women's groups played an important role, as well as the east/west political tension. Not to be outdone by its rivals, the United States signed on to the UN Decade for Women once the socialist bloc appeared to be taking the lead. For example, Kristen Ghodsee explains that "as it became clear that there would be an international conference at the UN on women's issues, American politicians, fearing that communist women would hijack the deliberations with an anti-capitalist agenda, became actively involved in constructing a definition of 'appropriate' women's issues for the U.S. delegates" (Ghodsee 2010, 4).

In addition, during the UN Decade for Women, the Soviet position of "Peace" swayed agendas and pushed controversial issues, such as support for the PLO, calling out Zionism as a form of racism, and challenging apartheid in South Africa. The unequivocal support for women's rights from the socialist bloc pushed the United States to engage (and legitimate) the UN women's rights process when it had been reluctant. This push also, of course, generated momentum within the UN machinery. Yet accounts of the development of women's rights at the UN often discount the generative role of the socialist bloc countries.

In returning to the UN periodization, I challenge the idea that global women's rights evolved in "homogenous empty time," Benedict Anderson's term for an abstract yet collective time/place in which people made a conceptual grasp of "the nation" (Anderson 1991). This time/place dimension was key, he argues, to the development of nationalism. Anderson explains that "an American will never meet, or even know, the names of more than a handful of his fellow-Americans. He has no idea of what they are up to at any one time. But he has complete confidence in their steady, anonymous, simultaneous activity" (26). I use Anderson's concept to make a similar argument about global women's rights. The "sisterhood" nation embodied in global women's rights operates as an imagined community that has a story of its emergence (i.e., the phases) and has a set of norms and even vernacular. It is the assumed feminist homogenous empty time of the evolution of global women's rights that leads to an evaluation of women's rights and activism based on the specific experience of the imagined community invoked by the UN periodization. Thus, the periodization is used as an evaluative tool to measure the timing, presence, or strength of national women's rights activities.

For example, feminisms in former state socialist contexts have been presumably "slow to emerge," "absent," and "not in sync" (Einhorn 2006; Holmgren 1995; Slavova 2006). Such claims are based on the periodization (evolution) of women's rights, particularly with the Beijing conference being an important point of historical reference. This periodization sets up postsocialist feminism as behind and constructs a "temporal lag" for second world women's activism. Maria Todorova explains in the case of Balkan nationalisms that a temporal lag is "when new arrivals are positioned in the starting block of a race already underway" (Todorova 2005, 145). Similarly, women's activism is often seen as suffering from a temporal lag—feminists from the former East are behind and/or producing ill-shaped forms of the standard (i.e., suffering false consciousness). Certainly, there was a learning curve for women unexperienced with the UN system who were engaged suddenly with that apparatus. Similarly, the global women's rights agenda was indeed already under way by the time postsocialism emerged as a new time/place. However, a simple notion of "catching up" should be challenged because the gap between second world difference and global women's rights is not simply remedied by "joining in" or latching on to already existing programs. There is a need for translation but also for generating alternative, if parallel, timelines. For instance, in many of the former state socialist countries there is, in fact, ongoing thinking about national feminist timelines as a mode of intellectual and political work.[5] And it is from these timelines that feminists are rethinking their relationship with "the global."

To consider this further, I refer to Partha Chaterjee's concept of heterogeneous time to complicate the assumed meanings tied to the chronology of global women's rights. In a critique of Benedict Anderson, Partha Chatterjee explains that "empty homogenous time is not located anywhere in real space—it is utopian. The real space of modern life consists of heterotopia. Time here is heterogeneous, unevenly dense" (Chatterjee 2005, 927–28). The uneven and plural aspect of Chatterjee's heterogeneous time opens up reflections on the opportunities and contradictions of the standard periodization of global women's rights.

I analyze two dimensions of the heterogeneous time of the UN periodization of women's rights to highlight a lingering disjuncture between the former second world and "the global." One dimension relates to understandings of political versus cultural difference in the expansion of women's rights norms within the CSW. The second dimension relates to the contradictory relationship of the socialist bloc to "the global" during the late Cold War and the implications of that contradiction for postsocialist engagement with the global agenda at the 1995 Beijing world conference. I first revisit the periodization of the UN women's rights agenda, looking specifically at the idea of political versus cultural differences in the context of expanding women's rights norms. Then I analyze the 1995 Beijing conference in terms of the heterogeneous temporalities of the postsocialist condition.

Political and Cultural Difference in the Periodization of Global Women's Rights

WOMEN'S LEGAL EQUALITY: PHASE 1 (1945–1962)

The Sub-commission on the Status of Women was established in 1946 and given the mandate to "submit proposals, recommendations and reports to the Commission on Human Rights regarding the status of women" (Boutros-Ghali 1995, 12). This subcommission was quickly upgraded to commission status as the CSW. It reported to the Economic and Social Council of the UN Secretariat. One of its first actions was to establish a global survey of the status of women. Its members proposed an annual survey of laws pertaining to the status of women entitled "Questionnaire on the Legal Status and Treatment of Women." The survey was the first fact-finding endeavor regarding women's rights at the UN (some survey work was done in the League of Nations, but it was quickly seen as outdated and insufficient). The strategy of fact-finding was used to frame and validate resolutions proposed by the CSW, and it is a strategy that has been used repeatedly throughout the evolution of the women's rights agenda at the UN.

The questionnaire emphasized four areas of concern: political rights of women; legal rights of women both as individuals and family members; access of girls and women to education and training; and working life (Pietilä 2007, 21). The data collected from these surveys served as the foundation for several conventions that would be used to advance women's equal rights, including the 1951 Convention Concerning the Equal Remuneration for Men and Women Workers for Work of Equal Value, the 1952 Convention on the Political Rights of Women, the 1957 Convention on the Nationality of Married Women, and the 1960 UNESCO International Convention Against Discrimination in Education (Pietilä 2007). These conventions also had an impact on the 1967 Declaration on the Elimination of Discrimination Against Women, which was adapted in 1979 as CEDAW.[6]

The development of women's rights in phase 1 emphasized the legal positions of women within their countries. For example, the area of suffrage was given special attention. The political right to vote was viewed as the epitome of women's equality. However, there were serious impediments to achieving universal suffrage. Some countries in the world were still under colonial rule and not democratic. Therefore, as Devaki Jain points out, "in such countries there was no scope for suffrage for women" (Jain 2005, 24). With the rise of anticolonial movements and the admission of newly liberated countries into the UN, the meaning of women's rights was broadened within the CSW. For women who had participated in liberation movements, "the concept of women's equality [went] beyond legal equality in civil and political rights to equal participation in nation-building, social and economic development, the strengthening of civic responsibilities, and the overall improvement of the status of women" (25). By the end of phase 1, the CSW had established a strong vision of women's legal equality, and this reflected the influence of a first world agenda for women's rights. However, the meaning of the term "women's status" was about to undergo an important expansion.

During phase 1 a normative categorization and positioning of countries emerged within the UN. Western countries (the United States and Western Europe) emphasized women's civil and political rights, while state socialist countries emphasized women's social and economic rights. "The West argued that there was a denial of civil and political rights in the East and the East argued that there was deep inequality in the West linked to economic injustice" (Jain 2005, 29). The political split between east and west was never discussed as a cultural difference. Instead, the difference between them was based on political ideologies. It was a point of pride that the Soviet Union could proclaim political and legal equality for its citizens, while the United States seemed to lag behind.[7]

In conjunction with the east/west political split, there was a growing concern for the role of religious and cultural traditions as impediments to women's status. The role of culture in defining or inhibiting women's rights largely came through the recognition of countries outside the east/west political divide. The fact that state socialism was viewed in terms not of culture but of ideology is important because, as the CSW moved beyond a concern for women's political equality, the first/third world tension became a central normative mechanism in the evolution of global women's rights agendas.

DEVELOPMENT IS A WOMEN'S ISSUE: PHASE 2 (1962–1975)

Phase 2 in the evolution of a women's rights agenda at the UN marks two important shifts. As a result of anticolonial movements, the UN took on new political projects that focused on economic development. The First UN Development Decade (1960–1970) and the "international development strategy" focused on the advancement of underdeveloped economies by using the principle of trickle-down economics. At the same time, new political blocs formed within the UN. The Non-Aligned Movement held its first summit in 1961 in Belgrade as a result of the leadership of India, Egypt, and Yugoslavia. The countries that grouped themselves in the Non-Aligned Movement opposed alignment with either of the Great Power alliances (Willetts 1978). In addition, a group of developing nations formed the Group of Seventy-Seven, which was the largest intergovernmental political bloc in the UN in 1964. The Group of Seventy-Seven "provides the means for the countries of the South to articulate and promote their collective economic interests and enhance their joint negotiating capacity."[8]

These changes altered political dynamics and signaled a shift toward economic development priorities. At first, women specifically were not mentioned in relation to development. Some members in the CSW believed that "development was not really a women's issue and that too much attention to economic development would divert the commission from its primary goal of securing women's equal rights" (Jain 2005, 35). However, these views began to shift as the second UN Development Decade (1970s) took shape.[9] Women's involvement in the Non-Aligned Movement challenged orientalist and sexist views of third world women and "modernization." In particular, events outside the CSW were important to linking women's rights and development. Danish economist Ester Boserup's book *Women's Role in Economic Development* (1970) is often cited as one of the most influential strides toward taking women more seriously within development paradigms. The data she presents in the book show how women's labor contributes to national economic productivity. Then, in 1972, the Interregional Meeting of Experts on the Integration of Women in Development helped to advance WID, a new approach to development. The Interregional Meeting of Experts "emphasized the integration of planning for women in overall policy formulation at national and regional levels rather than dealing with women's development issues in isolation" (Jain 2005, 53). This shift in emphasis was reinforced at the UN World Food Conference (1974) and the UN World Population Conference (1974).

These events from outside of the CSW slowly pushed it to pick up the issue of development as a women's issue. By 1970, there was growing criticism of the trickle-down strategy of the UN Development Decade as well. The power blocs now competing with those of the United States and the USSR were able to present their critiques of global inequalities and what some argued was neocolonialism. This work led to the Declaration on a New International Economic Order and the Charter of Economic Rights and Duties in States of 1974. Women's NGOs across the developing world were also taking shape and would play a significant role in the evolution of the UN women's rights agenda (Huston 1979; Moghadam 2005; Rupp 1998; UN Development Fund for Women 1985).

THE UN DECADE FOR WOMEN: PHASE 3 (1975–1985)

Phase 3 is marked by the full institutionalization of women's rights within the UN with the establishing of a global women's rights agenda. There were conflicts along the way, but the decade is viewed as a progressive movement toward greater coordination and alliances between women across the globe. The first World Conference on Women, the International Women's Year in Mexico City (1975), launched this movement. The preparatory process for the conference was truncated, and it was clear that there was a severe lack of data about the world's women (Fraser 1987, 21). After plenary sessions and committee meetings, a World Plan of Action was drafted and proposed. The World Plan of Action was meant as a road map for the UN Decade for Women, with the specific themes of "equality, development and peace." In addition, the more radical Declaration of Mexico was adopted, despite opposition. This declaration included politically contentious concerns such as for Zionism and apartheid and was aligned with the principles of the Declaration on a New International Economic Order.

The World Plan of Action recommended the setting up of government machineries in order to collect data and evaluate progress toward the goals of the World Plan of Action. In addition, two more global conferences were scheduled to mark the five-year intervals of the UN Decade for Women. In 1980 the second World Conference on Women was held in Copenhagen. This conference is often described as riddled with conflict, with the political tensions of the Cold War and the racialized tensions between the first and third world (Moghadam 2005, 6). These tensions were understood as falling along political and cultural differences. While the Cold War continued to shape and filter the contributions of representatives from the state socialist countries, many first world women of color in the United States and Europe built bridges with women in the third world. Similarly, socialist women's organizations networked with women in the global south.[10]

This decade is also described as a time when national and transnational NGOs gained momentum. While official declarations such as the World Plan of Action and the Forward Looking Strategies represented the commitments of governments, there was a flourishing of women's networks that represented the demand for those governments to live up to their commitments (Jain 2005, 123). Many of these organizations had an impact on the outcome of UN doctrine. For example, the network DAWN had its first meeting in Bangalore, India, in 1984 as part of the preparatory process for the Nairobi world conference. The network criticized the "ladders approach" of the UN questionnaire sent out to help countries prepare for Nairobi. They argued that it only measured "the disparities between men and women in a select set of indicators such as education, employment, and health and works to bring up to the same level as men as a way of achieving equality" (96). What the questionnaire did not get at were the links between macroeconomic policies, such as export-led strategies for growth, and increased poverty and the expansion of informal economies. A plan prepared in Bangalore, "Development, Crises, and Alternative Visions," was referenced at the Conference of Non-Aligned and other Developing Countries on the "Role of Women in Development" in 1985 (97). Like DAWN, a cadre of NGOs was growing and now had experience at the global level. At each of the UN world conferences there were parallel tribunes where NGOs gathered. While NGOs had always been a part of the UN process in a consultative role, their collaborative influence grew over the course of the decade.

By the end of the UN Decade for Women, much had changed and evolved. In 1979 CEDAW was voted on. In 1985 the Forward Looking Strategies provided a road map for the advancement of women to the year 2000. Substantively, women's rights expanded beyond legal equality to include issues of development. This was reflected in the new agencies that were created within the UN to collect research on women's issues (the UN International Research and Training Institute for the Advancement for Women) and create development projects geared toward women (the UN Development Fund for Women). From its first days as a mere subcommission, the CSW had evolved into a powerful force for women's rights. According to Fraser, "the last half of the Decade for Women saw a critical mass of women much more pragmatic, professional, and political. They knew how to use the U.N. system to place women's issues on the agenda of every world meeting" (Fraser 1987, 159).

This narrative of the evolution of women's rights at the UN describes the UN Decade for Women as a time of emerging and competing interests and growing momentum. Yet for many state socialist countries this period is one of contradictions. While some state socialist government representatives played an important role in the UN process and forged global connections with third world women, criticism of state socialist gender equality was not a part of women's rights discourse at the UN. Rather, the rights and achievements that women enjoyed in state socialism were presented as always already reflected in UN doctrine. While documents like CEDAW and the Forward Looking Strategies were used to push governments to live up to the idea of women's equality, state socialist governments used them as political ammunition against the West. It was rare to use such documents as leverage against state socialist governments to improve the conditions for women within the socialist bloc.[11]

In particular, there were two contradictions between the state socialist sexual contract and doctrine for women's rights that came out of the UN Decade for Women. First, from the perspective of state socialist states these documents reflected policy that was already enshrined in their national legislation. Thus, the political impact of the documents was blunted because it was assumed that state socialist women's equality *predated* these documents (Racioppi and

O'Sullivan 1995). This inversion created a challenge for state socialist representatives to engage their states on women's issues using the momentum created
through the UN process. This challenge was not the same across the region, of
course (see Ghodsee 2012). However, while some socialist women may have
persuaded their states to respond to their concerns, this activism was not part
of the metadiscourse at the UN such that a critical state socialist perspective
registered there. Such critical views could have emerged through shadow reports, such as those produced by NGOs for CEDAW, but they were not created
during the state socialist period.

Second, many of the ideals embodied in CEDAW and the Forward Looking
Strategies emphasized the disadvantages women experience as a result of
being treated differently as women and thus advanced an implicit gender critique. Yet the state socialist sexual contract was premised on maintaining the
idea of women's sexual difference. The Marxist-informed Soviet solution to
the "woman question" was never a critique of gender; the socialist critique
of women's inequality was rooted in a critique of capitalism (Racioppi and
O'Sullivan 1995; Zimmerman 2010). In an inversion of Simone de Beauvoir's
critical declaration of the second sex, state socialist ideology relied on an essentialized view of sexual difference. This classification of women's sexual difference was the register in which state socialism structured equality. Thus, the
source of women's oppression was not socially proscribed gender norms but
the economic disadvantages they suffered under capitalist systems. Once a socialist economic system was established, it was believed that inequalities of all
kinds would cease to exist. This position allowed state socialist governments to
use women's rights as political ammunition against the West and obscured the
gendered impact of those systems.

On a practical level, state socialist equality policies promoted women's
employment, protections and provisions for motherhood (such as some state
support for children and childhood), quota systems for political representation, and access to higher education. These achievements should not be un-
derstated. Yet along with these achievements women were burdened with a
double shift and segregated into gender-specific fields (Holmgren 2013). Soviet
rhetoric emphasized women's achievements as workers and mothers *for the
state* (Wood 1997). For example, an official compilation of Soviet legislation
from the late 1970s includes this comment: "Recognizing for women not only
the role of workers, but also their social role of motherhood, as well as their
part in public and state affairs, the Soviet state, besides the general norms of law,
enacts special norms granting women additional rights and privileges" (Belyakova et al. 1978, 15). The special norms included providing women with work

appropriate "to the female sex," increasing protections for pregnant women, nursing mothers, and women with children under one year of age, increasing social maternity relief, and implementing legal protections for women's equality in "all areas of social life" (15). By establishing equality through a classification of women's sexual difference, such norms in fact established women's status as a second sex: "The special norms of law compiled in the Collection take into account the anatomic and physiological features of the female organism with a view to protect it, and also the social role of women as conditioned by such features in childbirth and the care of young children" (17). This view of essential sexual difference was never challenged within state socialism, despite the fact that women were encouraged to participate in fields typically associated with masculinity/men, such as the piloting of fighter planes, science, or medicine.

This aspect of state socialist gender inequality that was due to the absence of a gender critique was never included in the conversations that occurred during the UN Decade for Women. Instead, state socialist representatives were the torchbearers for state socialism's brand of sex equality. This stance supported the importance of wage labor for women's rights and thus bolstered some of the activism of women in the global south. However, in the wake of the historically important statements for women's rights that accompanied the events of the UN Decade for women, state socialist political rhetoric indicated that these states were starting to pull from their traditional stance on women's equality. Starting in the late 1980s during the perestroika period, Mikhail Gorbachev critiqued the Soviet approach to equality and initiated a political backlash against women's equality that continued into the post-Soviet period. Gorbachev argued that women, and society, suffered from too much equality and that the Soviet model had taken away from women's natural duties as mothers. In his reflections on the goals of perestroika, he explained that the USSR had over-emancipated women.

> This is a paradoxical result of our sincere and politically justified desire to make women equal with men in everything. Now, in the course of perestroika, we have begun to overcome this shortcoming. That is why we are now holding heated debates in the press, in public organizations, at work and at home, about the question of what we should do to make it possible for women to return to their purely womanly mission. Further democratization of society, which is the pivot and guarantor of perestroika, is impossible without enhancing the role of women, without their active and specifically female involvement, and without their commitment to all our reform efforts. (Gorbachev 1987, 117)

With a critique of the Soviet equality model, Gorbachev recycled essentialist gender roles in a new political package. Gorbachev did not invent essentialized sexual difference but reinvigorated it in the name of perestroika. Thus, a turn to neotraditionalism continued in and through the processes of transition in the 1990s in Russian and other former state socialist states (Goscilo 1996; Watson 1993; Zdravomyslova and Temkina 1996). Polish feminist Agnieszka Graff claims that the postsocialist backlash against feminism in Poland was only partly an American import and was a national response to earlier state-sanctioned political projects as well (Graff 2003).[12] In many postsocialist national discourses, the turn to neotraditionalism was a backlash against the state socialist version of "equality."

An important contradiction emerges when juxtaposing the standard UN periodization with that of the state socialist timeline I have described. The UN Decade for Women is generally regarded as the major vehicle for generating a global women's rights agenda. Yet the actual experiences of many women in state socialist countries were not fully represented. Moreover, the momentum created by the Decade's events—at the governmental and nongovernmental level—cannot be assumed to be part of the state socialist evolution toward achieving women's rights. To the contrary, at the very moment when there is a liberalization of political and economic discourses, there is an official political *pullback* from the very ideals embodied by the Forward Looking Strategies and CEDAW. Thus, in many state socialist contexts, women experienced a double silencing. Women did not have an independent voice at the level of the UN, *and* their views were often silenced in the dominant dissident discourses, despite the fact that they were very active in those movements (Einhorn 1991; Penn 2006).

Writings such as *Zhenshchina i Rossii Al'manakh* (Woman and Russia almanac) were considered "the first free feminist publication[s] in the Soviet Union" (Mamonova 1984, viii). Published in the Soviet Union in 1979, this publication gave voice to women's experiences of everyday life and expressed visions for peace, including opposition to the war in Afghanistan. According to Tatyana Mamonova, these were viewpoints that were cut out from dissident publications (xiii). This context of double silencing is important for evaluating the impact of the "violence against women" discourse that occurred in the interim period between the end of the UN Decade for Women and the 1995 Beijing conference.

In the period between 1985 and 1995, profound political and social changes occurred in the countries of the former second world. The myriad responses to those changes in the region did not seamlessly track onto the already existing discourses that had been evolving at the global level. In profound ways, the evolution of a women's rights agenda at the UN was not coterminous with the evolution of women's democratic activism in the (former) second world. While the ideological meanings attached to the three worlds of the Cold War have much less significance today, in 1995 the former second world "joined" the global conversation from a distinct albeit not always recognized location.

ALL ROADS LEAD TO BEIJING: PHASE 4 (1986–1995)

The significance of the fourth World Conference on Women in Beijing in 1995 is important looking back and looking forward. The Beijing conference represents the apex of organizing for women's rights at the global level. It was the largest global conference on women, and the Beijing Declaration and Platform for Action is still the most significant global statement of women's rights. It had six thousand delegates from member states, and it had four thousand or more representatives of NGOs and thirty thousand participants at the associated NGO Forum in Huairou (Jain 2005, 143). While there were certainly disagreements about issues, the kind of networking and dialogue that was able to occur was fairly spectacular given how many participants there were. The World Plan of Action was drafted throughout the preparatory process; much of the work for creating the document was done prior to the summer of 1995. According to Noeleen Heyzer, the UN Development Fund for Women's director at the time, "if you think about the 50,000 who went to Beijing you could almost triple that number for the preparatory process. What was being generated was political will" (14). In many respects, the conference is viewed as the culmination of an evolutionary process that started in 1945 with the establishment of the UN. In some regards, it was all preparation for Beijing—the pinnacle moment. This too is reflected by the fact that subsequent assessments of global women's rights are identified by the incremental review of the Beijing document (e.g., Beijing+5, +10, +15).[13]

While Beijing symbolizes the culmination of an evolutionary process, it also marks a period of change. By the early 1990s, a significant number of new states joined the UN. The entrance of new states created myriad political shifts. Importantly, there was no longer a socialist bloc. As Devaki Jain describes it, "the Socialist bloc had supported approaches that required a strong state, a thrust toward public provision of basic services, and a more equitable global economic program such as the NIEO [Declaration on a New International Economic Order]" (Jain 2005, 103). But with the dissolution of Soviet hegemony, new blocs emerged, including the European Union and Commonwealth of Independent States (CIS). In addition to shifting power alliances, most of the newly independent states validated the neoliberal economic development strategies of the Bretton Woods institutions by undergoing rapid transitions toward market economies. At a time when many governments and activists were heightening their criticism of the World Bank and International Monetary Fund, most former state socialist states extended their tacit consent by taking out loans and adopting neoliberal economic approaches. Thus, as the first post–Cold War global conference on women, the Beijing conference coincided with the demise of socialist political solidarity and the implementation of economic transition policies.

The absence of the old geopolitical battles should have added to the penultimate character of the conference: after decades of feminist organizing and the toppling of the east/west divide, the Beijing conference was supposed to be a unified statement for women's rights. A plethora of newly independent organizations and state representatives now could take part in the process. Yet the making of that historic context was not entirely available for post–state socialist representatives. The preparations for Beijing were rooted in the UN Decade for Women, and thus there was an important divide between that era and the post-1989 period. While the interests of women in former state socialist states were not radically different from those of women in other parts of the world, there was a disjuncture between a newly emerging "second world difference" and "the global." This disjuncture was evident in the preparatory process as well as at the conventions.

While new autonomous organizing was under way in former socialist countries, there was very little connection between the state socialist engagement with the UN process during the Decade for Women and those new organizations. For example, in the following commentary by an important Russian women's organization, it is evident that many felt ill prepared as representatives in the UN process in comparison to others.

> Women's organizations of all kinds prepared for this meeting earlier, not just a few months but a few years, beginning with the 3rd World Conference on the status of women in Nairobi. Many of them arrived early with prepared documents and their strategies on advancing them. Our official delegation in New York was especially young and inexperienced and did not manage to have an impact on the formulation of the Platform for Action, which then was discussed at the 4th World Conference [on Women]. NGOs also were not ready to actively participate in the work creating the documents and so everything was dependent on the participation of the government representatives. (Information Center of the Independent Forum, n.d.)

This quote is from a document by Informatsionnii Tsentr Nezavisimogo Forum (Information Center of the Independent Forum), an autonomous women's network that emerged in Russia after the first Russian Independent Women's Forum in 1991. The statement reveals how, once representatives got to Beijing they realized that there had been a long preparatory process, dating back to the third world conference in Nairobi. It was a shock for them to realize that the Platform for Action largely had been agreed on prior to the conference.[14] Unlike many other NGOs who had years of experience (and influence) at the global level, this was the first time that autonomous organizations from former state socialist countries participated in the UN process.

Thus, Beijing represented the emergence of their global organizing and networking rather than an apex of years of experience. As Svetlana Konstantinova, one of the Russian representatives at the Beijing conference, states, "the Russian groups, which are taking their first steps towards women's liberation and the feminization of our emerging democracy, are becoming a part of the global women's community—with its ideology, special language, style of leadership, and vision for the future. The Beijing conference contributed greatly to that process" (Konstantinova 1996).

This disjuncture led to significant frustrations for some representatives from the former Eastern Bloc and USSR that went beyond the sense of a need to "catch up." Rather, some were frustrated with the lack of time and space that was provided for second world women to express their concerns based on their experiences. This frustration is reflected in the document "Statement from a Non-Region," which was presented by a collective of representatives from former socialist countries (Nowicka 1995).[15] This group consisted of more than four hundred women representing eighty NGOs from nineteen countries. In this statement, the authors express their frustrations with the absence of their concerns in the Platform for Action: "Our group of countries is a Non-Region, because there is no recognizable political or geographic definition for the region composed of countries in Central and Eastern Europe and the former Soviet Union" (Nowika 1995). Indeed, the problem was not one of "catching up" but a problem of intelligibility.

The concept of the "nonregion" was produced by the disjuncture between postsocialism and "the global" at Beijing. By the time of this conference, there was not a consolidated or homogenous postsocialist position/perspective. Thus, the "statement from a nonregion" exemplifies the lack of discursive space given to postsocialist representatives in which to formulate and articulate the emerging views from that diverse region. One emerging view was a theorizing of "transition." Even though state socialism was not the same across Central and Eastern Europe and the USSR, there were enough similarities to those systems and the transitions under way in them to enable the presentation of transition as a complex and contested terrain. As the "nonregion" statement declares, "we could not contribute in drafting in the early stages of the process and believe that the description of the impact of the transition to democracy on women is inadequate" (Nowika 1995).[16] While the authors acknowledge the importance of the Beijing Declaration and Platform for Action for their "nonregion," they explain that some of the language does not effectively address the specific challenges they face.[17] "We disagree with the description of the feminization of poverty as a short-term consequence of the political, economic and social transformation. Our most serious problem is the consistent and drastic decline in the status of women. Women face problems with unemployment, environmental disasters, armed conflict, increased violence and trafficking in women" (Nowicka 1995). Despite its obvious meaning, for many women the term "transition" was not simply a temporary marker but a concept that defined the complexity of their particular postsocialist positions. The discrimination and social neotraditionalism that women faced were not just the result of an insufficient or incomplete implementation of democracy or capitalism. While new and dramatically different economic policies were undertaken across the region, many observed that the actual policies tied to democracy and capitalism were simultaneously perpetuating and compounding gender inequality.

This more complex understanding of transition was not reflected in the Beijing Declaration and Platform for Action. While the term "transition" was included, it was not presented, as a critical feminist position—in ways similar to but different from—the other two dominant metageographical positions represented in UN discourse: namely "developing countries" and "industrialized countries." Because the concept of transition was not thought of as a distinguishing characteristic of the unique context of postsocialism, it was seen as a temporary qualification and thus did not carry a readable difference. Yet for some the concept of transition was beginning to describe the new order of things. The term "transition" was not just about temporality but was about the quality and characteristic of the diverse post-socialist political and economic arrangements that were becoming permanent.

The inability to "see" second world difference was not just a problem of timing. The tendency to not see difference was tied to the obscuring of the myriad, complex, and uneven differences of the second world by the political-culture divide constructed by Cold War rhetoric. Second world political difference became irrelevant with the end of state socialism. And because the second world was a political "other" rather than cultural other to the first world, many assumed that "transition" was a neutral process.[18] Thus, it is important to consider how such norms informed and ultimately structured women's rights priorities at the UN. Arguably, development and "violence against women" were the two most important registers along which women's rights emerged through and out of the Cold War. In the evolution of those registers, the tension between the first and third worlds was equally as powerful as, if not more powerful than, the first world/second world tension. The issue of development tracked along cultural/racialized divides, and the socialist bloc supported the "development" position throughout the UN Decade for Women. Indeed, the political expediency of the "violence against women" agenda was attributed to its ability to neutralize the cultural divides present during the Cold War. A lingering question remains, though, of why the second world was never presented/ understood as a cultural difference. This is an important question to briefly consider because second world difference continues to be misrepresented or forgotten in global women's rights discourses (Suchland 2011).

In the early seventies, feminists argued that traditional development paradigms failed because they did not consider or respond to the important roles women played in their national economies. Ester Boserup's work is often credited with advancing this argument. Boserup argues that development can take away the traditional power that women have in their societies when their economic roles are "modernized." One example she gives is of the introduction of plows. Men took over the plows and thus displaced the hoeing that women had performed. Introducing modern practices such as private property also made women dependent on men because only they could receive bank loans (Tinker 1976). These are just two examples of the kind of challenges the WID approach made to dominant development paradigms.

The WID field brought women into the conversation about development. The category "women and development" also functioned as a discourse that challenged the ethnocentrism and presumed neutrality of standard development programs. The women and development agenda presented criticism of western stereotypes of gender norms imposed on developing countries (Kabeer 1994; Mohanty 1988). It was the specific turn to look at women that revealed the importance of culture in creating effective development strategies. In her statement about the adverse impact of development on women at the 1975 World Conference of the International Women's Year, Irene Tinker argued that "because Western stereotypes of appropriate roles and occupations for women tend to be exported with aid, modernization continually increases the gap between women's and men's ability to cope with the modern world"

(Tinker 1976, 33). By ignoring how women are culturally situated, these western stereotypes can do more harm than good.

Thus, an implicit dimension of the WID discourse was the emphasis on the *cultural* context in which development existed. Of course, this was an important intervention. But an unintended consequence was that "developing countries" were marked as places where culture mattered, whereas "modern" countries were marked as places where the "Western ideal of 'equality for all'" was not culturally signified (Tinker 1976, 33). The underlying message was that development strategies needed to adapt to culture in order to advance women's equality, whereas women's equality is advanced in "modern" countries by demanding that governments live up to the inherent ideals of the existing culture. For example, "violence against women" may be represented in the West as an outcome of patriarchal men, while "violence against women" in developing countries is presented as the outcome of culture (Gunning 1998; Volpp 2001). Through the process of incorporating the WID approach at the UN, the developing world functioned as a discourse about cultural difference that never challenged the presumably culturally neutral "West."

The term "culture" was a political designation even if not always explicitly used. So euphemistic terms such as "subsistence economies" or "traditional economies" were juxtaposed to "modern economies" or "industrialized economies." Such categories carried implicit assumptions about what constituted "women's status." For example, how should researchers measure women's social position? What indicators should be used? One indicator that was used was the proportion of women in the paid labor force. From a western perspective, the extent of paid labor (and the assumed freedom from domestic labor) was seen as an indication of women's status. However, research showed how "labor force participation of mothers and the distribution of household tasks are not sexist issues" the world over (Buvinic 1976, 3). Furthermore, given the different values assigned to different work, how could women's status in the labor force be measured? Buvinic gives the example of the high rate of women's participation in Poland, Argentina, Peru, and Chile. She asks, "Is it accurate to infer, on the basis of these 'professional participation' statistics, that for example, Argentinean women have a higher status than U.S. women?" (Buvinic 1976, 4).

An important dimension of this evolving discourse on development was that the second world was *not* part of the critique of western stereotypes. Because the state socialist economies were industrialized, there was an assumption that their economic context was not culturally different from that of the capitalist industrial countries. The official statements of the USSR, for example, validated this assumption by proclaiming that women had achieved full equality under state socialism. There was no need to alter western measurements of the status of women in society for the state socialist context. While the socialist bloc supported the efforts of third world countries and the csw at the un, their position did not challenge the ethnocentrism of some women's rights norms. And, as a result, state socialist economies were not projected as a cultural difference in need of translation; this assumption continued into the postsocialist period. Such assumptions about the former second and third worlds continue to impact the way "the global" is studied and represented (Roman 2006; Slavova 2006). As Silke Roth argues, "despite the previous conflicts between women from the Global North and Global South, for example during the un conferences, it was not taken into consideration that differing experiences of living under (former) state socialism and in democratic capitalist (welfare) states might impact on the communication between eastern and western women" (Roth 2007, 464). The former state socialist states (with some important and interesting exceptions) continue to be sidelined or misrepresented in western feminist knowledge production.[19]

Second World Difference beyond the Temporal Lag

With the end of state socialism, the excitement at the grassroots level for engaging the global women's rights agenda was not matched at the governmental level in terms of support. While official political gestures were made, funds were not readily allocated to the grassroots. The lack of national budgetary commitments to the burgeoning women's movements in the region was exacerbated by the absence of an economic infrastructure that could compensate for that lack. In Russia "there was no such thing as direct mail, people do not have checkbooks, and credit cards are not widely used"—all of which are crucial to social movement organizing (Sperling 1998). If nongovernmental participants were going to participate in the un process, they needed external support. There were some attempts by outside donors to collaborate with and include former state socialist groups. For example, the Eurasia Foundation (with funding from usaid) "contributed enormously by providing money for different U.S. organizations to organize research and training seminars in Russia prior to the conference" (Konstantinova 1996). Other international sources funded the participation of women from the former socialist bloc.[20]

For Russian representatives, the emergence of new gender discourses in the perestroika and post-Soviet periods were the "preparatory" context for the

Beijing conference and not the UN Decade for Women. There is evidence that Russia was not an outlier in this way (Novikova 2006). There are also important different experiences in the region, including the role of the European Union in countries that hoped to one day become members (Hašková 2005; Regulska and Grabowska 2012). As I turn to the specific experience of Russian gender/feminist discourse (1988–95), it is important to clarify that it does not serve as an analogy for the entire region. Russia is a part of the postsocialist region and so in this way is one experience of second world difference. But I am aware that it does not and should not represent the myriad experiences within the postsocialist.

The state socialist emancipation project did many positive things for women in the name of women's equality, such as extending education to most if not all women. I highlight some of the shortcomings of the Soviet sexual contract not to invoke a cold war–style delegitimation of state socialism but rather to make explicit what was left out of the dominant global women's rights discourse. A more nuanced understanding of state socialism is important to translating the metageographical disjuncture articulated by the "Statement from a Non-Region." What we now know of "real existing socialism" is that women were highly educated, highly employed, and saddled by a double if not triple burden (Gal and Kligman 2000; Popa 2003; Voronina 1993).[21] In addition to their paid labor, women were unquestionably the primary caretakers of children and the domestic sphere, which included the daily challenge of procuring household items. By the end of the state socialist experiment, many citizens had become deeply suspicious of the rhetoric of equality because of the tremendous burdens these so-called rights had created; rights had become burdens (Slavova 2006).

The Soviet practice of equality that submitted women to domestic and civil burdens haunts contemporary relationships to the concepts of equality and the welfare state. Ironically, the pathologies of state socialism have tarnished the very language that is supposed to replace the now voided Soviet rhetoric. For some, there is a lingering resistance to terms such as "equality" and "emancipation" and an inclination toward a claim for independence. For example, Russian feminist Anastasia Posadskaya-Vanderbek argues that concepts such as "equal opportunity" and "independence" have a strong cultural resonance (Posadskaya-Vanderbek 1997). While the term "equality" may be irreparably damaged from the Soviet experience, there are important uses for it in the post-Soviet context. Starting in the late perestroika period there was a growing backlash against Soviet "equality." And, although "real existing socialism" did not provide complete gender equality, the rhetoric of "equality" nevertheless was uncontested. That is no longer the case.

Russian feminists such as Olga Voronina suggest that the move toward democratization, started during the perestroika period and carried through the post-Soviet period, has actually challenged Soviet advances for women in society. Ironically, the move toward greater freedoms and democracy has coincided with a reduction in women's social status and an undermining of the state's bureaucratic commitment to women's rights. While Soviet sex equality valorized women's sexual difference—and in this respect the essentialism used by Gorbachev reflected that norm—the difference in the post-Soviet context is that this valorization is not attached to an ethos of women's rights. Women's so-called equality is not used politically as an indication of the success/health of the state writ large, as was done during the Soviet period. Thus, as Nadezhda Azhgikhina argues, the failure of the newly democratic Russian state to ensure women's rights is tied to the rhetorical and practical devaluing of equality in the post-Soviet context. This devaluing is tied to a new valorization of the antifeminist capitalist West. She explains: "The reason for it is most likely rooted in the image of capitalism impressed on the minds of both the young leaders of reform and the average Russian citizen. The modern world has long since passed through the stage of initial accumulation of capital, disregard for the social sphere and the peak of patriarchal ideas—all the things that many people in our country have always associated with 'capitalist paradise'" (Azhgikhina 1998, 16). The implementation of democracy and capitalism has ushered in a reification of patriarchal values in Russia infused with understandings of western masculinist capitalism.

A particular post-Soviet paradox grew out of this context of backlash. The introduction of democracy in fact ushered in the abandonment of a political commitment to the rhetoric of women's equality. At the same time, there was a pressing need to insert women's concerns in the processes of democratization and marketization. The roots of this paradox were actually in the late perestroika period, when voices for democratization gained greater political and social credence. Azhgikina argues that women's issues were not central to those discussions. "Women who had stood in the front ranks of demonstrations for democracy and demanded that the memory of the victims of Stalin's terror be honored, or who had collected signatures on petitions to free Andrei Sakharov from internal exile and open Russia's borders—these women found themselves shoved aside by loud-voiced men. Dissident thought, which had captured people's minds, did not accept consideration of women. And women themselves followed the line taken by the democratic newspapers of the period: It was better for men to be in charge" (Azhgikhina 2000, 224). The tension between the political discourse of democratization and the marginalization of women engaging that democratic process sharpened with the introduction of post-Soviet institutions.

While women's representation in formal politics declined with the end of state socialism, women have been politically active, particularly in what is known as the third sector. In fact, these activities predate the collapse of the USSR. I have already mentioned Tatyana Mamonova, who was exiled for writing the *Women and Russia Almanac*. Years later, an independent discourse on women's issues arose in the perestroika period. The intellectual collective "Lotus" (League for Emancipation from Sexual Stereotypes) was formed in 1988 with Olga Voronina, Valentina Konstantinova, Natasha Zakharova, and Anastasia Posadskaya (Posadskaya 1994, 2). This core group would later be the nucleus of the Center for Gender Studies in Moscow. The group focused on women's status in the USSR and a commitment to independent research on women—something almost entirely absent in the Soviet Union. The Center was established prior to the collapse of the USSR. In that same time period, in Leningrad (St. Petersburg) Olga Lipovskaya initiated the Free Association of Feminist Organizations, in collaboration with Natalia Filippova in Moscow, in order to develop "women's, gender and feminist studies as part of Soviet scholarship" (Voronina 1994, 51). These developments in the perestroika period were central to the rise of "academic feminism" in Russia (Zdravomyslova and Temkina 2002).

In addition to these intellectual activities, women organized all kinds of associations. In fact, in the early 1990s there were estimates that more than fifty thousand nonprofit organizations had emerged in Russia (Ruffin, McCarter, and Upjohn 1996, 4). Many of those organizations were run by women and/or focused on women's issues. The activities of these organizations ranged widely in terms of their focus as well as in their feminist orientation. With few exceptions, Russian women and their organizations eschewed the language of feminism to describe their work (Holmgren 1995; Sperling 1999). There were and continue to be reservations about the term "feminism." Often erroneously associated with foreign influences, feminists garner negative stereotypes.[22] But feminism is also associated with an approach to equality that was delegitimized by the failure of state socialism to carry it out. As I described earlier, the language of equality and emancipation—key state socialist sex equality items—are deeply fraught in the post-Soviet context. Thus, it is important to see the particular discursive challenges, in addition to the formidable institutional challenges, that women's organizing faced in the late perestroika and post-Soviet periods, particularly as we look at the entrance of many of these organizations and women into the global women's rights machinery.

In March 1991, just months before the attempted coup in Moscow and the final blow to the Soviet Union, the first Independent Women's Forum in Russia took place in Dubna. The forum was organized by an academic collective at the Moscow Center for Gender Studies and brought together a range of organizations in order to develop a stronger network across Russia and the evolving region.[23] In looking at the summary documents from the forum, one can make several important observations about the ideas discussed and the language used to discuss them. The summary account (*itogovyi otchet*) describes the significance of the forum in terms of its development as an independent initiative of women's groups. Unlike the past, when women's organizations were organized "from the top" (*sverkhu*), the forum is said to be an expression of the widespread, but largely hidden, existence of women's organizations. The summary document states: "For the longest time in our country, a network of women's organizations formulated from the top existed and worked. Today, independent women's groups are forming with the aim to decide important and urgent matters that are mounting in front of them. So far these groups exist separate from each other but are quickly learning about each other" (*Pervogo Nezavisimogo Zhenskogo Foruma* 1991).

The document reflects an emphasis placed on the origins of the forum. It did not emerge from the official top but from the women who, with their own interests and initiative, pushed for it. This piece of the forum was very important given the context of women's groups in the Soviet Union. Women's political participation was filtered through official organs of the state. The organizations were an outlet but also a device to politicize women, which largely meant energizing them as agents for state socialist (production) goals. In the early Soviet period there were official women's departments (*zhenodtel*), but they were disbanded by Stalin when the "women's question" was put to rest. Starting in the late 1950s, Khrushchev reinstated social organizations in an attempt to politically engage women and to generally promote greater public involvement (Browning 1987). The organizations were conceived of as political but described as "independent," "spontaneous," and "ad hoc" (57).

Genia Browning's research on the *zhensovety*, the women-only socialist social organizations, argues that the groups did not operate as independent organizations but that there was a great range of activities that took place across the USSR (Browning 1987). While there may have been exceptions to the politicized nature of the *zhensovety*, it is clear that at the 1991 Dubna conference there was an important distinction between the official "top" women's organizations and the ones germinating from below. Interestingly, there was some synergy between the old *zhensovety* and the new independent organizations at Dubna. The summary document explains that activists at the *zhensovet* of the Unified Institute for Nuclear Research in Dubna had pushed the idea for the forum (*Pervogo Nezavisimogo Zhenskogo Foruma* 1991). In addition, former *zhensovet* cells transformed into informal organizations. For example, the *zhensovet* from Voronezh became NeZhDi (Don't Wait), and the *zhensovet* in Novocherkassk became Soyuz Zhenshchiny Dona (Union of Women of the Don) (Abubikirova et al. 1998, 3). While individual activists within *zhensovety* may have acted independently, overall the system was not viewed as relevant to women. "After decades of political manipulation, when the women's movement was an integral part of the totalitarian state system, women have finally decided to get themselves organized and discuss the issues that concern them" (Posadskaya 1993, 6).

In addition to distinguishing the forum as built on independent initiative, the goals of the forum were also important. As my earlier quotations indicated, the organizers recognized that there were diverse groups all over the Soviet Union but that they were not aware of each other. The organizers believed that there was a women's movement but it did not see itself as one because groups operated in isolation from one another. Thus, an important goal of the conference was to create a network (*set'*) to link the groups. It was the lack of a structure and the need to collect and organize the separate groups that was a primary focus. While the final document (*itogovyi dokument*) of the forum does provide a set of thematic concerns that were agreed on at the conference, the discussion at the beginning of the summary emphasizes that the purpose of the forum was not to create a single voice. Rather, in the groups' coming together as a network, the power of the women's movement would be revealed: "In the process of the preliminary discussions of the organizing committee in Moscow, the concept of the forum came up. The centerpiece of the concept was the idea of 'seeing the strength' of women and women's organizations and the real activism happening in different spheres but unaware of themselves as participants of a national women's movement. Therefore, the organizing committee thought the strength of the project was not on making suggestions for new principles, a platform or other activist positions" (*Pervogo Nezavisimogo Zhenskogo Foruma* 1991).

As the quote reveals, a great deal of importance was placed on not forcing any ideological or political coherence between groups at that historical moment. This desire is further illustrated by the terms used to name the organizations, including "informal organizations" (*neformal'nyi organizatsii*) and "independent organizations" (*nezavisimyi organizatsii*). These terms rhetorically emphasize that they are not premised on any ideological or political program.

Posadkskaya emphasized the importance of independence in her comments at the forum when she explained that it was most important for informal groups of women who were looking at their own problems to listen and be heard by other groups. These groups could then promote women's views on a range of social problems in the broader society. The link between these groups needed to be premised on an independent structure (*Pervogo Nezavisimogo Zhenskogo Foruma* 1991). A questionnaire was distributed to participants at the forum in order to document their views and activities, which would then be distributed in the network. This bottom-up approach to "collectivizing" the organizations was another indication of the organizers' sense of the importance of not imposing ideas from the top.[24]

Thematically the forum produced a broad and very critical statement about the "social-economic, political, and cultural discrimination of women" (*Pervogo Nezavisimogo Zhenskogo Foruma* 1991). The overarching theme of the forum was "Democracy without women is not democracy" (*demokratiia minus zhenshchina—ne demokratiia*). Historically it is important to note that this theme was created in the midst of the collapse of the USSR; it was not a response to Russia's post-Soviet political arrangement. The democracy that the forum was responding to was the project of *demokratizatsiia* (democratization) that Gorbachev had promoted. At this point in 1991 the Communist Party apparatus was still in place, although weakened. In fact, there was great suspicion of the activities of the forum. In her account of the forum, Anastasia Posadskaya recalls how attempts were made to shut down the forum by publishing politicized remarks about the organizers. These efforts did not work, of course, but at the start of the forum she noticed the presence of KGB officers. Clearly there was still suspicion of independent organizing despite the rhetoric of democracy that was circulating at that time. The first Dubna forum was a response to and germinated from that perestroika context.

As a result of the forum, five suggestions were put forward on the themes of human rights, politics, new economic conditions, the family, and the sphere of culture and education. The first point stated that while the USSR had ratified CEDAW in 1981, its principles had not been promoted. It stated that ignoring women's interests was undemocratic and there should be parity in the political representation of women at all levels of government. Some remarkable suggestions were given for improving women's economic role, including the creation of a depository for commercial information for women entrepreneurs, a state fund for the development of women-owned businesses, and the formulation of a training system for women in business. Finally, the forum document declared that there were widespread stereotypes of women that presented them as sexual objects and negatively impact their position in the family and society. It was suggested that there needed to be a public campaign against these images and a program to educate the public (including children in school). These and many more arguments were made in the final document presented at the end of the Dubna conference. This experience set the stage for the second Dubna conference as the political context was radically altered.

The declaration that democracy without women was not democracy was a response to Soviet *demokratizatsiia*, but unfortunately it foreshadowed post-Soviet Russian democracy as well. By the time of the second Independent Women's Forum in November 1992 there was optimism and energy for the future as well as concern for what post-Soviet democracy was bringing. The motto of the forum, "From problems to strategies" (*ot problem k strategii*), signaled a turn to thinking about tactics for advancing the women's movement. The language of "women's movement" (*zhenskoe dvishenie*) was used in the summary document, but national demarcation was rarely provided. While many of the organizations were Russian and the forum was in Russia, there was also an underlying sense of connection and relevance across the former state socialist sphere.[25] As with the first forum, the concept of "independent" informed the spirit of the second forum. The meaning of the "women's movement" was not grounded in a restricted platform but was based on the ideal of women's independent actions on behalf of women's issues. This is illustrated in the forum document: "The politics of the organization of the Forum consisted of making an open tribune like the previous one and for new women's organizations, initiatives and individual women who are looking for an answer to the 'women's question,' independent of their material position. The Forum gave participants that ability to come regardless of their visibility in different feminist forms and independent of their religious, political, or national differences" (*Materialyi Vtorogo Nezavisimogo Zhenskogo Foruma* 1992).

The notion of independence was discussed in Anastasia Posadskaya's comments as well. During the USSR the meaning of independence was associated with being unaligned with official top-down politics. Now that that structure was gone, what was the concept of independence based one? Independence from whom? Posadskaya explains that women's organizations are inherently political because they challenged the sexist pathologies of their state: not one political party or group had a program to address the status of women in society, women were practically excluded from the process of political decision-making at all levels of power, women's social position only was viewed as the byproduct of some other national goal, whether it be socialism, perestroika or democratization (*Materialyi Vtorogo Nezavisimogo Zhenskogo Foruma* 1992).

Thus, independence does not so much exclude women's activities from politics as it qualifies their intent to truly address women's issues, regardless of the rhetoric of socialism, perestroika, or democratization. Posadskaya argued that women must learn how to use the current political structure despite the fact that women's social activism had been manipulated for such a long time (i.e., in the *zhensovety*). Lingering resistance to engaging "the political" should not keep women from engaging in contemporary political structures.

Within this concept of independence an important tension existed. In Posadskaya's comments there is a concern that the emerging voice of the women's movement engage in the official political arena, while at the same time she expresses concern that the independent women's movement not claim a unified voice. She asserts that it is "especially important that the independent women's movement does not speak for all women, does not appropriate itself as the whole all-Russian organization of women, but presents itself as an open tribune for any women's organization and any women who have their answer to the 'women's question'" (*Materialyi Vtorogo Nezavisimogo Zhenskogo Foruma* 1992). This desire to remain open and independent influenced the first strategic emphases, including the creation of a network, the publishing of a "who is who in the women's movement" catalogue, and the publishing of an alternative national report on the status of women.[26]

This tension between pluralism and political expediency is not unique to the post-Soviet sphere, but it is crucial for understanding the experience of some post–state socialist representatives at the Beijing conference. At the second forum in Russia, there was greater recognition and connection to a global women's rights agenda. For example, Posadskaya remarks that there must be a strategy at different levels, including the national, regional, and city levels, and the global level: "Most importantly, we must leave this forum, with our individual strength, and make our place in the global women's society which has the right to their voice in this period of establishing a new world order" (*Materialyi Vtorogo Nezavisimogo Zhenskogo Foruma* 1992). There is also more global women's rights language in this forum's documents, including references to *trening* (training), to violence against women and gender violence (*gendernii nasiliia*), and to establishing an effective "national mechanism" for monitoring the status of women in society and the inclusion of the Center for Women's Global Leadership call for "sixteen days of action against violence," which was a clear example of the link between Russia and "the global." But with the turn to "the global," Russian and other former state socialist women faced a new context that was largely unknown to them. The tension between pluralism and expediency that I have highlighted in Posadskaya's comments thus provides insight as to why second world representatives felt left out, in a symbolic if not a substantive way, at the Beijing conference—which was three years after the 1992 Dubna forum.

The deep cultural and historical relevance of claiming an independent women's movement, in all the meanings I have explained above, set up many of the representatives from the former second world in a contradictory "place" vis-à-vis the politics of Beijing. On a practical level, the Beijing conference and the Platform for Action was the outcome of direct and unified organizing on behalf of national or regional interests. The strategies for lobbying at the global level were learned through the UN Decade for Women (1975–85), and we know that most representatives from the former second world were not privy to that experience. Just as women's "independent" consciousness was expressing itself outside the yoke of state socialism, women were met with a global women's rights agenda that had evolved through metageography (particularly the first/third world divide) and now did not have a clear place for them. This point is about not just a lack of skills or resources but a discursive disjuncture. This disjuncture was between a global movement to universalize women's rights norms and the particular post–state socialist inclination to "independence" that included a desire to avoid such universalizing. Elena Kochkina expressed this view in a conference in Moscow soon after Beijing: "The shortcomings of the Beijing document, from our viewpoint, are its high-level of universality and the absence of those problems, priorities and strategies that reflect the situation in Russia as a country living through a period of transition. Our future lies in reconstructing the historical emergence of both universal human rights and of the rights of women, and in defining where the specifically post-Soviet paradigm begins" (Kochkina 1995, 45). The centrifugal tendencies of women's organizing did not mesh with the centripetal forces of the global women's rights agenda. Clearly there was a concern for creating some unifying forces, as there was an emphasis on creating networks that would link the many and diverse women's organizations and initiatives across the Russian and broader region. Yet, in the beginning, that network was not conceived of as a strategy for enumerating a thematically (or politically) driven movement.

Thus, in addition to the tendency to not see the second world within global arenas such as the UN, and in addition to the practical "joining in" that women's organizations needed to do, the historical and conceptual context of women's self-identified independent organizing also contributed to a disconnect between feminist homogenous empty time and postsocialist difference. This tension between the global apparatus of transnational feminist networking and local independent women's organizations has been a central focus of concern in feminist scholarship (Guenther 2011; Lang 1997; Sloat 2005). This tension has not been resolved and, in the context of "violence against women," has served to displace economic approaches to antitrafficking.

4 / LOST IN TRANSITION / POSTSOCIALIST TRAFFICKING AND THE ERASURE OF SYSTEMIC VIOLENCE

The fourth wave of trafficking emerged as a new phenomenon just as the global agenda against "violence against women" achieved discursive and political dominance. As I outlined in chapter 2, the identification of postsocialist victims of trafficking facilitated a deepening of political commitments toward a prosecutorial approach to antitrafficking. Was it a forgone conclusion that post–Cold War trafficking discourse would prioritize prosecution at the expense of economic interventions? The analysis I advance in this chapter reveals how the idea and experience of transition became disconnected from global criticism of neoliberal economic policies. This disconnect between the concept/experience of transition and criticisms of real existing capitalism was an important reason why trafficking was not grasped as a problem of precarious labor. Thus, the discourse of transition is essential to understanding contemporary commitments and approaches to antitrafficking.

Despite the presence of critical perspectives of transition in the former second world in the 1990s, the concept of transition did not become a register of critique. Rather, the concept of transition was used to promote particular economic policies as necessary and inevitable.[1] In contrast, activists and intellectuals in the majority (third) world had already critiqued development policies

FIGURE 4.1. An infamous Soviet consumer line due to shortages. ©Peter Turnley/Corbis.

and contested the concept/experience of development (Escobar 1995; Kabeer 1994; Sen 1999; Uvin 1998). A critique of the teleology and capitalocentrism of development was not widely seen as relevant in the early postsocialist transition period (Gibson-Graham 1996). In American scholarship, there was a fierce debate in the 1990s regarding the concept of transition and the way some used it as a method for studying postsocialism. Critics argued that "transitologists" assumed too much (transition to what?) and were myopically focused on a set of categories to measure social change. While these robust intellectual debates have made an impact on how postsocialism is studied, the idea of transition remains very powerful in most political and academic settings. The end of socialist projects in the USSR and Eastern Bloc helped to delegitimate alternatives to capitalism and validated the notion that there ever was one. In its circulation, the concept of transition fueled metanarratives about "the market" and normalized radical transformations to labor.

The fourth wave of trafficking that ensued after the dismantling of socialism in the former USSR and Eastern Bloc could have been politicized as a symptom of failed or contested economic policies and certainly connected to systemic global dynamics such as migration practices, visa regimes, and the international division of labor. Yet a critical economic critique of the fourth wave of trafficking did not have wide policy circulation. I suggest in this chapter that this is because a static and quite uncritical view of transition was used as the backdrop for the problem of sex trafficking. In the post–Cold War era, the idea of transition (as opposed to development) allowed for some bodies to be recognized as the proper victims of globalization—that is, victims who ultimately do not raise a challenge to the underlying violence of capitalism that needs to be taken seriously.

Trafficking as aberration exemplifies what Slavoj Žižek calls subjective violence—that is, violence that is made visible (Žižek 2008). According to Žižek, subjective violence is made visible by its positioning against an obscured objective violence. He states: "Subjective violence is experienced as such against the background of a non-violent zero level" (2). I understand the distinction between subjective and objective violence to be about a politics of intelligibility, rather than materially different forms of violence. Similarly, I suggest that in the post–Cold War era human trafficking operates as visible, subjective violence. The politicization of postsocialist sex trafficking allowed certain bodies/experiences to be visible and, consequently, shaped understandings of unacceptable violence.[2]

Indeed, in U.S. antitrafficking law, the language of "severe forms of trafficking" is used to define trafficking. This odd qualification of trafficking reveals that there are acceptable forms of violence but they do not warrant the same level of recognition or redress. The terms "severe" and "trafficking" are made equivalent, and thus (only) forms of violence that are considered severe are made visible. In the wake of the Cold War, the twin discourses of "violence against women" and transnational crime made trafficking visible. Neither discourse centrally addressed the economic dimensions of the issue. Forced labor was not new in 1989 but took on a new discursive life. Human trafficking (especially sex trafficking) became visible, while other forms of violence due to global capitalism became normalized.

By the mid-1990s, there was growing recognition of the persistence of social hierarchy and the mixed outcomes of postsocialist transformations (Bradshaw and Stenning 2004; Burawoy and Krotov 1993; Funk and Mueller 1993). However, despite this recognition the concept of transition did not readily convey a critique of political economy.[3] To the contrary, the term "transition" is now commonly used as a rhetorical if not also normative replacement for the highly criticized idea of development. In the mid- to late 1990s, when governments and activists began responding to human trafficking, advocacy groups and researchers were making connections between economic transition and the phenomenon of human trafficking. At the time, the issue was primarily taken up by select local organizations focused on "violence against women" advocacy.

Politicizing trafficking as a form of "violence against women" was critical for the political recognition of the problem of sex trafficking in Russia and other postsocialist states. Advocacy organizations that provided services to victims of domestic violence and rape were the first to acknowledge the problem of trafficking in the region. Furthermore, international donors and governments tended to support advocacy organizations that fit in with the 3Ps framework. The conceptual and practical link between sex trafficking and "violence against women" has shaped how violence is politicized in the postsocialist context. Namely, the discrimination, disadvantages, and violence that ensued from economic restructuring became visible as "violence against women." While many Russian advocates and others in the region understand "violence against women" simultaneously as an economic, political, and social problem, overall the naming of violence (*nasilie*) tended to have a confining effect. That is, the politicization of "violence against women" displaced economic understandings of structural violence.

A clear indication of this dynamic in Russia is the fact that the recognition of sexual harassment as *nasilie na rabote* (violence at work) has been accompanied by its common dismissal as a manifestation of gender discrimination in the new market economy. Furthermore, sexual harassment is not viewed as an issue attendant to sex trafficking, despite that link to violence. I suggest that the naming of gender discrimination and precarious labor as violence has depoliticized the economic dimensions of both. The reasons for this dynamic are complex, and it is not reducible to being explained as a global phenomenon of neoliberalism or a co-opting of second wave feminism (Fraser 2009). The story of antitrafficking advocacy in Russia is one that includes the brave efforts of local organizations responding to the physical and psychological violence that women experience in their everyday lives and in the survival circuits of new economic conditions. It is also a story of political and financial investments that have prioritized certain approaches to women's rights that have not typically considered how postsocialist women's groups have been formulating their own agendas. The early western concern that postsocialist states successfully transition to capitalism and democracy was later joined by a concern for the Natasha sex trafficking victim. There was a glaring disconnect between the two: the very policies that were being promoted for economic transition never became the focus for the role they played in fueling sex trafficking.

The Western advisors were marketing themselves as the intellectual saviors of
the benighted East by putting the scientific prestige of neoclassical economics
behind one of the most cockamamie social engineering schemes (voucher
privatization) of the twentieth century.
—DAVID ELLERMAN, World Bank economist (2005)

Traditional comparative economics, which dates back at least to the discussions of
market socialism in the 1930s, studies under what circumstances either the plan or
the market delivers greater economic efficiency. By the time socialism collapsed in
Eastern Europe and the Soviet Union, this question lost much of its appeal. Socialism
produced misery and inefficiency, not to mention mass murder by several communist
dictators who practiced it. Capitalism, in contrast, typically produced growth and
wealth. If capitalism is triumphant, is comparative economics dead?
—SIMEON DJANKOV ET AL., The new comparative economics (2003)

In order for postsocialist trafficking to be understood as an aberration, the
broader context of economic transition had to be normalized and depoliticized in terms of political economy. This normalization was made possible
because of how the concept of transition was used to index specific policies
that supported "shock therapy," or what some critics would come to call "market fundamentalism" (Gowan 1995; Stiglitz 2002). World-historical assumptions, such as Francis Fukuyama's "end of history" proclamation, presented the
ideological collapse of state socialism as a clear-cut starting point rather than a
complex experience and unstable reference point for transition (Sakwa 1999).
In addition, the concept of transition was used to describe a temporary context
of vulnerability, a necessary "growing pain" on the way toward market capitalism, or as a path out of a period of crisis. These associations with transition
made it easier to discount criticisms of economic policies because transition
was always already necessary and temporary. Both the inevitability and tem-
porariness attached to "transition" immunized it from critiques of structural
adjustment and austerity that had already emerged across the globe.

The dismantling of state socialism was presented as a short-term strategy
by those advocating shock therapy (or a "big bang" approach). Even in those
countries where a more gradual approach ultimately was taken, as in Russia,
the concept of transition was used to justify the necessity of authoritarian
economic change (Rutland 2014). As Johanna Bockman's research reveals,
the defining characteristic of neoliberal transition was its reliance on a small,
powerful centralized state and a "reaffirmation of the hierarchal control of

managers and owners, while simultaneously attacking workers" (Bockman 2011, 207). The strong-arm tactics of transition were executed by the "central planners" of capitalism, also known as "market Bolsheviks" (Bockman 2011, 264; Ellerman 2003; Glinski and Reddaway 1999; Kostera 1995; Sirotkin 2006).[4] Ultimately, the authoritarian and antidemocratic measures of transition were glossed over by the ideological meanings of transition that came to discursive dominance.

While the experiences with and beliefs about transition varied across the region, a metanarrative of transition developed and contributed to the depoliticization of postsocialist economic reform. The techniques of transition were widely debated, yet the meaning of transition narrowed in on the irrefutable fact that socialism had failed and the belief that only (a certain form of) capitalism could replace it. It is now clear that the concept of transition is not temporally limited, for many of the countries that have undergone marketization are still classified as transition economies. In this respect, the idea of transition can be a permanent descriptor that maintains (the memory of) the forced dichotomy between capitalism and failed socialism and thus precludes recognition of the possibility and existence of viable alternatives to neoliberal capitalist formations. The term "transition" also glosses over the fact that different forms of neoliberal governance have been adopted in the region, including the more authoritarian neoliberalism of Russia.

Yet the concept of transition was used in quite different ways as part of a discourse on reforming state socialism before 1989. The direction of transition was not necessarily toward capitalism but toward some form of market socialism or hybrid system. Neoclassical economists within state socialism had long debated how to improve their systems using the shared tools of neoclassical economics toward the goals of market socialism (Bockman 2011). Bockman makes it clear that "socialists advocated 'transition' for decades, whether from capitalism, or from state socialism to a market economy within socialism" (202).

For example, "laissez-faire socialism" was created in Yugoslavia, the New Economic Mechanism (beginning in 1968) moved the Hungarian economy toward a mixed system, and Solidarity-led self-management committees were created in Poland. Other Eastern Bloc countries, including Czechoslovakia, instituted legal changes to allow for joint ventures with foreign enterprises (Appel 2004). In the Soviet Union, economists such as Leonid Abalkin claimed, with supporting arguments, that "the market is by no means an exclusive property of the capitalist system alone" (Abalkin 1989, 8). Under Gorbachev's leadership, the Soviet Union altered its laws on entrepreneurship, allowing workers cooperative ownership of enterprises. Cooperative ownership was a widespread phenomenon in state socialist countries and showed that via "the decentralizing socialist reforms over the years and decades before 1990, the workers, managers, and local communities had developed a range of de facto property rights (or 'use rights') over their enterprises" (Ellerman 2003, 14).

While Cold War political rhetoric presented a simplistic dichotomy between capitalism and socialism, the reality was that "actually existing socialism" in many countries included some measure of integration in the global economy and of private ownership. After 1989, elites deployed a new dichotomy between market capitalism and failed socialism in order to advance their national programs of transnational neoliberalism (Appel 2004; Bockman 2011; Greskovitz 1998; Harvey 2005; Kalb 2009; Weiner 2007). The open-ended and dynamic meanings tied to the idea of transition that existed within state socialism abruptly evaporated when "transition" came to mean imposing market capitalism by any means possible. Normative debates about transition transformed into narrow technical discussions about the speed and sequence of reform. The main rubrics of transition that were focused on were privatization, price reform, hard budget constraints, stabilization, and market institutions (Kołodko 2000; Nordhaus 1990). A flood of books, articles, and policy papers discussed how quickly and in what order reform should happen, at the expense of pre-1989 discussions of hybrid models.

The previously dynamic concept of transition turned into a referent for globally sanctioned neoliberal capitalist practices. Political elites and policy-makers then used this narrative of transition as a way to defuse quite contentious policies. For example, if there was a main fetish of transition it was the privatization of state assets. Grzegorz Kołodko has critically claimed that the entire concept of transition is based on the "correct assumption" that allocation through a free market, unlike central planning, guarantees higher efficiency, rising output, and better living standards and that concept is "the driving force behind the desire to transform the socialist system" (Kołodko 2000, 155). As such, many viewed the privatization of state-owned enterprises as the most direct and fastest way to that free market. Methods of privatization were debated at a technical level in terms of how to go about it, as in the case of the voucher programs instituted in Czechoslovakia, Poland, and Russia. Yet behind the process of privatization was a thoroughly antidemocratic and antiworker scheme that disabled citizens' rights. Market Bolsheviks insisted that privatization required the reclaiming of state assets from workers in the name of efficiency.

David Lipton, Jeffery Sachs, Stanley Fischer, and Janos Kornai, influential proponents of this approach, detailed in their map for Polish transition that "in many cases, workers wonder what the fuss is about, because of course *they* own the firms. Privatization should begin by establishing that the central government owns the enterprises and has the exclusive power to engage in privatization" (Lipton et al. 1990, 128). In response to such views, the World Bank critic and former insider David Ellerman has passionately argued that options that were presented by those active within reforming state socialism (as in Yugoslavia, Hungary, Poland, and Russia) and even by the European Bank for Reconstruction and Development were whisked away by national elites and economic advisors who envisioned privatization as a zero-sum process.

> The alternative to institutional shock therapy and market Bolshevism—the counterfactual—would have been to formalize the nearest approximation to the de facto property rights that would be accepted as socially fair and thus continue the decentralizing thrust going "straight to the market." If that alternative approach had been taken, then people would have encountered the market as something that would recognize and formalize the capabilities they had already developed and would allow them to do even better. Instead, the market Bolsheviks designed the "market reforms" with the exact opposite purpose to deny the de facto property rights accumulated during the "communist past," to righteously wipe the slate clean by renationalizing all companies of any size, and to start afresh with formal property rights deliberately unrelated to the previous "vestiges of communism." (Ellerman 2003, 15)

The neoliberal approach to privatization, that is, the disempowerment of workers and citizens in the name of efficient marketization, became the silent backdrop to elite-driven privatization. This happened not only in Poland but also in Hungary, Russia, Yugoslavia, and Czechoslovakia. Bockman explains that "because Eastern Europe did not have capitalists to create capitalism, and workers were deemed inadequate owners of the means of production, technocrats and political elites sought to create new actors interested in a new neoliberal system (Bockman 2011, 209).

Despite the existence of critical voices, including World Bank economists such as Ellerman (who later "retired" from the bank), those who pushed a notion of transition as a necessary and total break from socialism muted the underlying antidemocratic processes at work. For market Bolsheviks, the concept of transition referred to rejection of socialism and the drive to create a blank slate for a new market system. In that process, speed was often viewed as paramount. Slow or gradual reform was associated with long-term goals that included some dimension of worker cooperatives or small-scale ("piecemeal") privatization. Gradual reform was also suspect because it opened the door to "turning back" or a supposed loss of will. Speed was paramount in order to capitalize (in more ways than one) on the window of opportunity presented by the demise of the political hegemony of the Communist Party. Economist Padma Desai, a commentator on the "plan to market" transition, expressed this common perception: "Low speed" reformers could have been countries that embraced "market socialism." However, this approach had been generally discredited, and rightly so, fairly early on, and the countries making the transition have generally abandoned the illusion that such an approach makes any sense" (Desai 1997, 5).

Thus, speed was equated with a specific type of privatization process. In the case of Russia, a "mass privatization program" was orchestrated after the recentralization of state-owned enterprises beginning in 1991. Then those assets were transferred to the State Committee for the Management of State Property, which then distributed privatization coupons or vouchers to the general public (World Bank 2003). In the end, mass privatization was the quickest route to oligarchy in many contexts (Sakwa 2014).

Hilary Appel's analysis of privatization in Czechoslovakia and Russia suggests the same ideological importance placed on speed. Appel states: "the advocates of radical privatization and economic liberalization more generally argued that the government must take advantage of the revolutionary moment in the 'period of extraordinary politics,' during which great change was possible" (Appel 2004, 113). The advocates Appel is referring to include national elites such as Leszek Balcerowicz in Poland, Dušan Tříska in Czechoslovakia, and Egor Gaidar in Russia, as well as advisors from international financial institutions (i.e., World Bank and IMF) and important economists in the West. Appel contends that foreign advisors influenced the evolution of thinking on reform programs and created conditions that favored the adoption of a particular economic paradigm. "However, rather than crudely imposing privatization on unwilling officials, they promoted leaders already predisposed to liberal economic reform" (16).

Some elites saw the inefficiency of the state socialist system as a reason to seek the "fastest" route and criticized alternatives as inherently flawed (see Gaidar 2003).[5] Bockman summarizes what happened this way: "The new elites presented their options as technocratic change or decline into [this] chaos. Then they rejected market socialist options, presenting a seemingly narrow but actually authoritarian understanding of neoclassical economics to support neoliberalism" (Bockman 2011, 214). Importantly, the international financial institutions and western political figures identified these indigenous leaders as "liberal reformers" (that is, anticommunists) when in fact they were proponents of a specific ethos of market Bolshevism.

The oversimplified dichotomy between so-called liberal reformers and protectors of the communist past short-circuited the debate over the meaning and policies of transition. A neoliberal *idea* of transition fed the metanarrative of capitalist hegemony and "There is no alternative" at a historical moment when market socialism potentially could have expanded. In effect, the discourse of transition resuscitated beliefs about economic development and capitalocentrism that had been strongly criticized from the perspective of the majority (third) world. By the early 1990s, when transition programs began, a growing body of literature had already advanced criticisms of development and articulated postdevelopment perspectives (Escobar 1992; 1995; Gibson-Graham 1996; Latouche 1993). Yet critiques of the failures or hardships of transition policies often looped back into debates about the mechanics of transition or the misdeeds of particular national elites.[6] While popular anticapitalist anger erupted, it did not transform into anticapitalist discourse (Fleming 2012; Ost 2005).

The answer to the question of why a sustained critique of "transition" did not evolve in the 1990s is complicated to untangle. Obviously the role of political elites in shaping the discourse of transition was important, as I have discussed. In addition, Paul Kubicek argues, throughout the region unions were unable to coalesce as either a political or economic force (Kubicek 2004).[7] He asserts that the demise of unions in the postsocialist region, rather than being unique to the region, was tied to structural economic changes that have undermined the position of unions across the globe. Other scholars argue that we must destabilize the concept of loss in order to understand the complex context in which socioeconomic change was experienced by the people living through transition (Stenning 2005; Weiner 2007). In particular, what kinds of assumptions are embedded in a question like the one I am posing about why an anticapitalist discourse did not emerge in response to transition? It may be that the deleterious effects of transition, or the losses of state socialism, should be analyzed as experienced in fluid and relative ways (Shevchenko 2009; Weiner 2007). Certainly I agree with this nuanced approach to "transition." While I am alert to the generalizations I may be relying on, my analysis of loss is still important for understanding the absence of a critical economic discourse for postsocialist trafficking—an absence that has had profound implications for the people living in the postsocialist region, and globally, who are invested in and subject to the contemporary antitrafficking carceral regime.

Another important dynamic at play in the absence of critical political economic responses to transition is the contentious relationship between the forgetting and the remembering of state socialism (Marciniak 2009). For many, the socialist past remains a "disavowed reality" that shapes nostalgia for, as well as the silencing of, the experiences of state socialism (Marciniak 2009, 176; Etkind 2013; Todorova and Gille 2010; Velikonja 2009; Žižek 2005). As such, the idea of transition has operated not only as an economic category but as a denunciation of totalitarian violence (Eyal 2000). In this sense, the violence perpetrated by the communist state remained a referent for post-1989 interpretations of socioeconomic crises (Shevchenko 2009).[8] Many of the deleterious outcomes of privatization were expected "growing pains" and did not register as the violence of capitalism and were juxtaposed to (and haunted by) totalitarian violence and late socialism's crisis of scarcity (see fig. 4.1). As the quotation from Simeon Djankov and his coauthors in the epigraph to this section illustrates, the end of state socialism was associated with the end of any alternative to capitalism and the demise of a system that had produced "mass murder." The death of comparative economics was understood as a triumph over totalitarian violence.

The focus on the "old" violence of totalitarianism both sustained a discourse of crisis in which (neoliberal) transition was validated and obscured the violence of new capitalist arrangements. As Michael Fleming provocatively argues in relation to the Polish experience, "the shift from socialism to postsocialism has witnessed the nonintentional structural violence of the market replace the intentional violence of the state as the dominant form of violence" (Fleming 2012, 483). However, the implications of this metanarrative of transition extend beyond the postsocialist region. The inability of a critical discourse of transition to take hold, given the existence of anti- or postdevelopment voices, actually points to how the concept of transition has come to *replace* that of development since 1989. The emergence of postsocialist transition in 1989 resuscitated "old" beliefs in teleological capitalist development at a time when they had been challenged in other geopolitical contexts (see table 4.1). Only fairly recently have scholars of transition economies joined postdevelopment interventions, shedding light on the existence and future of alternatives to capitalist practices (Smith and Stenning 2006; Williams 2005; Williams and Round 2007a; 2007b; Williams, Round, and Rogers 2013).

A critical resignification of the concept of transition is unlikely to evolve in the ways that engagements with postdevelopment have challenged the dominant meaning of development. Rather, the concept of transition can now be seen as a post-1989 global approach to "development." The concept of transition

TABLE 4.1. Aspects of Transition and Development Discourses: A Comparison

Point of Comparison	Transition	Development
Presupposition	Progress narrative	Progress narrative
Target	Disavowal of socialist modernity	Disavowal of premodernity
Historical referent	Postsocialist	Postcolonial
Economic appeal	Economic intervention to dismantle state socialism (i.e., failed alternative to capitalism)	Economic intervention to modernize subsistence-based economies and/or reorder colonial-based economic arrangement
Policies	"Structural adjustment programs"; privatization; liberalization of market	"Structural adjustment programs"; Foreign Direct Investment; liberalization of market

may still be associated with postsocialist economic transformations but is also used outside that context in complex ways. An interesting example of this is how the term "transition" transformed for the very groups who had tried to launch a critical discourse of it. As I discussed in chapter 3, the authors of the statement from the "nonregion" circulated a critical discourse of transition. That effort had a limited impact at the UN but did spur further activity in the region. For example, some of the original voices for the "nonregion" created the advocacy network KARAT Coalition. Their website explains their mission and "HerStory," including their experience at the Beijing conference in 1995.[9] No longer referring to the term "transition," the KARAT Coalition is now situated in a complex position not reducible to the old east/west insider/outsider dichotomy. Poland, as well as other postsocialist EU member states, are still considered "new member states" and thus hold a qualified status. Yet many of these states also are considered "new donor countries" in respect to the EU neighborhood and the global south.

As a reflection of this new position, Joanna Szabunko started a thematic program on "gender and development" in 2005. In an interview she explained that the program is both a response to the position of new EU member states as donor countries and as a strategy to advance a gendered analysis of social and economic justice.[10] I asked Szabunko if there is any relevance to the term "transition" now. She stated that the term is associated with a narrow understanding of development, democratization, and market capitalism—in fact, governments now push the experience with transition as one that is to be promoted in development programs.[11] This exporting of the concept of transition to advance development illustrates how the discourse on transition has resuscitated old beliefs about development. But this dynamic remains complicated in terms of representing women's issues in the former "nonregion." On the KARAT Coalition's website the program "Gender and Development" is described as follows: "While promoting gender equality and women's rights in development cooperation KARAT places an emphasis on the needs of women from the developing countries, especially countries from the Region as these are often overlooked in the context of development targeting 'traditional' developing countries (in the development jargon known as the 'South'). We strive to link the development perspectives of women from the East, North and South."[12]

Clearly, there is a silencing of women's issues from "the region" because of the positioning of the EU vis-à-vis its economically weaker neighborhood. In this way, there is a loss of a critical perspective unique to the "nonregion." At the same time, states now part of the EU are in a privileged position. This further complicates the rebranding of the term "transition" for critical socioeconomic interventions.[13]

There are other examples of the concept of transition being exported to regions beyond the former second world. For example, in 1990 the World Bank initiated the journal *Transition Newsletter* to cover the events in the postsocialist region. Most of this journal's issues in the 1990s served as area studies reports on economic policy and outcomes in the formerly planned economies. Over time the journal incorporated countries previously categorized as developing in the majority (third) world. To reflect this shift, in 2004 the journal was renamed *Beyond Transition*.[14] Another example is the Transition Studies Network, which was founded in 2002 and produces the journal *Transition Studies Review*. The Network began as a regionally based group of experts from the Central Eastern European University Cooperation. However, starting in 2005, "a worldwide regional approach looking to Asia, Latin America, Eurasia and Great Middle East has been implemented."[15]

In another example from Russia, the former Soviet Institute of Economy of the World Socialist System of the Academy of Science underwent a change of name to the Department for International Economic and Political Studies within the Institute of Economy (Russian Academy of Sciences). The name change was expected. However, a symbolic indication of the ideological impact of the neoliberal concept of transition is reflected in the journal the Department started in

2004, *World of Transformations* (Mir Peremen). The root of the words "transition" (*perekhod*) and "transformation" (*peremen*) is the same, so there is a close resemblance. In the editor's discussion of the journal's mission, Ruslan Grinberg (who was also a contributor to the World Bank journal mentioned above) used a variety of terms, including *peremen, perkhod*, and *transformatsiia*. The meanings of these terms reference the underlying raison d'être of the journal. Grinberg explains: "Having rejected communist dogmas, as well as those of command and administrative autarchic economy, the peoples of the former Socialist bloc with great hardship are mastering the rules of pluralistic democracy and civilized market economy. . . . Grandiose transformation does not imply a return to 'old good' pre-socialist times, but rather a movement towards 'normality'" (Grinberg 2004). He goes on to write that the journal is filling an "information niche" to document and comment on *peremen*.

All of these examples suggest that, while the term "transition" was closely associated with postsocialist economic transformations, the term is now used to demarcate a growing stratum of peripheral economies. Furthermore, the term "transition" specifically denotes an assumed and uncontested economic paradigm. The post-1989 discourse of transition and its geographic expansion solidified this paradigm on a global scale. It was in this context of transition that the fourth wave of trafficking was interpreted.

Girls without Inhibitions: Precarity and Femininity in the New Economy

The state socialist sexual contract ensured that most women had access to education and employment. While is it important not to understate the significance of the social engineering of women's labor participation, over time that right to employment also became a burden for many women (Fodor 2004; Slavova 2006; Zimmermann 2010). The social provisioning promised by the state to relieve women of the bourgeois tasks of domesticity never fully materialized. Rather, the socialist sexual contract ensured that women would carry the weight of domestic labor and pick up the slack of an economy of scarcity. The burden of state socialist employment led some women to want to opt out of the new capitalist labor force. Romanticized visions of an economically comfortable domestic life helped fuel that desire. As it turned out, most did not have the luxury to do so. With economic restructuring, new freedoms and opportunities became available, but the immense social vulnerabilities that resulted dampened any unqualified statement about an increase in quality of life.

The immediate impact of transition on women's economic well-being was mixed across the region (Fodor 1997; Funk and Mueller 1993; Ghodsee 2005; True 2003; Weiner 2007). There were opportunities, successes, losses, and new constraints as a result of the dismantling of state socialism. However, one common experience across the region was the proliferation of neotraditional views of gender. Gender-neutral language of transition was contradicted by cultural discourses sexualizing women's labor and bodies in the new masculine market (Gal and Kligman 2000; True 2003; Yurchak 2003). While women's groups and institutions such as the UN recognized the gendered impact of transition, the economic dimension of new and reified forms of discrimination was overshadowed by an emphasis on gender violence (Hemment 2007). By the early 2000s, the anti–"violence against women" agenda dominated the focus on gender and transition.

The specificity of postsocialist experiences is not distinct from economic globalization, but it is important to highlight dynamics common to the second world. In feminist literature on migration, women's labor, and globalization there has been an emphasis on survival circuits within and between the global north and south. This work is important but not always sufficient for grasping postsocialist formations. Experiences with colonialism, economic exploitation, and development have distinct localities. While I think that Grewal and Kaplan's formulation of "scattered hegemonies" is analytically most precise, at the same time, less is known of state socialism and postsocialist transition within transnational feminist theorizing. This section provides a partial overview of the economic context of postsocialist transition and Russian women's labor. I do not want to generalize across the region on the basis of the Russian experience—nor do I provide a comprehensive view of the Russian experience. My purpose, rather, is to convey a general idea of the specific economic context of postsocialist precarious labor.

It may be helpful to have a general sense of "where" Russia is in terms of global economic standards. What is life like in a second world economy? The categorization of "second world" was largely a political designation but also correlates with some economic characteristics. There is a range within this broad (if also problematic) categorization of "second world" too—life in Moscow, Irkusk, Bishkek, and Chişinău is not the same. In particular, scholars have detailed the "multicolored" economies of socialism, a concept used to describe the multiplicity of the Soviet system (Stenning et al. 2010, 69). The notion of a "rainbow" economy articulates the myriad economies (formal, informal, and subsistence) that have contributed to the total welfare of the family within the Soviet system. This hybrid system was characteristic for the many millions of people living in the urban centers developed by state socialism. It also continues to characterize an ongoing hybridity of new capitalist and dilapidating Soviet development. As Katarzyna Marciniak explains in the context of Łódź, Poland, this "post-socialist hybridity" is a landscape of the new promise of mobility and consumerism against the backdrop of socialist ruins (Marciniak 2009, 175).

In the case of Russia, we can grasp this hybridity by looking at the trajectory of its Human Development Index score.[16] In 1987 Soviet Russia scored .920, and in 1995 the score had fallen to .769 (Babenko 2009). With the economic crisis of 1998 the score dropped further, but it started to improve in 2000. Russia's 2012 score was .788—considered "high human development" by the UN.[17] According to Mikhail Babenko, life expectancy and per capita GDP in purchasing power parity are the two Human Development Index measurements that pushed Russia's index down (Babenko 2009). The relatively high score in 1987 reflects the extent of Soviet development, while the dip in the score and its slow increase indicate socioeconomic loss as well as some growth.

The formal economy underwent dramatic changes during the 1990s, intensifying the need for informal and subsistence economies. This was because the early stages of transition to capitalism (1990s) created a steep drop in the basic standards of life for the majority of citizens. In Russia, early attempts at shock therapy were abandoned for gradualism. The turn to gradualism ultimately slowed the rate of job shedding in comparison to other transition economies. Job loss was primarily the result of privatization, as state-owned enterprises were eliminated or restructured for the sake of efficiency. Job loss was also due to the fact that the state bureaucracy—that behemoth of the "service economy"—was radically downsized. Job shedding profoundly impacted the rate of unemployment. While the Russian economy stagnated and industry declined in the early transition years, massive labor shedding did not take place until the mid- to late 1990s. Despite clear production declines, "Russian firms continued to resist downsizing the labor force and attempted to retain workers through pay cuts, wage delays, work stoppages, restricted work hours, mandatory leaves, and non-monetary benefits" (Glass 2008, 760). As Russian industries transformed and labor force participation fluctuated, unemployment grew.

In her study of women's labor force participation in Bulgaria, Hungary, Poland, and Russia, Christy Glass notes that between 1993 and 2000 the jobless rate nearly doubled in Poland and in Russia nearly tripled (Glass 2008, 766).[18] The unemployment rates between men and women have shifted over time and are difficult to measure in an absolute way. At points Russian men may make up the majority who are officially unemployed, but a majority of those working in the informal economy also tend to be women (Liborakina 2002). In one study of Russian female unemployment in the early 1990s, women made up more than half of the unemployed from 1991 to 1994, with the highest percentage in 1992 (72 percent).

While women's rate of unemployment now tends to be equal to that of men in Russia, this is due less to gender equality policy than to the impact of demographic processes, such as men's high mortality rate and depopulation (Zubarevich 2003, 12). Zubarevich argues that the "equality" of unemployment is tied to the fact that men do not compete for the low-paid and unprestigious jobs that women are willing to take. "As a result, gender problems are being masked by differences in mechanisms used by men and women to adapt themselves to new labor market conditions" (12). For example, during the first decade of transition, women accepted worse working conditions in order to gain employment and as a result experienced declining labor mobility (Zubarevich 2003). So, while employment rates can give some measure of economic well-being, they must also be seen in the context of shifting labor values, declining wages, and reduced social provisioning.[19] Precarious postsocialist labor conditions included diminished wages, working without wages in order to keep employed, job loss, downward mobility, loss of social provisioning, and shifting labor values—this all in addition to the uncertainty of new capitalist markets and industries.

At the same time as these economic shifts, patriarchal beliefs about gender that were never altered by the state socialist emancipation project came into full fashion (Fodor 2004, 787). Speaking of Eastern Europe, Éva Fodor has argued that "now that the regime has collapsed, its positive effects are expected to disappear and male domination to emerge with a vengeance because its depth and shape were not fundamentally altered during the forty-odd years of communist rule" (787). Similarly, observers of post-Soviet economic transformations in Russia have described the introduction of market capitalism as a process of masculinization. Having had the Soviet economy feminized by failure, a turn to the market was a turn to a new masculinized market (Meshcherkina 2000; Kay 2006; Yurchak 2003). In reference to Russia and Ukraine, Tat'iana Zhurzhenko argues, "the introduction of the feminine is viewed as a refusal of the rational progression of a market economy and liberal society" (Zhurzhenko 1999, 167). Not only was the market marked as masculine and thus the proper domain for men but also women were sexualized within that market (Alchuk 2006; Borenstein 2008; Ibroscheva 2013; Holmgren 2013).

The emergence of postsocialist human trafficking is a reflection of and embedded in new economic opportunities, constraints, and adaptive strategies, such as labor migration within and across the old Soviet and Eastern Bloc borders and a reliance on informal survival circuits. Sex trafficking in particular represents the combined processes of the political economy of the dismantling of state socialism, the sexualization of women, and their labor in postsocialist societies and the global market in "Slavic women" (Agathangelou 2004; Glajar and Radulescu 2004). Certainly, it is important to recognize that women seek out economic opportunities that capitalize on this sexual economy (Johnson 2007; Taraban 2007).

Yet, even if capitalizing on these opportunities, deeper dynamics are still at play. This tension between emerging opportunities and the gendered and economic dynamics that produce them is vividly depicted in artist Tanja Ostojić's project *Looking for a Husband with EU Passport*.[20] Ostojić posted a nude portrait of herself online to solicit marriage invitations. The photo is a bleak, even tragic, depiction of the artist, with her head shaved to the skull and pubic hair removed. This image is in perverse contrast to the solicitation to contact hot-tanja@hotmail.com. It was a haunting photograph that received over five hundred queries. After hundreds of email correspondences, the project continued with a public performance of her meeting with a German man (also an artist) and eventual marriage to him. After six years, they divorced (also as a performance art piece). Ostojić captures the exclusions that are created by the transition to capitalism and how women's sexuality circulates as a commodity if also as a means to inclusion. The artist also starkly depicts the commodification of postsocialist femininity.

Indeed, new opportunities emerged in the postsocialist context because femininity became a desired commodity that was marketed by a racialized and patriarchal practice of capitalism and buttressed by a cultural turn to neotraditionalism. This commodification of femininity is portrayed in David Redmon and Ashley Sabin's film *Girl Model* (2011). This documentary focuses on Russian girls who are recruited as models for the Japanese market. Leaving their desolate lives in rural Russia, they hope for monetary returns for their beauty, so desired in certain markets. The global demand for a certain ideal Slavic femininity is then compounded by neotraditional norms that emphasize women's sexuality. Describing the problem of neotraditionalism, Janet Johnson and Jean Robinson explain how "the use of the image of a sexed nude woman to sell journals, products, and even politicians has been assimilated into mainstream culture through the region. In contrast to a liberatory ideology that embraces women's sexual empowerment, the cult of beauty and sexiness has become key to the new market economy" (Johnson and Robinson 2007, 11). Ironically, neotraditionalism sexualized rather than domesticated women's sexuality—despite the state's promulgation of pronatalist policies.[21]

The gendering of the new market economy was not about returning women to the home (even if some had idealized that option) but about segregating them into feminized sectors of the economy and often sexualizing their labor. While the gendered division of labor of the Soviet period laid important groundwork for job segregation in the post-Soviet period, post-Soviet restructuring established "traditional" capitalist job segregation. For example, few women now work in the trade, banking, and finance sectors of the economy—sectors that are more prestigious and masculinized. There is also an increase of women in the service sector, where jobs are feminized and paid less (Maltseva and Roschin 2006). In addition, women's activity in the informal economy and domestic sphere during the state socialist period took on an added urgency and necessity with transition (Khotkina 2001). As recent scholarship reveals, the gendered divisions in the informal labor market reflect and reinforce the gender divisions of domestic labor (Williams et al. 2013, 124). These trends are not unique to Russia, of course, but coincide with global restructuring and the expansion of the informal economy and of gendered and racialized intimate labor (Agustín 2007; Boris and Salazar Parreñas 2010; Cabezas 2009; Keough 2003).[22]

Changes in occupational segregation have also made a significant impact on the relative economic standing of men and women. According to Katarina Katz, the market economy has exacerbated the prejudice, discrimination, and inequality that the Soviet order held for women (Katz 2001). The masculine market revalorized traditional gender roles that furthered the social expectation that women perform certain types of work and that they are the primary caretakers of the home and children. While occupational segregation may have existed under state socialism, its material impact is exacerbated in the market system. This is evident in women's relative wages. In one account, female average wages were 56 percent of male average wages in 1999 and 50 percent by the mid-2000s (Zubarevich 2003). "The reason for gender inequality in the remuneration of labour is the existing branch segregation and professional (above all vertical) discrimination" (13). While this study notes regional differences, the trend during the first decade of transition shows that women lost ground in terms of relative wages to men (Gerber and Mayorova 2006).

As the responsibility for social services (such as maternity leave and child care support) has shifted from the state to employers and states have promoted pronatalist policies, women have often been seen as less desirable employees. There are times when men are viewed as a higher risk than women because of health issues, such as alcoholism and drug addiction, and violations of labor discipline (Zavyalova and Kosheleva 2010, 346). Despite this, men continue to dominate the majority of managerial and administrative positions (Zavyalova and Kosheleva 2010). In addition, business remains a masculinized economic sphere in Russia, impacting whether and how women enter certain professions (Mazzarino 2013; Salmenniemi, Karhunen, and Kosonen 2011; Fieldon and Davidson 2010). As Elena Zavyalova and Sofia Kosheleva argue, women's place in the Russian economy is constrained—they are more likely than men to be highly educated but less likely to be promoted beyond midlevel management. "Women's prospects for career advancement have not changed much during the reform period, either qualitatively or quantitatively. Women are assigned the role of a relatively cheap and sufficiently skilled workforce, . . . are virtually excluded from public administration, face the 'glass ceiling' in promotion to executive positions in industry, and are forced to take the entrepreneurship and self-employment route if they want to achieve higher levels of independence and responsibility for their careers" (Zavyalova and Kosheleva 2010, 344).

Indeed, women are responding to these aforementioned constraints by pursuing a variety of entrepreneurial strategies. While the dominant view of entrepreneurship is masculinized, a variety of *biznesladies* proliferate in the formal and informal private business sector—including babushkas selling World War II paraphernalia, young women selling marriage, migrant shuttle traders, and small enterprise owners.

In fact, women are the owners of a significant proportion of Russia's small and medium-sized businesses. Sergei Katyrin, vice president of the Russian Commerce and Industry Chamber, stated that women are in charge of 40 percent of small and medium-sized business ventures in Russia. Furthermore, Tatyana Gvilava, director of the Russian-Arab business council and president of the Women and Business Association, stated that business ventures headed by women show more dynamic growth (with rates up to 170 percent) than male-owned ones ("Business Ladies Increasing in Russia" 2004). The presence of women business owners is a testament to their abilities and drive. However, as Zavyalova and Kosheleva reveal in their research, women's entrepreneurship is also an indication of the sexism they face in the workplace. Thus, the positive growth in female entrepreneurship attests both to women's participation in the new capitalist economy and to the discrimination they face within it

("Biznes Zhenshchinam k Litsy" 1996; Salmenniemi, Karhunen, and Kosonen 2011; Sandul 2002; Tiers 2002; and see Burdeau 2001; Welter, Smallbone, and Isakova 2006).

Through the process of transition, women have faced and adapted to precarious labor. As in the global trends, informal and intimate labor has expanded. Boris and Salazar Parreñas explain that "intimate labor remains a primary source of livelihood, which women increasingly gain by being paid for it in the marketplace rather than through performing it within heterosexual marriage in exchange for support" (2010, 8). The intimate labors most associated with post-Soviet women include sexual labor (via sex trafficking) and mail-order marriage (Johnson 2007). Yet sex and marriage are not the only forms of intimate labor that have expanded as a result of transition—many have migrated in order to obtain care work, "entertainment" labor such as dancing or hostessing, and domestic work (Agathangelou 2004, Kaşka 2006; Keough 2006).

Another form of intimate labor in the Russian context has been the refashioned job of the secretary "without inhibitions" (*bez komplekov*). In the 1990s, one of the most common and blatant displays of the sexualization of women's work was found in advertisements for such positions. Various Russian newspapers were known for listing job advertisements by sex. It was not uncommon to see an advertisement that requested only female candidates under the age of twenty-five, with long legs, and *bez komplekov*.[23] Figure 4.2 gives a graphic depiction of a specific mold for this secretarial position. In 1994, the special court of the Judicial Chamber on Information Disputes in Moscow (which at that time was tied to the office of the president) reviewed a challenge to the publication of job advertisements that were gender exclusive. The case was filed against *Izvestia* (News), *Finansovaya Izvestia* (Financial news), and *Ekonomika i Zhizn* (Economics and Life) for printing job ads that specified that men only need apply or for female applicants "without inhibitions" listed in separate sections. The court ultimately decided that the advertisements were a breach of Russian constitutional law (Human Rights Watch 1995). However, the prohibition of these sexualized job advertisements did not necessarily correlate with a shift in behavior toward female workers. A 2008 court dismissal of a sexual harassment case indicates the ongoing presence of harassment and how it is largely dismissed in Russia. The judge's dismissal of the case stated: "without sexual harassment we would have no children" (Bloomfield 2008).

It seems quite obvious that sexual harassment would have become an important issue in the context of women's sexualized labor and the masculinized market. Yet criticism of sexual harassment (*seksual'noe domogatel'stvo*) has

FIGURE 4.2. Who can measure up? Courtesy of All Russian Anecdotes, http://vseanekdotu.

had little traction in Russia. Some women's groups and scholars have raised the issue, but it has not received attention as an acute problem of discrimination. One reason for the lack of attention and even derision toward the issue relates to the fact that sexual harassment is associated with western political correctness. In Russia, as in other state socialist contexts, the workplace or public sphere was not gendered masculine. Women were expected to fulfill the feminine duties of motherhood and caring, but this norm was not based on a gendered division of the public and private spheres. In contrast, in the United States, where the concept of sexual harassment first emerged, sexual harassment referred to sexist behavior that emerged because women breached the gendered divide between public and private spheres. As women entered the paid labor force, the workplace (i.e., men) had to adapt to their presence. However, Russian women were never barred from paid labor because of the gendered division between public and private spheres. Sexism in the workplace was explained in another register. That register most often is tied to proper sexual behavior or sexual morality and not sexism.[24]

Without the calculus of this specific gendered public/private divide, sexual harassment is viewed as the result of sexual rather than sexist behavior in Russia.[25] Even then, sexual harassment is not widely regarded as a legitimate issue given the valorization of the sexualization of women—something that is widely embraced as an advance from the asexual Soviet times and that distinguishes

Russia from western political correctness. In an interview with Alexander Kletsin, one of the few Russian scholars to conduct research on sexual harassment, he said that it was a "nonissue" in Russia. Confused, I asked why, and he explained that the topic for his research was tied to the MacArthur funding he had received. His view was that sexual harassment was an American issue and not indigenous to Russia.[26] Supporting this, but from a critical perspective, Russian sociologists Elena Zdravomyslova and Anna Temkina argue that flirting at work in Russia is considered a "normal gender relationship" and that the erotic character of that relationship is viewed not as a deficiency but as a positive element of Russian culture (Zdravomyslova and Temkina 1999, 62). The real and perceived demographic imbalance of men and women is used as reasoning to promote the biological determinism for sexual harassment as well. As I have been told many times by Russians of all kinds, women desire and enjoy being sexually harassed—it makes them feel like women.

Women challenging sexist behavior in Russia commonly use this kind of essentialism as well. For example, in 2012 Iuliia Koliadina and Ol'ga Boltneva generated a high-profile media campaign against "impudent" Russian men. Their group, called Rosnakhal (a combination of the words "Russian" and "impudent"), brought attention to street harassment. They produced a short video that showed men harassing Iuliia on Moscow streets, documented with a hidden camera. In most cases, men would not take her refusal of their attention and harangued her for it. The YouTube video received nearly two million hits in just three months and spurred debate in Russia's Duma (Parliament).[27] Both women refuse to be called feminists and maintain that they love men ("Skrytnaia kamera zapechatlela khishchnykh muzhchin" 2012). Rather, they want the stronger sex (men) to respect the weaker sex (women). Their terminology for critiquing harassment reveals an essentialist gender order and resistance to calling sexualized behavior sexist. Terms that avoid the feminist language of sexism, such as "impudent" (*nakhal*), "rude" (*grubost'*) and "pestering" (*pristavanie*), are used.

This somewhat ironic politicization of harassment has broken the reigning silence on the issue. It has been some time since sexual harassment was taken up as a serious issue. One of the first post-Soviet Russian public responses to sexual harassment was Valerii Vikulov's organization DIANA (Khotkina 1996; Strokan 1995). Vikulov was a journalist working at the Moscow newspaper *Vse Dlia Vas* (Everything for you) in the early 1990s when he started to receive complaints from female employees about the lack of professionalism in the workplace. He and his wife started an organization that compiled a list of enterprises that had a record of sexual harassment against women. A list of over three hundred firms, or one in three firms in Moscow, was compiled into a document (*Obshchestvo i Zazhchity Zhenshchin ot Seksual'nykh Presledovanii na Rabote*). The lack of professionalism that female employees complained about was tied to the sexualization of women in the workplace. Rather than view women as potential assets to a growing firm or as having their own career goals, women were often relegated to the post of "secretary."

In contrast, Russian feminist scholar Zoya Khotkina believes that the issue of sexual harassment is a problem of economic discrimination. She claims that while exact numbers for the rate of sexual harassment in Russia are difficult to find, the fact that women are seeking jobs through newspaper advertisements using the qualification "without intimacy" (*krome intima*) suggests that this practice is still fairly widespread. A series of news articles in the late 1990s indicated that while a court of the Judicial Chamber had outlawed sexist job advertisements in 1994, women's work was still sexualized in many of the burgeoning sectors of the economy (Hunt 1997; Ivanova 1998; Nadezhdina 2000; Shelkovnikova 1999; Tracy 1999). Supporting this, Elena Khiltova, head of the International Federation of Business and Professional Women in St. Petersburg, acknowledges that sexual harassment of working women is a common practice in Russia and that it remains silenced.[28] In our conversation, she explained that there is too much embarrassment for women to come forward.[29]

Violence against Women: Framing Postsocialist Precarity

The economic restructuring of state socialist systems had a profound, if uneven, impact on people's lives and their well-being (Stenning et al. 2010). Certainly, the economic dimensions of postsocialist transition played a critical role in the emergence of trafficking within and across the region. Forces such as the instability and transformation of labor markets, the upending of social provisioning, the revaluing of labor and commodities, and the opening of borders created new opportunities as well as pathways to precarious labor practices. These forces should be considered within specific national contexts as well as in relation to economic forces such as deindustrialization in the global north, informalization, flexibilization, EU currency practices, transnational migration regimes, and global labor trends (such as intimate labor). The specificity of postsocialist transition, as well as its relationship to regional and global dynamics, is not simply a backdrop to but is the stage for trafficking. Trafficking is not an aberration to these dynamics but is part of them. While not solely determining of whether trafficking occurs, these (and other) economic dynamics were not seized on to frame postsocialist trafficking. In this section, I explore how the category "violence against women" circulated in the Russian context to both politicize violence *and* depoliticize economic understandings of that violence. This process of marking violence in specific ways is illustrated by the radically different levels of attention sex trafficking and sexual harassment receive in Russia, despite the fact that they are interlinked in the context of the neotraditional capitalist transition.[30]

The dynamics that have silenced the problem of sexual harassment are in fact some of the same ones that have brought sex trafficking into focus. Local organizations focused on violence against women were some of the few to give voice to the issues of sexual harassment and sex trafficking, as well as interpersonal violence, when such issues were silenced under state socialism (Fábián 2010; Johnson 2004, 2009; Zabelina 2002). Local advocacy work was enabled and validated because of the global resonance of the agenda of combating gender violence. While women's advocacy in the postsocialist region does not exclusively focus on "violence against women," it has received the most attention from foreign donors, local advocacy groups, and feminist scholars (Nikolic-Ristanovic 2002). This attention reflects the success of the global movement to address gender violence as well as the importance of combating gender violence in postsocialist states where it was previously neglected.

In Russia and other countries in the region, local organizations connected with transnational advocacy networks in order to advance national agendas against gender violence (Fábián 2010; Hrycak 2010; Johnson 2009; Keck and Sikkink 1998).[31] Drawing on the global paradigm, advocates in the region often conceptualize "violence against women" as a composite category that includes issues such as sexual harassment, domestic violence, rape, and sex trafficking. In some cases, organizations have adapted the language of "violence against women" so as to include an economic emphasis that has not been integral to either foreign donors or the UN conceptualization of "violence against women" (Fábián 2014; Ghodsee 2003; Hemment 2004; Hrycak 2012). Adapting the definition of "violence against women" in some cases has been a response by the women seeking help as victims. For example, Julie Hemment describes in her ethnographic work that women seeking help have an elastic and economic understanding of violence. She states: "Women who do call to speak about gendered violence frequently relate it to a range of other materially-based issues that commonly include unemployment, unpaid wages, impoverishment and cramped living spaces" (Hemment 1999, 36).

Hemment explains that "state and economic violence are at the heart of many of the 'problems' that Russian people identify as most urgent" (Hemment

1999, 37). Yet the discourse of "violence against women" does not capture such problems, nor are most of the organizations set up to address them. Local organizations largely do not engage a critical economic lens on violence—regardless of the form of violence. This is in part due to the way the global framework for "violence against women" influenced *how* this concept came to discursive life in postsocialism (particularly through monetary support). As a result of the foregrounding of interpersonal and bodily violence, the socioeconomic violence of transition receded to the background. There also continues to be an emphasis on a juridical response to violence rather than, or in addition to, a welfare response. This dynamic is not just a symptom of the hegemonic discourses imposed on local activists—though this is also at play, and research suggests that local organizations continue to negotiate the power differentials between donors and receivers (Sundstrum 2002). The success of the "violence against women" agenda also reflects neoliberal governmental practices of recognizing violence only through the apparatus of the carceral state. This catch-22 of gender violence advocacy has been highlighted by feminists for some time (Bumiller 2008). In the Russian context, the politicization of "violence against women" also was taken up as a corrective to a legal and cultural context where violence had been primarily viewed in relation to an abusive state. Thus, the composite category of "violence against women" facilitated an important discourse on violence that garnered legitimation outside the ethos of state socialism while at the same time playing into the new neoliberal Russian state.[32]

Sex trafficking and sexual harassment are categorized as forms of "violence against women" because they are viewed as specific gendered manifestations of violence.[33] This emphasis on gender violence explains why sexual harassment has received little attention, while domestic violence and sex trafficking have received much more. Sexual harassment rarely involves physical violence, yet it is routinely discussed as a form of violence. While physical violence is not necessarily associated with sexual harassment, the little politicization it has had relies on the language and imagery of sexual violence.

Some opinion polls on the prevalence of harassment conceptualized it as sexual advances by a boss or coworker. For example, sociologist Alexander Kletsin conducted the first survey research on the topic in 1996–98, looking at women in St. Petersburg (Kletsin 1998). His results suggest that from 1996 to 1997, 35 percent of women experienced some form of sexual harassment at work (48). Around the same time frame, a poll taken in Nizhny Novgorod found that 75 percent of the female respondents had been subject to sexual harassment at some point, while another newspaper poll in St. Petersburg stated that 39 percent of the respondents (75 percent of whom were women) had been subject to sexual harassment (Kuvshchinova 2002).[34] An article in the popular Russian weekly *Argumenty i Fakty* (Arguments and facts) published in 1998 claimed that one in three women in Russia were sexually harassed (Ponarina 2000). More recently, the Russian newspaper *Chastnyie Korrespondent* (Private Correspondent) gave the figure that 30 percent of women experience sexual harassment at work (Sukhov 2012).

However, the polling information presents a confusing picture of the extent of the problem, and given that the definition of sexual harassment is not precise, it is difficult to know exactly what is being measured. Legal cases are also not a helpful measure of the prevalence of harassment because so few citizens use the courts to solve the problem of discrimination.[35] According the the limited data I gathered, prior to 1990 there were twenty to twenty-five legal cases regarding sexual harassment, at the beginning of 1990 there were two to three cases, and in 1994 there were no cases.[36] Since then, very few if any have been filed under Russia's sexual harassment law, Criminal Code Statute 133. There are also no federal statistics gathered on the topic. So, despite the juridical frame for politicizing (and framing) "violence against women," in the Russian context sexual harassment remains a nonissue.[37]

A mixture of legal and social factors contributes to the reluctance of female workers to speak out about their experiences with sexual harassment. For one, the Russian legal system has yet to prove an effective channel for challenging sex discrimination (American Bar Association's Central European and Eurasian Law Initiative 2006). Activists and scholars have shown that the legal system struggles to properly process cases of sexual violence, such as rape and domestic violence, where criminalizing evidence can be more visible (Attwood 1997; Johnson 2001, 2004; Post 2000; Zabadykina 2000; Zabeliina 1996). The reluctance of legal professionals to take harassment claims seriously is even stronger because the evidence is harder to corroborate.[38]

In response to this legal context, a conference on workplace sexual harassment took place in 1995 and was supported by the American Bar Association's Central European and Eurasian Law Initiative, and the Moscow Center for Gender Studies.[39] This was one of many initiatives by the American Bar Association to build legal capacity in Russia to address women's rights. The participants in the conference ranged from women's crisis center representatives and academics to politicians and lawyers. Liudmila Zavadskaya, Russian Duma deputy and member of the Women of Russia political bloc (1993–95), spoke at the conference, as well as Aleksei Ignatov, a professor of law and member of the research/consulting group for the Russian Supreme Court. Also in attendance was Zoya Khotkina, who has written articles on the issue and worked on economics more broadly as well. The focus of the program was on Russia's legal system and its capacity to address women's legal rights. This focus was part of foreign (U.S.) "democracy assistance" to women's organizations. In her periodization of funding for Russian women's groups, Janet Johnson explains that this American Bar Association initiative was part of a first wave of assistance (1998–2001) that would later dry up (Johnson 2009, 61).

At the conference, the term "sexual persecution" (*seksual'noe presledovanie*) was used interchangeably with "sexual harassment." This language reflects the common conceptualization of harassment as sexual violence that predominated during the conference (Khotkina 1996). In fact, despite the title of the program, the term *seksual'noe domogatel'stvo* generally was not used. Rather, sexual persecution (*seksual'noe presledovanie*) was the preferred terminology. An important reason for this linguistic practice was the fact that representatives from women's crisis centers played an important role in the program. Given the advocacy focus of the crisis centers to aid victims of sexual violence, it is easy to see how violence served as the substantive connection between harassment and sexual violence. The political currency of "violence against women," originating both from within the American Bar Association and from Russian feminist scholars and activists, facilitated a discussion of harassment. Without the language or terminology of violence against women, the problem of sexual harassment would not have received the little attention it did get. Speaking to this point, Khotkina made a prescient point about naming discrimination in the closing epigraph to the conference publication: "A problem without a name does not have a chance to be resolved. In order for society to know about sexual harassment, they must learn that it is not just a problem of saleswomen [*prodavshchits*] or secretaries in offices, but the encroachment on women's human rights" (125).

Another reason for the slippage between terms is that "sexual harassment" continues to be situated in Russian law as a sex crime and associated with other sex crimes such as rape. Statute 133 refers to compulsion (*ponuzhdenie*) to engage in sexual acts. The statute is not new and has been included in Russian criminal law, in some form, since before the Soviet Union (Suchland 2008). In Soviet law, compulsion was described as a crime against women and the result of their socioeconomic vulnerability. The revised criminal code of the Russian Federation took out the socioeconomic piece and inserted gender-neutral language. Instead of crafting a new legal category explicitly to address workplace sex discrimination, the statute carries on as de jure sexual harassment (*seksual'noe domogat'stva*). It has now become an obscurity: most legal professionals are not familiar with the statute (Nadezhdina 2000). This fact was also discussed at the 1995 conference. If the recent proposal by United Russia for amending the Russian Administrative Code is passed, sexual harassment may finally gain legal traction (Sokolova 2012).[40]

Thus, sexual violence was already a framework for a set of laws regarding women prior to post–Cold War discussions of "violence against women." This history is an important reason why sexual harassment and sexual violence remain legally coupled. The growth in activism against gender violence also furthered this connection. For example, the postsocialist articulation of sexual harassment as a form of "violence against women" in Russia is revealed in the expression "sexual violence at work" (*seksualnoe nasilie na rabote*). This connection is also seen in the way that the terms "sexual harassment" and "sexual persecution" get used interchangeably. The term "sexual violence at work" was created by crisis centers as a translation of the programatic language of "violence against women"—and it fits well in the Russian context, where sexual harassment is legally understood as a sex crime. The phrase "violence against women at work" reveals the enabling and disabling effects of the language of "violence against women" to frame and adjudicate different forms of violence and discrimination that are tied to economic and not sexual violence. The problem of sexual harassment still is largely not criticized in terms of neoliberal transition and the masculine market. One important explanation is that the discourse of "violence against women" did not enable such engagements.

The language of "violence against women" was valuable for articulating forms of violence that had been silenced under state socialism. Yet I suggest that the classification of sexual harassment as a form of "violence against women" in Russia has constrained critical discourse on the economic dynamics of violence. This is also seen in how the "violence against women" framework helped legitimate the problem of sex trafficking in Russia.[41]

Women's crisis centers were the first to respond to victims of trafficking. In the early 1990s, these organizations were not equipped or prepared to help trafficking victims. Antitrafficking had not been a part of their original focus. According to Marina Pisklakova Parker, founder and director of the Moscow-based organization ANNA (National Centre for the Prevention of Violence), the organization was ill prepared to deal with the calls from trafficked women on their domestic violence hotline.[42] The needs of a rape or domestic violence survivor are similar but not equivalent to those of a trafficking victim. In addition, these women are often in complex economic situations, needing legal help with migration laws, if not potentially still vulnerable to those involved in their trafficking. Years before Russia's first official antitrafficking organization was created, women's crisis centers managed and began to document victims of trafficking.

In what was likely the first conference on trafficking in Russia in 1997, Natalia Khodyreva, founder and director of the St. Petersburg Psychological Crisis Center for Women, explained: "Since 1994 we have been gathering information in the field of trafficking of Russian women for prostitution" ("Trafficking of NIS Women Abroad" 1997). Khodyreva is now an outspoken antitrafficking advocate and helped build the Angel Coalition, which was started in 2000 as a network of antitrafficking NGOs.[43] In addition, Natalia Abubikirova, the first executive director of the Association of Crisis Centers for Women "Stop Violence," explained in a 2004 conference on human trafficking in Russia that many in their network of organizations had been working on combating trafficking since 1997. The Angel Coalition and the Association of Crisis Centers have been the two largest networks of antitrafficking advocacy in Russia. Both networks had their beginnings with domestic violence advocacy in the early 1990s.

Outside Russia, one of the first organizations to advocate on behalf of trafficked women was the Dutch organization Foundation against Trafficking in Women, which was founded in 1987 and advocated for Asian and other "third world" women trafficked into Holland's sex industry. As I discussed in chapter 2, by the early 1990s there was already political movement on the issue in Europe. The Council of Europe had commissioned a report on "the traffic in women," and Lucia Brussa's report came out in 1991. Because Western Europe was the most common (and closest) destination for postsocialist trafficking, and labor migration in general, actors there were some of the first to articulate sex trafficking as a new post–Cold War dynamic. The Dutch NGO Foundation against Trafficking in Women was also instrumental in setting up the first European antitrafficking network, LaStrada. (In 2007 the Foundation against Trafficking in Women underwent a name change to CoMensha; it continues to be a part of the European Network against Human Trafficking.)

In Russia, the issue of sex trafficking was picked up by women's crisis centers in a somewhat delayed way, given the fact that victims from the former state socialist region received attention in Europe and the United States earlier on. In Eastern Europe, there was a simultaneity to the emergence of the problem, its recognition, and the formulation of a response to it. For example, Trijntje Kootstra, one of the founding members of La Strada, explained that the activists first involved in the project took a pragmatic approach.[44] There was no time to really reflect on how to frame trafficking as an issue because they were in the middle of a transition process that was not entirely visible. Their first response was to pressure governments and the media to pay attention to the issue and to provide services to victims. Another original member of La-Strada working in Poland, Stana Buchowska, explained that at first the media and governments refused to recognize the problem but that it later became a sensationalized issue.[45] In separate interviews, both activists also talked about how the Beijing Platform for Action was an important but insufficient document for their work at the time. While the document broadly validated their work to national governments, it was insufficient for specifically combating trafficking. Since the mid-1990s, when La Strada was establishing its roots across the region, the organization has gained a more critical perspective regarding the dominant approaches to trafficking (Uhl 2010).[46] For example, Marieke van Doorninck, the public affairs advisor for La Strada Holland, now works on lobbying for antitrafficking legislation that respects women's right to migration for work and formulating economic tools for prevention.[47] But this more critical position evolved over time. At first, it was difficult to both bear witness to and respond to the problem of trafficking.

By the time organizations in the region engaged transnational institutions about trafficking, the discourses of "violence against women" and transnational crime were already firmly in place. The predominance of this understanding of trafficking was evident in the documentary *Bought and Sold* (1997), which is regarded as the first to depict the fourth wave of trafficking. The film debuted in Moscow in 1997 at the conference "Trafficking of NIS Women Abroad," also regarded as the first coordinated antitrafficking conference in Russia.[48] The creator of the documentary, the Global Survival Network, was joined by the International League for Human Rights (New York) and Syostri (a women's crisis center in Moscow) and was financially supported by the Soros Foundation.

Documentation from the conference reveals that there was considerable momentum behind the two major global frameworks for sex trafficking—"violence against women" and transnational crime and corruption. President Clinton previously had initiated U.S. efforts to address "violence against women" and in March 1998 issued an executive order on the new global crisis of "violence against women." One indication of the discursive momentum behind the frame for trafficking is that Theresa Loar, the senior coordinator for international women's issues for the U.S. Department of State, presented at the conference. Her message focused on the "3 PS" that would come to define U.S. antitrafficking law. Michael Platzer, from the UN Crime Prevention Branch in Vienna, was also present. Conference transcripts indicate that trafficking was being addressed within new UN efforts to combat organized crime.

This was because, it was said, "the UN has become increasingly concerned with the violence against and trafficking of migrant workers and women by criminal organizations, resulting in a special mandate from the Secretary General to address this issue through the UN Center Against Transnational Crime" ("Trafficking of NIS Women Abroad" 1997). The presence of and comments by Loar and Platzer suggest that the dominant approaches to antitrafficking were already solidified by the 1997 conference, despite the fact that the U.S. TVPA and the UN Convention to Combat Transnational Organized Crime would not appear until late 2000. However, additional views were expressed at the conference. In particular I want to highlight the comments by the participants who emphasized the economic chaos that had ensued during postsocialist transition and how it related to the rise of trafficking.

It is important to note that in 1997 the Russian government was giving very little official attention or resources to human trafficking. In fact, officials were known for eschewing the topic because these human rights violations, according to them, largely occurred outside of the Russian territory. Many did not see cause to get involved in the poor decisions of migrant laborers. Neither was the issue of prostitution particularly important. In fact, there was still a desire for "open" discussion and display of sexuality, including sex work, as part of an ongoing sexual *glasnost'* that had begun in the late 1980s. Thus, the Russian government was not compelled to see human trafficking as a domestic issue, nor was there public or political debate about sex work as an indigenous market. Comments from Liudmila Zavadskaya, deputy minister of justice, indicate this trend in Russian officialdom, though her comments suggest greater sympathy toward controlling trafficking as criminal behavior.[49] Zavadskaya made the important point that greater interagency cooperation was needed, including increased awareness within the Foreign Ministry as it worked with the Ministry of Justice.

A very different set of comments came from Olga Samarina, then deputy director of the Department for Family, Women and Children within the Ministry of Labor. Her remarks, which are fully documented in the conference transcripts, focus on the "socioeconomic conditions pushing women toward a search for employment abroad" ("Trafficking of NIS Women Abroad" 1997). Samarina provides the only structural analysis of trafficking from a gendered perspective on economic transition. The picture she depicts is precise and quite powerful. The socioeconomic position of women in Russia is the primary focus of her remarks. She states that, in the move toward a market economy, women have experienced greater discrimination, a loss in their competitive abilities, and reduction in employment opportunities. Women now earn less and are crowded in the lower paying sectors of the economy. Women constitute a majority of the unemployed (she quotes 63 percent) and "constitute almost 80 percent of parents left without a job raising underage children and children handicapped since childhood" (Trafficking of NIS Women Abroad 1997). All of these socioeconomic causes are central for understanding why women seek employment abroad. Samarina suggests that antitrafficking efforts must address the employment and discrimination problems that women face in Russia. Some of her suggestions include altering social policy to support and regulate women's wages and providing maternal aid to families with children; strengthening of social security for part-time, temporary, and contractual workers; expanding entrepreneurial opportunities and training in finance and professional development geared toward women; and a temporary job bank for women facing the threat of being laid off ("Trafficking of NIS Women Abroad" 1997).

Samarina's comments and suggestions are remarkable for how they so directly link trafficking with socioeconomic conditions—conditions that are in flux and can be altered. No other speaker really targeted women's economic status as a method of antitrafficking. In reference to sex trafficking, Gillian Caldwell said, "This reality is a direct result of the fact that the economic status of women has declined dramatically in the transition to a market economy. Trafficking must be seen as part of the worldwide feminization of poverty and of labor migration" ("Trafficking of NIS Women Abroad" 1997). Yet, despite this statement, the documentary she helped produce does not frame sex trafficking in this way. The antitrafficking message of *Bought and Sold* is focused on the criminal dimensions and provides no criticism/analysis of the economic policies of postsocialist transition. The emphasis on the criminal dimension of trafficking has influenced "prevention" strategies and promoted an emphasis on educating potential victims of trafficking to help them avoid becoming abused migrants. Attempts to avoid the creation of trafficking victims are not equivalent to mitigating the causes of trafficking. Yet this line of advocacy, focused on education as a method of prevention and thus reduction of trafficking, is precisely what was developed most in Russia and across the region. In addition to increasing capacity for prosecution, a majority of antitrafficking efforts have relied on the hope that fewer people will get trafficked if they understand the risks of migration. Ultimately, these priorities allowed the socioeconomic strategies that Samarina suggested in 1997 to slip through the cracks.[50]

For further evidence of the dynamic to displace the socioeconomic dimensions, we can turn to the presentations of two other important representatives at the conference. Natalia Khodyreva, director of the St. Petersburg Psychological Center for Women, discussed how her organization had worked with trafficking victims since 1994. As an activist engaged with the issue early on, Khodyreva holds an important perspective coming from within the Russian Federation. Her comments focused on the need to provide outreach education in order to prevent women from becoming trafficked, in particular addressing cultural stereotypes about migration, work abroad, and prostitution. For someone involved with direct services to survivors of violence, these priorities make a lot of sense. She, and the many other crisis centers who became involved in antitrafficking, engage the issue of trafficking ex post facto—they work with victims. And it is from that antitrafficking perspective that Khodyreva and others have directed their attention toward preventing victimization rather than addressing the root causes of trafficking. Because sex trafficking was first addressed in Russia by women's crisis centers and has remained primarily an advocacy issue affiliated with "violence against women," there is an ongoing tendency to prioritize victim prevention rather than trafficking prevention.

The focus on victim services is an expected outcome given the origins of where antitrafficking advocacy emerged. At the same time, many crisis center advocates did have a handle on the socioeconomic dimensions of violence, but the immediacy of their work—and the demands from their donors—focused their attention in ways that did not provide an opportunity to develop additional projects (Hemment 2007; Johnson 2009). However, we could expect a U.S. policy advisor on international women's rights to interject a socioeconomic lens on sex trafficking. Yet at the 1997 conference in Moscow, Theresa Loar's comments present the largely (already) consolidated vantage point of the United States on trafficking and how to combat it. She states: "Our interagency working group intends to attack trafficking in women with a variety of measures with an interdisciplinary, coordinated approach involving participants from law enforcement, judges, migration authorities, medical and social workers and members of grassroots organizations" ("Trafficking of NIS Women Abroad" 1997). These efforts are categorized as the 3 PS: prevention, protection, and prosecution. In her comments on prevention there is not a single mention of addressing root socioeconomic dynamics. Rather, there is an emphasis on changing laws. More stringent laws and frequent prosecution of trafficking criminals is viewed as a key component of preventing further trafficking. In addition to greater and more coordinated laws, Loar focuses on education as a method of prevention, including diplomacy programs to "better publicize the dangers associated with trafficking in human beings" and a "pilot information campaign designed to combat the trafficking of women in Eastern Europe and the newly independent state of the former Soviet Union" ("Trafficking of NIS Women Abroad" 1997).

Education programs and building law enforcement capacity are very important. However, these tools are not sufficient for the prevention of trafficking. Furthermore, there is growing criticism of prevention campaigns for the messages they send about migration and what is "normal" behavior (Andrijasevic 2007; Davidson 2006). Some campaigns rely on racialized and sexualized beliefs about women that are problematic and reinforce their precarity (Andrijasevic 2007; 2010; Hua 2011). While media campaigns are intended to warn the public of potential victimization, they do not abate the need or desire to migrate but help regulate and criminalize migrant laborers. As Julietta Hua argues, "representing potential victims as hailing from specific places and thus looking a particular way not only threatens to overlook other possible victims, but it also helps reproduce connections between ideals of sexual normalcy/ deviancy with national belonging and helps naturalize visual cues with racial categories and cultural communities" (Hua 2011, 71). Education programs are not value free. Nor are law enforcement interventions. Some scholars and activists question the benevolence of a law enforcement response to trafficking— particularly from the perspective of victims of trafficking (Gallagher and Pearson 2010). In this context of qualified progress toward combating trafficking, it is even more crucial to reevaluate what has not been theorized as much—the economic dimensions of trafficking.

On that front, Russian scholar Elena Tiuriukanova worked on the issue of human trafficking approaching it from an analysis of migration.[51] She conducted a considerable amount of research on migration, human trafficking, and forced labor in Russia. In addition, Tiuriukanova collaborated with Russian government agencies, international nongovernmental agencies, and international intergovernmental agencies. Her position as one of the main scholars on the topic in Russia is illustrated by the fact that she was the principal investigator for the report *Human Trafficking in the Russian Federation*, a massive inventory and analysis of data, resources, and actions taken to combat trafficking in the Russian Federation (Tiuriukanova 2006b). The project was coordinated by several UN departments, the ILO, the IOM, and the Canadian International Development Fund. She did not speak at the 1997 conference "Trafficking of NIS Women Abroad," but she was present.

One of the most compelling arguments Tiuriukanova's consistently presents in her work is that human trafficking and forced labor are significant problems within the Russian Federation especially in relation to irregular migration from the CIS. More than 12 million migrants enter Russia a year, mostly from the CIS region, with which Russia has had a visa-free arrangement (Tiuriukanova 2006b, 34).[52] With the Russian government's goal to double GDP in conjunction with its demographic crisis, there will only be increased reliance on migrant-based development (34). This reliance on migrant labor exists within the broader economic context in Russia, where the informal economy may constitute at least 22.4 percent of the country's GDP. It seems self-evident, then, that "trafficking for labor exploitation is the most common type of human trafficking in the Russian Federation" (35).[53] Combating human trafficking is incredibly difficult as a result of the liberal migration arrangement among the CIS countries and the relative lack of attention labor trafficking has received.

THE ONGOING FOCUS on "Natasha"—the woman who is sex trafficked to a foreign land—as the victim of trafficking has narrowed advocacy and understandings of human trafficking in Russia and illustrates the political and policy disconnect between the existing antitrafficking effort and the recognition of trafficking's roots in political economy. One key reason why Russian officials and Russian law have not paid sufficient attention to internal or CIS trafficking has been that political attention to trafficking from Western Europe and the United States was focused on the "Natasha" victim of trafficking from the start.[54] In particular, sex trafficking, not human trafficking, captured the attention of public policy discussions in the West. Since the first government reports on trafficking there has been more attention to labor trafficking. However, the intense focus on sex trafficking has had a lasting political impact on policy and the public imagination. In the 1990s, the face of trafficking was that of a young woman forced into sexual labor. This image illustrates not just who victims of trafficking are but what forms of violence are made intelligible by policy and social advocacy.

In Russia, as in other contexts, the normative shadow of sex trafficking has meant that "human trafficking using labor exploitation is often ignored and not regarded as a crime" (Tiuriukanova 2006b, 21). As a result, most legal cases that are processed are related to sex trafficking (Brennan 2008; Tiuriukanova 2008).[55] Yet labor migration to Russia is a growing phenomenon and one on which Russian economic development depends. There are an estimated 14 million labor migrants in Russia each year, with 80 percent coming from the former Soviet republics.[56] In many cases, there are no visa restrictions for entering Russia from a former Soviet republic. However, once in Russia labor migrants and their rights are often blatantly abused. While not viewed as trafficking victims at first because of the legality of their mobility, labor migrants can find themselves in forced or life-threatening conditions and facing restrictive citizenship regimes (Alexseev 2010; Bloch 2013).[57]

Another dimension of the bias toward a sexual violence frame for trafficking is that most organizations involved in antitrafficking are not invested in local sex workers' rights projects or sex markets, including migrants' rights. While antitrafficking organizations helped pass legislation to criminalize human trafficking and establish the legal and professional competency of law enforcement, their work is not tied to local sex workers' rights issues (Shapkina 2006). With important exceptions, advocacy on behalf of sex workers (*seks rabotnitsy*) in Russia is more recent if still quite limited. However, these organizations are not integrated into antitrafficking advocacy, nor were they part of the political or discursive evolution of the problem of trafficking in Russia.[58] In fact, my interviews reflect what other scholars have revealed: the prostitution debate that is so central to the western/global evolution of antitrafficking legislation was not indigenous to Russian feminist organizations (Johnson 2009; Shapkina 2006).[59] Rather, foreign donors and some Russian state officials imposed the divide between the abolitionist and sex workers' rights approaches.

The disconnect between concern for antitrafficking and the recognition of it as part of indigenous labor markets in Russia—both for sexual and manual labor—reveals the ongoing limitation of the "violence against women" and transnational crime frameworks. This disconnect also obscures the structural violence created by postsocialist transformations. The trumpeting of human trafficking as *the* post–Cold War human rights issue has hidden what is most obvious: the triumph of capitalist forms of violence.

Part III. Economies of Violence

Current descriptions of trafficking are not devoid of an economic vernacular. In fact, the triumph of the carceral antitrafficking approach has enabled a neoliberal economism in human trafficking discourse. Terms such as "supply," "demand," and "market" are common categories used in this logic, and they indicate a shift to a more structural view of trafficking. Yet this economism is deeply problematic. The term "economism" is often associated with critiques of Marxism (Funk 2012). It is a term used to critique the Marxist tendency to reduce complex hierarchies to class relations. However, I deploy the term to describe a *particular* economic logic that informs analyses of human trafficking (Molland 2010). While some of the new market-based work has brought attention to issues such as the significance of the informal economy and the relationship between the recent global financial crisis and social vulnerabilities, the logic of neoliberalism is reappropriated in this discourse and ultimately put into practice in antitrafficking efforts. This final part analyzes current trends in antitrafficking advocacy and attempts to advance an economic approach to the issue.

In recent years, there has been a shift in focus from the individual victim to the market of trafficking. But this shift does not remedy the shortcomings I have discussed. The market is yet another metaphor for speaking of individuals—the rational agent *homo economicus* animates the illicit market of trafficking. A key assumption of this approach is that individuals (victims and traffickers) exist in a measurable and rational market. Trafficking is not just viewed as a criminal act but also as a rational economic endeavor that is distinguishable from the licit economy. Ultimately, the tendency to see and measure trafficking as separate brackets understandings of it as embedded in or even as a byproduct of everyday economic practices and relationships. The failure to see this embedded economic character of trafficking is a major blind spot in the approaches of the dominant governmental and nongovernmental agencies working to combat human trafficking.

The turn to standardized data collection is viewed as an important strategy to generate concern and resources for antitrafficking. Specifically, experts attempt to quantify trafficking as a measureable market—in terms of workers/victims, profit making, and lost wages. In order to do this, profit estimates are based on estimates of the number of victims of trafficking. Sidestepping the politics of naming victims of trafficking, these estimates of profit simplify the economic relationships that function to produce exploitative labor. Furthermore, the quantification of profits generated by trafficking presents an imprecise measure of the magnitude of the problem. The complex and at times problematic methods used to generate profit estimates fail to address normative questions about human rights and labor exploitation. The magnitude of the problem and the size of the profit do not alter *how* we approach antitrafficking. Standardized data collection may have less to do with strategies of antitrafficking and more to do with influencing political commitment.

Conceptually, the focus on estimating profits generated by trafficking does not move us toward a more accurate measure of the ethical magnitude of human trafficking but supports a general trend toward a business model understanding of and approach to antitrafficking. In particular, antitrafficking agendas have increasingly focused on "demand reduction." Demand reduction strategies seek to reduce the purchasing of products that rely on slave labor. For example, there are campaigns to dissuade men from buying sex in public education programs such as "John schools" or criminalizing the purchasing of sex, as with the Swedish Sex Purchase Act. Both strategies are based on a particular understanding of sex trafficking as a business and are believed to cut down on the demand for sexual services and thus reduce sex trafficking. In response, sex workers' rights organizations have pushed back against these strategies because of the underlying conflation of demand for sex work with trafficking. Their critique of demand reduction strategies is based on a belief that people have the right to sexual labor. Ultimately, the positions and political strategies of both groups treat trafficking as a business and thus collude to promote a neoliberal economism in human trafficking discourse. With radically different ideologies, these agendas promote rather than critique the concept of the market and the right to entrepreneurship as the solution to trafficking.

The adoption of a market-based analysis of trafficking as the predominant economic approach has further obfuscated how global capitalism and government policies structure precarious labor. In chapter 5 I describe how trafficking is analyzed as a market. In the final chapter I present a brief look to alternative approaches. Human trafficking is a violation of human rights and should remain a juridical problem. But it is time to expand advocacy beyond a carceral understanding of human trafficking.

5 / FREEDOM AS CHOICE AND THE NEOLIBERAL
ECONOMISM OF TRAFFICKING DISCOURSE

Measuring the Trafficking Market

The effort to create greater clarity about the size of trafficking is a significant trend in the policy discourse on trafficking. While there have always been attempts to grasp the human magnitude of trafficking, more recently there have been attempts to estimate the revenues and profits generated by it. In the key documents that present these estimates it is assumed that trafficking can be monetarily quantified as a market and that rational economic actors inhabit that trafficking market. The illicit character of the economic behavior may make it difficult to collect accurate data; but beyond that qualification, the measurability of trafficking as a market is never questioned. In order to measure the profits generated by trafficking, the analysts must assume that those numbers (and behaviors) can be captured as distinct from the general market economy. In this way, the market metaphor brackets trafficking from the broader global economy. In addition to isolating the trafficking market from the general economy, there is the assumption that the profits and "wages" earned are the result of rational economic behaviors. The problem of human trafficking is viewed through the actions of *homo economicus*, leading either to cost-benefit analyses of the business of trafficking or to redirecting the labor of victims of trafficking.

In 2003 the UN estimated profit from trafficking to be between $7 billion and $10 billion annually (U.S. Department of State 2003, 9). Soon after that, the U.S. FBI gave an estimate of $9.5 billion in annual profit (13). Since 2005, the ILO has resolved the inconsistencies between estimates and methodologies. The ILO generated estimates for all forced labor, from which estimates of trafficking were drawn. The ILO distinguishes trafficked labor as a form of forced labor, so not all forced labor is trafficked. Trafficked labor is defined as that which is manifested by deceit, fraud, or threat. The 2005 ILO report estimated that forced labor trafficking creates profits of $3.8 billion and that the profits from commercial sexual exploitation due to trafficking are $27.8 billion (ILO 2005b). The total for all forced labor, including that due to trafficking, is $44.3 billion. A 2009 ILO report estimated the amount of lost earnings (termed "opportunity cost") for victims of forced labor to be $19.6 billion. In May 2014, the ILO released a new study on the profit of forced labor. The current estimate is three times the previous global estimate—$150.2 billion in annual profit from forced labor (ILO 2014).[1]

The size of these numbers is shocking and lends urgency to combating human trafficking. But the number values are not self-evident in terms of their size or meaning. Are the numbers shocking because they reflect a sense of the possible human magnitude of trafficking? Does this economism of human exploitation make that exploitation more concrete? Such questions raised by the profit estimates are not part of the official discourse, for example in the ILO reports. I reflect on these normative questions later. For now, I challenge the face value of the profit estimates. Most important, the profit estimates rely on a variety of other estimates that should be taken into consideration, such as estimates of the number of people trafficked into forced labor and forced commercial sexual exploitation and estimates of wages. In the case of the former, the profit estimate hits a core question/tension in the trafficking debate—that is, who is a victim of trafficking?

In order to calculate profits, therefore, an estimate of the human magnitude of trafficking must be used. In the 2005 ILO report, the profit estimates rely on a (presumed) stable population of victims. Yet the laborers—the population of victims that is used to generate the profit estimate—are not a closed population. Victims of trafficking traverse various labor markets and may even have their status as victims of trafficking alter throughout their working experiences. The question of how many people are victims of trafficking is an ongoing empirical and political debate among antitrafficking advocates (Kelly

2005). In the ILO research, a method called "capture-recapture" is used to estimate the number of people in forced labor.[2] The capture-recapture method most commonly is used to estimate unknown animal populations such as fish or birds. For example, there is no way to count how many fish live in a lake. With the capture-recapture method, it is assumed that the lake contains a fixed but unknown population of fish. Therefore, the likelihood of capturing a certain quantity of fish will be as likely the first and second time a sample is collected. In other words, the statistical probability is the same with the first capture and the recapture (also known as a binomial probability). Once that data is collected, a statistical model is used to estimate the total number.

The capture-recapture method was used to generate a global estimate of forced labor. Typically the ILO uses country-specific data to generate global estimates, but in the case of forced labor, country-specific data has not been available. The use of the capture-recapture method is a creative way to deal with this lack. Yet it is also a potentially problematic solution. The metaphor of the lake of fish conceptually matches the assumption that there is an isolated trafficking market, but it does not match reality. Trafficking victims are not always distinct fish in a lake of workers. The identification of victims of trafficking is one of the hardest aspects of combating and prosecuting trafficking (Gallagher and Pearson 2010; Goodey 2004; Soderlund 2005). The elusive undertaking of identifying victims of trafficking, particularly sex trafficking, is a major challenge to generating accurate estimates of it. Locating victims of trafficking is difficult for reasons that go beyond the criminal and/or hidden character of trafficking. Individual cases of trafficking often are not black and white in terms of (potential) victims' self-consciousness of their situations. The crime of trafficking requires the identification of trafficking victims, not only by a state agency of some sort but by the actual people who will claim victim status. It can be ignorance, defiance, or fear that keeps someone from being identified as a victim of trafficking. Compounding the psychological dimension is the fact that there is a fine line between smuggling and trafficking. Someone may have willingly agreed to be transported or hired through informal connections and ended up in a situation of trafficked labor. The contested and blurry distinction between smuggling and trafficking challenges the assumption that there is a clearly defined and stable population of trafficking victims.[3]

Thus it is problematic to say that there is a fixed population of trafficking victims, given that there is a dynamic relationship between trafficking and other forms of labor exploitation, as well as complex identities that are not reflected in the juridical category "victim of trafficking." Another dimension of the capture-recapture method that is potentially problematic is that a date range (1995–2004) was used to collect the population estimate. Thus the estimate is not an annual number. The 2005 ILO report estimated that there were 12.3 million people in forced labor, with 2.5 million due to trafficking. What that means is that during the period between 1995 and 2004 there were 2.5 million people trafficked, including new annual victims and those trafficked for different lengths of time during that date range.[4]

I am not trying to deflate the meaning of the numbers. However, given that these numbers are frequently reproduced in popular discourse, it is important to think about what assumptions are communicated when data are wielded. There is a rhetorical difference between the statement "2.5 million victims of trafficking" and the statement "2.5 million people trafficked between 1995 and 2004." Yet the estimate often circulates as a self-evident number and is not qualified by its methodological parameters. It is also the case that the estimate may be under- or overvalued because it is possible that people were unwillingly identified as victims, and it is likely that people remain unidentified as victims of trafficking. While some of the issues I raise here were addressed in the 2012 ILO global estimate, the estimates of profit still rely on estimates of the forced labor population.[5]

Reflecting on the implications of the capture-recapture method raises a set of important questions about the utility of separating smuggling from trafficking, about separating forced labor from trafficked labor, and about the relationship between scale and magnitude when it comes to human exploitation. Yet these questions are not part of the policy discourse on estimating forced labor and estimating the profits from trafficking. Rather, the assumptions about the magnitude of trafficked labor are rolled into the global estimates of the profits from trafficked labor. While the 2012 ILO population estimate uses survey data and thus is an improvement, more discussion is needed about the relationship between data collection methods and antitrafficking strategies. How do data collection methods link up to particular antitrafficking strategies? This is a question that begs further discussion. Yet, at the same time, regardless of their methods, the ILO reports contribute to the economizing of human trafficking by making lives (and violence) measurable, computable, or relatable but not necessarily better known, appreciated, or valued.

Estimates of global profit from forced labor in the 2005 and 2014 ILO reports provide an accounting of how much profit can be generated by labor exploitation. Because the 2005 profit estimate relies on earlier population estimates, the $44.3 billion amount reflects a date range and is not an annual profit estimate. However, the 2014 ILO estimate uses 2006 as a reference year, and thus $150.2 billion is a global estimated profit per year. In the 2005 and 2014 reports, the calculation of profits is based on an estimate of wages and a measurement of value added, which is the difference between the sale price and the production cost of a product.[6] Both figures are difficult to determine and change across various industries. In the 2005 report, commercial sexual exploitation is the only industry disaggregated in the profit estimates. All other forms of forced labor, such as agricultural, construction, and domestic work, are grouped together. For forced labor, data for value added and wages are drawn from the agricultural industry. This problematic methodology was corrected in the 2014 ILO report. To generate that estimate, country-specific surveys used in the 2012 ILO population estimate were used to generate estimates for wages and value added measurements in three sectors (domestic, nondomestic, and sexual exploitation).

While the mathematical maneuvering used to gain credible estimates suggests an evolution toward precision, a constrained aspect to this statistical understanding of trafficking remains. The algebra used to generate such estimates supports the dominant logic regarding antitrafficking. That is, plugging in the numbers to calculate the size (total profit) of human trafficking contributes to the view that it is a discernible market and thus separate from the formal economy. Furthermore, the estimates are statistical abstractions that further distance advocacy from the experiences that people have and the violence that runs through precarious labor. This is because the statistics do not lend a specific ethical response to trafficking. Statistics are norms abstracted from their referential objects, not strategies. In this way, statistics are purely formal, seemingly sterile, and can be used to any end. Thus the work to generate an economic grasp of trafficking can further carceral approaches or obscure critical economic analyses.[7] I suggest that they support a neoliberal mapping of trafficking in which rational actors need only shift their entrepreneurial energies to reduce violence and exploitation.

The more trafficking is categorized and measured, either through the metaphor of the market or through prosecution rates, the more it is viewed as distinct from the practices of formal (and legal) behavior. The more trafficking is viewed as an aberration, the less we address the complexities of trafficking and its embeddedness in global capitalism and social hierarchies. Trafficking does not exist as a market in and of itself prior to the existence of the legitimate markets of agriculture, construction, or domestic work. Trafficking is not toxic algae floating invasively in a lake. It is not something that can just be located, counted, and then removed from the clean waters of the market. It is in the water.

The 2014 ILO report gives us the astounding estimate that forced labor generates $150.2 billion in profit. I say the number is astounding because I personally cannot imagine what that amount means. The number sounds like a lot, and it bothers me. But my response is a general one and not dependent on a specific profit amount. The statistic operates as a self-referential norm—it seems our indignation is not indexed by the profit margins of slavery per se but by a prepackaged "outrage" that evaluates certain human rights violations. As feminist theorist Mary Beth Mader elucidates, statistics operate as norms that are "immanently self-referential; no genealogy, history, ancestry, or external standard matters for determining it. The norm purports to register whatever is the case at any given sampling point" (Mader 2011, 50).[8] The global estimates of forced labor profit reference the method and ratios used to generate that number— they do not signal appropriate levels of outrage, an ethical grasp of human exploitation, or a clear strategy for advocacy. What can we do with a figure like $150.2 billion?

These statistics beg the question: is there a relative scale for $150.2 billion in profits? Would additional figures provide a sense of what these dollar amounts mean? How does the annual estimated profit compare to other industries? Is this the cost of violence or of potential wages? In thinking through these questions, I wonder about relative scales, because statistics are impossible to comprehend without some comparison. With what do we compare $150.2 billion? The ILO estimates that of the total global profit from forced labor, $99 billion is annually generated from global forced sexual exploitation (ILO 2014, 27). If we treat forced sexual exploitation as a separate industry, how does it compare to other industries for annual profit? In 2010 the global apparel industry generated $2.560 trillion in profit. In 2010 the global banking and finance sector had a sluggish year and only generated $3.8 trillion in profit. The global agriculture industry produced $5 trillion in profit in 2013.[9] These numbers certainly overshadow the estimated profits of forced sexual exploitation or even the total estimate for forced labor. My point is not to downplay the magnitude or gravity of the problem of trafficking but to make the point that economizing trafficking does not clarify the problem.

If the scale of human trafficking is not determined by estimates of the profit, what function does the estimate serve? What does this ongoing commitment to viewing trafficking as a measurable market do for antitrafficking efforts? Certainly, the knowledge created by such reports can lend urgency and validation to antitrafficking advocacy. Human trafficking is often thought to be invisible, lurking in the shadows of society. Thus putting a dollar amount to trafficking makes it seem real and tangible. Yet economizing human trafficking has supported the dominant approaches to antitrafficking that obscure the role of political economy.[10] This economism turns people, practices, and violence into abstract numbers and thus distances antitrafficking advocates from those realities. The logic driving the ILO reports is present in other areas of trafficking advocacy. I turn next to two prominent voices often thought of as diametrically opposed—those advocating neoabolitionism and those advocating sex workers' rights. However, in both cases trafficking is economized as a business in which rational actors merely need to alter their actions.

Neoabolition: A Business Model Approach to Trafficking

While the trafficking market is viewed as a separate (and criminal) sphere, the deployment of the market metaphor also draws on a belief that it operates with the same rational order as those of legal markets. A business model approach to trafficking isolates particular components, such as supply and demand, profits and commodities, in order to understand trafficking as an industry. Underlying this approach is a belief in rational economic actors who seek to maximize their profits either at great risk to their lives or through illegal means. The rationality of these actors and their contexts are largely static. For example, rational actors are pushed and pulled by factors such as wealth and poverty. A woman is willing to take a job in a foreign country and risk leaving her familiar life because of the poverty of her location and the assumed relative wealth of the destination country. A trafficker is also a rational actor. Her rationality is embedded in a criminal mind but nonetheless directed toward the maximizing of profit. The trafficker's decisions are constrained by the risks of the business of trafficking. Trafficking certainly includes a variety of monetary exchanges, but a business model approach to trafficking oversimplifies the issue, reducing it to these rational exchanges, and displaces trafficking from the wider economic and social contexts in which it exists.[11]

An example of a business model approach to trafficking is the influential book by Siddharth Kara *Sex Trafficking: Inside the Business of Modern Slavery*.[12] In his book, Kara takes great care to think through the dynamics of sex trafficking as a business. The author is a researcher with business experience, an MBA from Columbia, and a passionate concern about the problem of sex trafficking. The book draws on his research consisting of hundreds of interviews conducted across the globe, including experiences that put him at danger in order to obtain information about the sex industry. In addition to this fieldwork, Kara uses semiacademic literature and major governmental and nongovernmental reports to craft his economic analysis. The majority of the eight chapters reflect his "personal mission" to understand how trafficking works in different parts of the world. Two chapters provide the primary economic analysis. In his writing and approach, Kara is influenced by the neoabolitionist antitrafficking movement most notably identified with Kevin Bales and his Free the Slaves project (Bales 1999). Kara thus deploys the language of slavery and sex slavery and does not traverse the contested territory of this language choice. Sex trafficking is the same as sex slavery, and prostitution is the same as sex slavery. There is no distinction made between sex workers and sex slaves or between sex workers and victims of trafficking. As Kara explains it, the "anatomy" of sex trafficking includes two components: slave trading and slavery (Kara 2009, 5).

Kara isolates three aspects of the business of sex trafficking, which include the size and growth of the industry, the revenues and profits from selling slaves, and the revenues and profits generated by the exploitation of sex slaves (Kara 2009, 16). He is most interested in understanding the third aspect, which he calls the sex-slave business. Kara's calculations of the profitability of the sex-slave business are much like the ILO estimates I previously analyzed. Kara uses a U.S. State Department estimate for the number of people trafficked into commercial sexual exploitation and from there derives a measure of the profits, disaggregated by region. With some tweaking of the numbers, he creates an estimate that the weighted average net profit margin for "slaveholders" to be almost 70 percent. Kara explains that no company comes close to this net profit margin, comparing figures for Google (29 percent), Microsoft (28.5 percent), and Exxon Mobil (10.8 percent) (19). His point with this comparison is that when labor, in particular sexual labor, is done by slaves, then the net profit margin goes up: "Slave labor makes profits soar" (22).

Kara concludes that sex slavery is an industry that we must try to understand in terms of its business operations in order to eliminate it. Grasping the supply and demand of sex slavery is key to understanding those operations. In a section on the supply of sex slaves, Kara touches on broad economic trends that have contributed to the supply of slaves. In particular, he references the intensification of globalization and the onset of the economic transition beginning in the early 1990s as having "helped make present-day slaves easy to procure, easy to transport, and easy to exploit in an increasing number of industries" (Kara 2009, 24). The cause of this easy supply is that there are now more people who are economically vulnerable and states provide less for their citizens. Importantly, Kara notes the role of the International Monetary Fund in exacerbating the economic collapse during the 1990s of the former state socialist economies and in the instability of East Asian markets. Kara also references the fact that the supply of sex slaves is fueled by the global predominance of patriarchy and the disenfranchisement of ethnic groups. While these points are important, he does not integrate them any further in his analysis. Kara does not take the next step to unpack how economic policies contribute to systemic social vulnerability, or how gender and race intersect with those policies to create patterns of vulnerability. He claims that "to ensure that the business of sex trafficking is eradicated in the long term, the conditions in the 'host organism,' that first gave rise to the infection—namely, poverty and economic globalization—must also be addressed" (6). But such blanket statements are a common feature of economic analyses of trafficking. Concepts like "poverty" and "globalization" are not hidden from view or denied, but they serve no function other than that of a general reference. Such variables are part of the necessary backdrop to the description of trafficking but are rarely if ever brought to the forefront of the analysis.

Kara is more interested in looking at the demand side of trafficking, in particular the business opportunities and risks that are at play. He argues that trafficking is fueled by male demand for cheap sexual services and the demand for profit. The connection between trafficking and prostitution is based on the notion that demand is elastic. Because demand is an elastic variable, if the price for services goes down, demand will go up (Kara 2009, 35). Thus, brothel owners seek out slave labor in order to drive down the price of services, which will then increase the demand for services. Slave labor increases demand as well as profit, which in turn increases the demand for slave labor. This cycle is key to Kara's analysis of why the sex trafficking industry continues to thrive. The solution to breaking the cycle, according to Kara, is to increase the cost of sexual services. He makes the provocative statement that consumer awareness of slave labor "is largely irrelevant to the magnitude of demand represented by sex slave consumers" (203). Only adjustments to the cost of sexual services will have an impact on male demand.

Kara's focus on demand is tied to adjustments to the risks investors in sexual slavery undertake. While trafficking is illegal, Kara explains that "until the market force of risk is increased radically, and as long as sex trafficking remains immensely profitable, the industry will flourish" (Kara 2009, 38). There are various costs to running a sex-slave business, including the cost of procuring sex slaves and operation costs. Kara focuses on a third cost, that of getting caught. He argues that the greater the cost of being caught, the lower the profitability of conducting a sex-slave business (207). Using an equation that weighs the cost of being caught, along with the probability of prosecution (and conviction), he generates a "real" penalty value. Currently, the real costs are "almost nil" (207). Kara recommends that the risk-reward economics of sex-slave operations be inverted. In other words, the costs associated with getting caught and prosecuted must make a sizable dent in the net profit of the business. Brothel owners and pimps must be charged larger fines than they currently face to have an impact on the fees for sexual services. If consumers in the United States have to pay $87 instead of $30 for sexual services, then the industry will collapse.

Kara wants to hit the business of trafficking at its most lucrative and vulnerable place. His analysis suggests that prevention will have less of an impact because trafficking is primarily fueled by economic determinants, so economic solutions must be sought. As I have suggested at various points in this book, an economic approach to trafficking has been neglected in favor of prosecution and prevention. Indeed, Kara's work encourages a shift to economic questions for policy and advocacy work. In addition, his specific proposal to increase penalties for trafficking is provocative and entirely reasonable. In fact, even if the intended outcome of reversing the risk-reward economics of trafficking did not occur, raising the financial penalty for trafficking would have an immense symbolic impact.

However, the focus on demand in Kara's business model approach relies on a rational actor model instead of a macroeconomic analysis. While he references the International Monetary Fund and the role of state economic policies and suggests they are important to any long-term solution, he opts instead for a solution that simplifies the problem of trafficking to individual actions. What Kara assumes here is that trafficking can be eliminated if the conditions for its market are less favorable. Yet the conditions for the market of trafficking cannot be separated from relationships, dynamics, and contexts that exist in and beyond trafficking. By isolating certain economic behaviors, Kara obscures how "sex-slave" businesses are tied into economic and social structures. Depending on the context, these businesses may be intricately tied to informal economies, caste systems, migration regimes, or imaginings of self and other. Adjustments to the "cost" of trafficking would not necessarily have an impact on these dynamics. Kara assumes that the sex-slave industry exists independently of such relationships, dynamics, and contexts.

Another problem with Kara's market solution to trafficking is that it feeds back into a juridical remedy. Kara's solution is to make the fines against traffickers more expensive and requires an even greater emphasis on a prosecutorial response to trafficking. Kara acknowledges that prosecution and conviction enforcement are necessary in order for his suggestion to work, but ensuring enforcement is only one aspect of why the juridical remedy is complicated. Most important, Kara never addresses the debate about who is a victim of trafficking. As I have discussed, identifying victims of trafficking is one of the most troubling and difficult aspects of legally pursuing trafficking. For Kara's plan to work, greater clarity would be needed about the differences between victim of trafficking, sex worker, subject of irregular migration, and subject of smuggling. Kara never enters this messy territory. Rather, he assumes that trafficking pervades the sex industry (this is signaled by his language choice of "sex-slave" industry) and presumably that all sex workers—even if not technically victims of trafficking—would benefit from his proposed market adjustment. Furthermore, Kara's plan does not take into consideration the costs associated with protecting victims. His determination to hit traffickers where it would hurt most seems to be at the expense of those who would be required to claim victim status in order to flip the risk-reward economics of trafficking. Surely the "cost" of trafficking for the perpetrator would need to be matched by the cost of protection for the victim of trafficking.

The Feminist Choice Model and the Politics of Demand

Business-minded activists like Kara are not the only ones who draw on a rational actor model of trafficking. Ironically, sex workers' rights advocates and organizations also can play into this economism. Emphasizing the choice to engage in sex work, this advocacy position can support rather than challenge a business model approach to trafficking. The sex workers' rights position did not evolve in response to trafficking but has become intertwined with the issue since the early 1990s. Initially, activists asserted that sex trade is a legitimate form of labor and that women who sell sexual services defy rather than embody patriarchal objectification (Pheterson 1989; Chapkis 1997; Nagle 1997). Self-proclaimed "sex positive" feminists argued that sex work is a form of labor like other income-generating labor and opposed antipornography and antiprostitution feminists like Andrea Dworkin and Kathleen Barry.[13] The feminist debate over prostitution/sex work, dubbed the "sex wars," was not coterminous with the recasting of sex trafficking as a form of "violence against women." However, as I discussed in chapter 1, this feminist debate about agency and sex work became the contentious centerpiece of the debate on sex trafficking.

Some sex workers' rights positions have provided some feminist economic perspective in discussions on sex trafficking. In contrast to the sexual slavery position, which emphasizes an ethical argument against sex work, the sex positive (or sex workers' rights) perspective focuses on women's ability to use their bodies as commodities. The sex workers' rights position forefronts women's economic agency; the antiprostitution position forefronts the commodification of female sexuality. When brought into the context of sex trafficking, it is the sex workers' rights perspective that introduces some sense of the economic dimensions of the issue. The antiprostitution perspective tends to focus on "violence against women" and the lack of consent in sex work.

But the economic perspective introduced by the sex workers' rights perspective has a limited impact on combating sex trafficking and is not a sufficient feminist economic intervention. The rights of sex workers do need protection, and groups such as the Global Network of Sex Work Projects and the European Network for HIV/STI Prevention and Health Promotion among Migrant Sex Workers have worked to advance them. The Global Network for Sex Work Projects strives to insert the voices and concerns of sex workers into the discourse and challenge the problematic approaches to sex trafficking that typically criminalize or pathologize them. Their website states: "The standard paradigms through which sex work is currently viewed—AIDS, trafficking, and violence against women—fail to fully address the human rights of sex workers. It is therefore crucial that sex workers represent their own realities and fully participate in dialogues and decision making about issues that affect them" (Global Network for Sex Work Projects Website).

The increased concern for trafficking has thus complicated efforts to advance sex workers' rights. For those advancing a neoabolitionist agenda, like Siddharth Kara and Kevin Bales, trafficking and prostitution are synonymous. The politicization of trafficking has reenergized antiprostitution sentiments and blurred the boundaries between criminal and legitimate activities in sex work industries. Thus, organizations working to advance the concerns of sex workers must contend with antitrafficking agendas that consider sex work to be the cause of trafficking. Antitrafficking efforts, such as police raids or "street outreach," often disregard the human rights concerns put forth by sex workers' rights organizations. In an effort to eradicate trafficking and find victims of trafficking, people in the sex trade are put under greater scrutiny.

This increased pressure on sex workers in turn has emphasized the need to locate choice and agency so as to distinguish victims from individual laborers. This is unfortunate, because the focus on choice creates a false dichotomy between victims and agents. The need to separate sex work and sex trafficking on the basis of choice and agency has foreclosed the possibility of making important connections between sexual labor, human rights violations, and desires for economic empowerment. Rather than opposing victims of trafficking to sex workers by creating a distinction based on choice, we should seek out the connections between them using entirely different terms.

Forging alternative terms for addressing sex trafficking and sex work has been difficult. In part, this is because sexual labor (selling sex for money), rather than the terms of precarious labor, is most often viewed as the source of the exploitation. Even in legal definitions of trafficking, sex trafficking is made distinct from other forms of human trafficking (as in the 2000 UN Optional Protocol to Prevent, Suppress and Punish Trafficking in Persons, Especially Women and Children). The wider context of sexual labor, including women's presence in informal economies, their displacement in postindustrial transformations, and the increased pressures on them to migrate, are not yet the focus.

While it is important to respect human agency and labor, the sex workers' rights advocacy position is a limited feminist *economic* response to the issue of trafficking. An advocacy position that emphasizes individual workers narrows feminist economic interventions to propositions for choice and rights—two concepts that play well into pernicious political agendas (Bumiller 2008; Smith 2005). Not unlike Kara's analysis of rational economic actors, a sex workers' rights perspective is concerned with the rational choices and agency of those laboring in the sexual services industry. What is missing is a feminist analysis of the larger economic dynamics and trends that structure economic opportunities, choices, and experiences. The fact that some choose to labor in the sex trade does not address the structural forces that fuel trafficking—such as immigration regimes, international development projects, and the political economy of intimate labor.

Feminist engagements with the structural dimensions of trafficking and precarious labor are necessary today. In many cases, women may lack not the ability to exercise rights but a just social and economic structure in which to make their lives. However, over the course of the past decade the fierce debate between the sex work positive and antiprostitution advocacy positions has made choice the feminist focus in the trafficking debates. The fact that women can choose to work in the sex trade, that their rights should be protected, and that they are not all victims of trafficking or sexual slavery should not shut down questioning of how and why this type of labor functions in its larger economic context. For example, what gendered and racialized relationships enable different forms of sexual labor? How are informal sexual industries, in addition to other forms of intimate labor, outcomes of transnational economic arrangements? As feminists, are we constrained by a political allegiance to a principle for or against sexual labor in order to address the injustices workers face when doing this labor?[14]

The sex workers' rights position makes a claim for why not all sex workers are victims of trafficking but does not address the relationship between sex trafficking and intimate labor industries. There may be sympathy toward victims of trafficking laboring in sex industries and an acknowledgment that they are doing so, but the advocacy position itself is not a response to trafficking.[15] If anything, sex work advocacy groups want/need to distance themselves from the issue of trafficking because of the negative impact antitrafficking efforts have on their work.[16] As the Global Network of Sex Work Projects (2011) explains, "the conflation of sex work and trafficking, migration and mobility is no accident. It is not a misunderstanding of terminology but is a conscious attempt to abolish prostitution and prevent people, in particular women, from migrating for sex work." Ironically, despite the fact that sex workers' rights advocacy organizations have been involved in antitrafficking policy formation, there is no critique of sex trafficking from the perspective of sex workers' rights per se. Rather, there is a desire to protect a nonvictim status for sex workers.

The allegiance to the concepts of choice and agency in the sex workers' rights position makes it difficult to link sex work advocacy and antitrafficking because of how troubling and complex those concepts are when it comes to trafficking. In this way, the sex workers' rights position may be an advocacy "dead end" for those concerned with trafficking. Ultimately, the sex workers' rights position advances the interests of certain workers while not addressing larger structural issues—whether they be macroeconomic or related to the "indentured mobility" that characterizes many migrants' lives (Salazar Parreñas 2011). A critique of trafficking from the perspective of sex workers' rights actually emphasizes the entrepreneurial, rational actor view of sex work. This reliance on a rational actor model is not unlike that used in the market-oriented approaches to trafficking I previously discussed. Unintentionally, the sex workers' rights discourse colludes with the economism in human trafficking discourse. What do business-minded neoabolitionists like Siddharth Kara and sex workers' rights organizations such as the Global Network of Sex Work Projects have in common? Both agendas draw on an economism of rights because they are rooted in belief in, rather than critique of, the operations of the market and the right to entrepreneurship.

The discussion about demand reduction is a place where we can see the differences but also similarities between the neoabolitionist business-model approach and the sex workers' rights approach. As stated before, Kara recommends that governments increase the cost of risk for traffickers by increasing the fines charged when they are prosecuted. Kara believes that with less demand for sexual services the practice of sex trafficking will diminish. Other examples of demand reduction strategies include the criminalization of purchasing sex, as with the Swedish Sex Purchase Act (passed in 1999) and "John Schools," which are programs for male clients caught soliciting. This approach has also been taken up in the celebrity world. In 2011, Demi Moore and Ashton Kutcher launched the "Real Men Don't Buy Girls" campaign, which aims to dissuade men from purchasing sex from underage girls.[17] All three of these strategies assume that demand for sex work alone causes sex trafficking. If men are not requesting sex for pay then the market for sex workers will decline.

In response to these strategies, sex workers' rights organizations have defended their labor and questioned the link made between sex work and sex trafficking. For example, in San Francisco the Sex Workers Outreach Project presented a School for Johns as a retort to the John Schools. The project consisted of a day of panels and workshops aimed at educating the public about the sex industry and providing proper etiquette for johns. According to Robyn Few of the project's national office, the San Francisco Police Department used the John Schools to shame clients and make money off of arrests. Furthermore, she explained that the department's John School "has done nothing to abate prostitution or get rid of clients" (School for Johns). Other organizations, such as the Global Network of Sex Work Projects, Creating Resources for Empowerment and Action, the Sexual Health and Rights Project, and the XTalk Project also have responded with briefing papers and research documents presenting arguments, with supporting evidence, for why sex work should be protected, why sex workers' rights are important, and why antitrafficking efforts should not criminalize the industry in an effort to reduce trafficking. There are strong arguments for and against demand reduction, but both positions are locked into a rational actor model of human trafficking.

The demand reduction strategy is part of a broader antitrafficking agenda that looks at the role of consumers and the power of their purchasing choices. Outside the arena of sexual and intimate services, consumers of other products and services are recognized as having the ability to reduce human trafficking by driving down the demand for commodities that have a "slavery footprint." This approach is illustrated in the 2011 U.S. TIP report, where the issue of consumer choice and demand reduction is raised.

> The demand for cheap goods, services, labor, and sex opens opportunities for the exploitation of vulnerable populations. And it is on this demand that human trafficking thrives. People are bought and sold as commodities within and across borders to satisfy demand from buyers. Poverty, unemployment, lack of opportunity, social upheaval, and political

instability facilitate traffickers' ability to recruit victims, but they do not in themselves cause trafficking. The economic reality is that human trafficking is driven by profits. If nobody paid for sex, sex trafficking would not exist. If nobody paid for goods produced with any amount of slavery, forced labor in manufacturing would be a thing of the past. Increasingly, antitrafficking actors are looking to combat modern slavery from the demand side rather than focusing on arrests and prosecutions (the supply side) alone. (U.S. Department of State 2011, 19)

As this quote illustrates, demand operates as an abstract concept that is largely decontextualized. Consumers have demand for cheap goods and services, and producers have demand for profits, but we do not understand what fuels that demand. The more specific details presented here, such as poverty, unemployment, lack of opportunity, and so on are provided for the victims of trafficking. It is assumed that the consumers and producers are not subject to those same pressures and that those same pressures may be linked to demand for cheap goods and more profit. Demand is abstracted from the wider political economy of intimate labor and thus escapes deeper theorization.

In addition, the foregoing quote reveals how the issues of poverty and unemployment are viewed as sources of vulnerability for victims of trafficking but are also decontextualized. And, ultimately, combating trafficking is not seen to be about addressing these issues of vulnerability but about altering consumer choices. The statement "if nobody paid for sex, sex trafficking would not exist" reveals a neoliberal economic approach to trafficking that privileges choice over structural change as a strategy to combat human trafficking. This catchphrase serves as the common battleground on which neoabolitionist and sex workers' rights advocates hash out their differences but also reveals their deeper commonalities. Consumer choice to not buy sex is pitted against sex workers' choice to pursue their employment. Both positions convey a limited vision of economic justice and human rights. Eliminating sex work does not challenge the dynamics that have led to the sex trafficking problem of today, and sex workers' rights are not protected when consent is the litmus test for precarious labor.[18]

This is not to say that demand reduction strategies have not promoted greater public awareness of how our lives are interconnected with human exploitation. It is hard not to be sympathetic to a campaign like "Real Men Don't Buy Girls"—especially when the narratives of sex trafficking emphasize the innocence of the victims and the aberration of its violence. I too would like to think that my consumer choices make a difference. I try to only buy fair trade chocolate. Doesn't that make a difference? This belief in ethical consumption was implemented in the United States in 2007 when the U.S. TIP report started to include a list of businesses that had been found to use slave labor. This list sustains the idea that there are good and bad choices in the market. Similarly, public awareness campaigns alerting consumers that there are ethical choices in the market are very common.

One example is a Salvation Army World Service poster that depicts children bottled in glass jars lining a store shelf.[19] The image suggests that child labor or exploitation is what is being purchased. It is an image that provocatively presents the connection between exploitation and consumerism, and is particularly geared toward a U.S. audience. Yet there is also something troubling about this demand-side approach. If we can choose to not buy the jars on that shelf and get different jars, won't they still be there, even if in fewer quantities? Where will the children go if the jars disappear because there is no demand for them? Will they be buying groceries of their liking and choosing as they stroll down wide isles of food with their mothers? Indeed, the jars decontextualize the bodies within them. As viewers of the image, we consume the anonymous bodies without an explicit link to the structural practices (racialized as well as transnational) that created the jars. The poster references the fact that every year fifty thousand women and children are brought into the United States to work as slaves. Will my refusal to purchase that jar of pickles make it one less—49,999? What assemblage of economic, social, and political forces remains intact even when there are fewer jars on the shelf?

I am sure that consumerism is in fact tied to human trafficking—but making better choices within the global market of consumer goods is not sufficient and may even give a false sense of living "slave free."[20] What do we mean by "slave free" when trafficked, smuggled, or indentured labor feed into the same products and the same services? The current formulation of demand reduction strategies tends to maintain the focus on the individual—the individual consumer and the individual victim of trafficking—rather than tackling contentious immigration policies, common labor practices in construction and agriculture industries, or illicit economies that are sustained by long-standing racial and class hierarchies. Many antitrafficking slogans include the phrase "not for sale," and images abound of female bodies with bar codes emblazoned on their foreheads or backs.[21] It is a powerful imaging, for sure. Humans should not be for sale. Nor should they be in the innumerable violent and precarious labor situations normalized in our current global system. Educating the public to not fuel slave labor requires far more radical changes than not buying sex work or choosing products on a slave-free list. I do not discount the importance of individual practices, but there is a dire need to move to a more expansive view of the political economy of trafficking and economies of violence.

The flipside of demand reduction projects in antitrafficking discourse is a supply-side strategy. This approach addresses potential victims of trafficking rather than the consumers of trafficked labor. Like the demand reduction programs, supply-side approaches focus on altering the behaviors of individual economic actors. Potential victims of trafficking are decontextualized from the economic and social contexts that structure their lives and are asked to avoid human trafficking or recuperate from it.

Entrepreneurship and Supply-Side Antitrafficking Programs

As I have discussed throughout this chapter, human trafficking is viewed as a distinguishable market by the major institutions invested in antitrafficking. There is a set of simplistic dichotomies—between the formal and informal economies, between impoverished and wealthy countries, between deceit and truth—that upholds the idea that trafficking is a separate market. It is widely documented that traffickers often come from the same economic context as victims of trafficking. Traffickers and victims of trafficking can share the same family, community, and nationality. Yet the dominant description of trafficking as a market relies on an economic distinction between perpetrators and victims that oversimplifies the hierarchies and dynamics at play. The 2002 U.S. TIP report provides an example of this oversimplification: "Economic and political instability greatly increase the likelihood that a country will become a source of trafficking victims. In countries with chronic unemployment, widespread poverty and a lack of economic opportunities, traffickers use promises of higher wages and good working conditions in foreign countries to lure people into their networks. Victims who want a better life for themselves and their families, are easily convinced by the trafficker's promises" (U.S. Department of State 2002, 1).

The statement presents an oversimplification that persists over a decade of TIP reports. Actors (traffickers and trafficking victims) create the trafficking market whereas the structural issues of chronic unemployment, poverty, and lack of economic opportunities are qualities pertaining to countries. While global economic disparities are certainly at play, few attempts are made to investigate the actual economic relationships between countries or the hierarchies within them that play into trafficking. There is an assumption that the wealthy countries exist independent of their relationships to other countries and vice versa, as well as an assumption that wealthy countries are productive independent of exploitative labor. The fiction that wealthy countries exist independent of exploitative labor is perpetuated by a trafficking discourse that views economic relationships through the simplified dichotomies of supply/demand and developed/underdeveloped. The global economy and its complex web of consumers, producers, sellers, and conveyers are flattened out into those who have and have not.

The dominant depiction of trafficking as a market driven by the forces of supply and demand has carried through the U.S. TIP reports since the first one in 2001. These reports also incorporate perspectives that complicate the simplified market analysis. In particular, stories of trafficking boxed to the side of the main text run through the TIP reports and often present complex pictures of trafficking. In addition to providing visual representations, through photographs and graphs, the "Victim Profiles" present stories of trafficking that highlight particular dynamics of trafficking. For example, the 2006 report contains a sidebar that discusses economic globalization and how it has opened up greater opportunities for labor exploitation because of the demand for cheap labor. The focus of the piece is on the importance of labor contracts for migrant laborers and proper regulation of those contracts (U.S. Department of State 2006, 7). In the same report, India's caste system is discussed as a contributing factor in bonded labor, which is a form of trafficking (15). A few pages later a picture of a billboard depicting a white woman in a bikini appears with the caption "A brothel in Cologne, Germany, displayed this banner on its building to lure World Cup soccer fans into the dehumanizing world of prostitution" (20).

The "Victim Profiles" are used to show that trafficking happens across the globe and is not determined by particular cultures or regions. This is explained in this caveat provided at the beginning of each report: "The victims' testimonies included in this report are meant to be representative only and do not include all forms of trafficking that occur. Any of these stories could take place anywhere in the world. They illustrate the many forms of trafficking and the wide variety of places in which they occur. No country is immune. Many of the victims' names have been changed in this report. Most uncaptioned photographs are not images of confirmed trafficking victims, but they show the myriad forms of exploitation that define trafficking and the variety of cultures in which trafficking victims are found" (U.S. Department of State 2011, 8).

The scenarios presented by the testimonies serve to reflect a universalism— trafficking happens everywhere. But that universalism conceals an oversimplified market analysis of trafficking. Rather than leading to an analytical breakthrough, the various examples serve as exposés that reflect a political necessity to unveil (reveal) trafficking wherever it lurks. The paradox is that the information provided in the side stories can shine light on dynamics of trafficking that are not taken up in the primary rationale of the TIP report. For example, the stories suggest that addressing immigration policy, combating unemployment, challenging racism, and other structural issues are in fact antitrafficking strategies. However, such strategies are not central to the U.S. approach to combating trafficking.

In the TIP reports, there is discussion of globalization, migration agreements, class and gender discrimination, and a host of dynamics that structure economic opportunities and relationships. But these issues are a backdrop and serve as embellishments to the primary text. They are not folded into the dominant approach to antitrafficking. This is the case with how the supply side of trafficking is treated. A supply-side analysis of trafficking considers the factors that push people into or make them vulnerable to human trafficking. For example, issues such as poverty, unemployment, and demand for immigrant labor are recognized in the text of the TIP reports as "supply side" factors. Yet addressing these issues is not the focus of supply-side approaches to the U.S. antitrafficking strategy. Poverty exists as a self-evident (unfortunate) fact that serves as a kind of backdrop to the primary actors and actions.

One place where we see that economic processes serve as a backdrop to the issues that are the focus of activity is the U.S. TIP country ranking system. The system ranks countries into three tiers based on their compliance with the U.S. TVPA's minimum standards. The minimum standards for the elimination of trafficking include the following: governments should prohibit severe forms of trafficking in persons and punish acts of trafficking; should prescribe punishments commensurate with the crimes of sex trafficking (including child sex trafficking) or with rape or kidnapping if trafficking includes these crimes; should prescribe punishments that are sufficiently stringent to deter and reflect the heinous nature of the offense; and should make serious and sustained efforts to eliminate severe forms of trafficking (U.S. TVPA 2000). In 2006 an additional "watch list" was created for Tier Two, distinguishing those countries whose ranking is under threat of dropping. The major focus of the minimum standards is on adequate legal provisions on trafficking. The criteria used to evaluate whether a country meets those minimum standards focus on law enforcement. Countries are evaluated in terms of their legal doctrine, data on investigations, prosecutions and convictions, victim protection in legal proceedings, public education programs, cooperation with other governments in investigations, monitoring of immigration and emigration patterns for severe forms of trafficking, and whether a country monitors its efforts in the above areas (U.S. TVPA 2000).

The U.S. TIP report measure of government activity on the issue of trafficking is entirely focused on legal interventions. The issue of prevention is mentioned, which could address the supply of trafficking victims and thus structural economic dynamics, but the emphasis is on educating the public to avoid getting into a trafficking scenario. Like the demand reduction approach, the public education programs geared toward reducing the supply of victims are based on the premise that people are rational actors. This assumption suggests that trafficking is the result of bad decision-making and focuses on transforming individuals rather than structures.

In the tier system, governments are not evaluated on their prevention strategies in terms of altering economic and social policies that have an impact on exploitative labor. Yet there could be a way to evaluate government policies as part of the minimum standards. Given that the TIP reports' acknowledgment that unemployment, poverty, and migration regimes contribute to the problem of human trafficking, why are such issues not part of the evaluation in the tier system? Understandably, public education programs are easier to execute than structural change. But the incongruence between the structural economic issues represented in the TIP reports and an evaluative system that is based on juridical responses reveals a major blind spot regarding—if not obfuscation of—government's role in antitrafficking and in the prevalence of exploitative labor.

Beyond the TIP reports, the U.S. government has provided millions of dollars in grant money toward antitrafficking efforts across the world. Between 2001 and 2005, the U.S. government granted $278 million to international antitrafficking programs.[22] That number significantly increased between 2005 and 2010, totaling $492.90 million in grants for international antitrafficking programs. While I do not have a percentage breakdown of the thematic areas these funds have been used for, the numbers are an indication of the important role U.S. government funding plays in shaping antitrafficking work around the world. The 3 PS, prevention, prosecution, and protection, are the thematic areas under which all U.S. expenditures are categorized. As I have noted, the Tier system is focused on prosecution and protection, with some mention of prevention. Supply-side approaches are considered part of prevention because they address potential victims of trafficking. Prevention programing focuses on educating the public about the existence of trafficking and warning people to make informed choices.

Antitrafficking prevention messages in the United States tend to focus on educating consumers/citizens about the victims who exist "beneath the surface" or in one's own backyard.[23] U.S.-funded antitrafficking prevention messages in other parts of the world caution the public about migration and irregular labor contracts, whereas in the United States they have focused on identifying foreigners who may be victims.[24] For example, the 2011 "Look Beneath the Surface" U.S. antitrafficking campaign presents the idea that victims of trafficking are all around us and that we can help identify them. The poster states: "A victim of trafficking may look like many of the people you help everyday. Ask the right questions and look for clues."[25] The underlying message is that individuals can act to save the life of a potential or actual trafficking victim. In contrast, USAID, in collaboration with MTV and others created a public service announcement, using the phrase "It could happen to any of us," for an Indonesian audience. The video presents a cautionary tale of deceit and dreams of employment. The underlying message is that individuals can act to avoid their own exploitation; "don't rush, ask questions" is the advice.[26]

The Indonesian MTV public service announcement is particularly compelling in visualizing the argument I am trying to make about structural economic issues serving as the backdrop to the actions of individuals. The subjects of the video are a young woman and a deceiving pimp. Their images are in photographic color, while the background is sketched, like a cartoon. The background is not animated; it does not move but is part of the context to the story. The only images that move are the people. The young woman is warned not to rush and to ask lots of questions about her potential employer. Her dreams of employment and a career end in a brothel. She is depicted in another scenario agreeing to work abroad and ends up being smuggled into an abusive domestic job. The advice given at that point is to "never give up your stuff," meaning passports, mobile numbers, and personal information. As a prevention tool, the video is educating the public about how trafficking works and attempts to give them tools to avoid it. But the video also reveals an underlying approach to prevention that focuses on individual actions and choices as the problem and solution to trafficking. However, the backdrop to trafficking needs to be animated and brought into the foreground of antitrafficking programing and into the theorization of trafficking as a contemporary violation of human rights.

Better choices can deter someone from being trafficked. This focus on individual actions and choices informs the promotion of entrepreneurship as part of prevention programs as well. As part of U.S.-funded prevention projects, there are a variety of programs that address people's economic needs. It is recognized that unemployment is a part of the "supply" of victims of trafficking

FIGURE 5.1. Young women work in garment factory in Moldova. Photo from *The Price of Sex 2004*, by Mimi Chakarova. www.mclight.com/gallery/113.html, ©Mimi Chakarova.

and that employment is an important part of the repatriation process for victims of trafficking ("victim reintegration"). For example, a 2004 USAID assessment report on antitrafficking in Eurasia states: "Another approach that has recently surfaced is to attack what is seen to be the primary root cause of the problem—a lack of viable job opportunities or economic alternatives at home. A new wave of programing has begun that attempts to train at-risk women to find jobs locally or to develop their own businesses, so that they will not need to risk migration abroad or within their countries of origin" (United States Agency for International Development 2004, 5).

Attacking the root causes of the problem is definitely needed. Yet there is a perverse contradiction in the report. At the beginning of the statement, poverty is recognized as an important cause of trafficking, but oddly, the solution is to find jobs in the same poverty-stricken context. This logical "jump" reveals an obvious gap in antitrafficking discourse—to theorize and address precarious labor and structural economic inequalities.

It is in contexts like Moldova, where there is widespread poverty and lack of economic opportunity, that this contradiction is most stark. If you take the journey through Mimi Chakarova's documentary photography project on Moldovan women, you can see the contexts in which people are living.[27] Many women who are trafficked have had jobs since they were sixteen years old—working long shifts in factories but never with enough money to buy what they toil to make. In Chakarova's photographs the deep underlying economies of violence seeps through, leaving a much darker and ominous reality than does our grasp of trafficking as an aberration. Figure 5.1 is a profound, if unlikely, rendering of human trafficking. This photograph depicts Olesa's life—she is the victim of trafficking referred to in this photograph, and here is the reality of her life, the backbone of global capitalism. Human trafficking rides along that backbone. The photo consolidates the victims and losers of global capitalism in one image and refuses any easy bifurcation.

Examples from former postsocialist states provide an illustration of the bitter contradiction of antitrafficking projects steeped in neoliberal economism. Some of these new projects have included provision of funds to NGOS working for "Improving Access to Employment and Training Alliance" in Moldova, for "Social and Occupational Integration Services" in Romania, and for "Improving Access to Employment for Young Women and Girls" in Russia. Without discounting the achievements of such programs, it is important to think about the rationale and implications of such entrepreneurship-based programs. Given the weak government investment in reducing the vulnerability of citizens in countries like Moldova, Romania, and Russia—and given the market Bolshevism that has evolved into authoritarian neoliberalism—it is troubling that NGOS now are asked to "empower" individuals to create their own employment in such contexts. Creating a more dynamic and active economy requires the innovation of citizens, but the singular focus on entrepreneurship training and promotion as an economic antitrafficking strategy perpetuates the myth that individuals alone can alter economies of violence.

CONCLUSION / ANTITRAFFICKING
BEYOND THE CARCERAL STATE

This book is an intervention into the current powerful framing devices for human trafficking that both expose trafficking and limit our understandings of it. The focus of my research has been on retracing the histories and geographies of how those frames came into dominance after the Cold War. At the same time, I am acutely aware of the need to move on, to take alternative roads and engage new strategies. Thus, I conclude the book with ideas for how to engage antitrafficking from a more critical position. Again, the impetus for doing so is *not* to downplay the violence of trafficking but to elevate recognition of the subterranean violence that both makes trafficking possible and is obscured when trafficking is viewed as a mere aberration. I think a key intervention is to start approaching human trafficking as a symptom of a multifaceted injustice rather than as a singular problem. There has been such intense focus on human trafficking as *the* problem, as *the* violation, that we have failed to see the entire picture.

Viewed as a symptom, we may approach antitrafficking from advocacy/policy platforms focused on immigration laws, labor rights, prison reform, global financial institutions, poverty alleviation in the context of urban decay, or even social services reform. These ideas are already on the minds of antitrafficking advocates. As I was writing this book, I began another project on U.S. domestic trafficking and interviewed activists and policy-makers in Texas and Ohio. In one of my conversations, a young antitrafficking activist in Austin, Texas, reflected that maybe the best antitrafficking strategy he could adopt would be to become a mentor for disadvantaged youth. I was struck by this simple revelation. In many ways, I think he is right. Not all paths to forced labor originate from the same source, but this example illustrates how in the context of a U.S. city antitrafficking advocates are making connections to structural (everyday) violence. While trafficking victims should be given special care as victims of trafficking, it is important to not isolate those victims from the wider contexts and specific communities in which they exist. We often go out of our way to find victims of trafficking—in the case of sex trafficking, police often hunt them down—while at the same time people who need support and advocacy surround us. There is now an opportunity to wield the affective power of the concept of "modern-day slavery" to reclaim the value of those who have been discarded, ignored, or written off, not just as the hidden victims of trafficking but as the dispossessed of our communities. This work requires local strategizing, in addition to making transnational linkages to migratory routes, global division of labor patterns, and the movement of money and resources by financial and government institutions.

Similarly, I suggest we rethink the strategy of emphasizing the concept of "violence against women" as a primary or sufficient activist category. I think it is important to see the inherent incompleteness of the term in order to contextualize violence and strike at the multidimensionality of racial, class, sexual, gendered, able-bodied, and national hierarchies. While the concept of "violence against women" now confers specific meanings—primarily certain acts of violence, such as rape, domestic violence, and sex trafficking—it should not convey a set understanding of why that violence happens, how it is constituted, what remedies are appropriate, and how to prevent it. There has been too much certainty that "violence against women" is just a symptom of patriarchy or that challenging *gender* norms alone will prevent violence. While this is undoubtedly part of the equation, it is only partial. For example, sexual violence against African American women was a strategy of the white supremacist backlash to the civil rights movement (McGuire 2010). The problem of domestic violence in Native American and Indigenous communities is inseparable from the ongoing projects of settler colonialism (Smith 2005). The mass killing of Mexican women on the U.S.-Mexico border is a tragic illustration of how economic arrangements (maquiladoras created in response to NAFTA) produce gendered and racialized violence (Fregoso and Bejarano 2010). The selling of Moldovan women into global sex trafficking is rooted in postsocialist restructuring and global demand for Eastern European women (*The Price of Sex* 2012). As these examples attest, the advocacy work against "violence against women" is not self-evident but requires gathering support from local organizing while forging coalitional agendas as well.

If we see human trafficking as a symptom of broader socioeconomic dynamics and problems, we see that the work of antitrafficking needs to expand from a single agenda focused on finding/helping victims to multiple coalitional agendas across precarity. The agendas invested in antitrafficking should include advocacy for the well-being of people laboring in industries (intimate labor, manual labor, immigrant labor, etc.) that are the sites of normalized violence. Some of these coalitional issues include support for the unionization of informal and intimate labor, protections for workers in industries dependent on nonstandard or illegal immigration, demanding a livable minimum wage, increasing access to health care, and supporting community programs that reach out to poor and disadvantaged youth. It will also be important to analyze the function that sex work fulfills in different societies and to address the ways it is used as a means to survive under the pressure of other forms of precarity—such as drug addiction, homelessness, urbanization and urban decay, development, transphobia and homophobia, and domestic violence. Addressing these underlying issues will only strengthen the coalitional project of antitrafficking. On another level of coalitional politics, there needs to be continued pressure on governments to generate just immigration policies and to rank human rights above corporate profit. Furthermore, how governments and intergovernmental institutions conceive of development and the programs they support in the name of economic growth sets the groundwork for the kinds of industries and labor that will flourish.

From the 3 Ps to the 3 Rs

With the foregoing suggestions in mind, an important first step in a radical shift to antitrafficking would be to expand the paradigm of the 3 Ps (prevention, protection, and prosecution) that continues to dominate U.S. and global policy. This reworking would allow us to put into place a new critical approach. Drawing on the broad ideas previously raised, I suggest a shift of focus toward these 3 Rs: rights, research, and responsibility.

The underlying ethos of any approach should be grounded in a commitment to rights—and not just as a juridical threshold but as a mark of what is truly at stake. The concept of prevention in the dominant paradigm has problematically focused on trying to prevent individual harm. A turn to rights shifts attention to structural processes and possible remedies. A focus on rights should include a commitment to labor rights, with an understanding that precarious labor is the wider sea in which contemporary trafficking flows. Rather than letting the magnitude of trafficking direct our ethical commitment to fighting exploitation, we can let the expanse of exploitation that supports trafficking become a primary focus. We may still need a juridical understanding of force, but that threshold should not serve as the sole domain of economies of violence or the arbiter of rights. As such, a commitment to labor rights could include support for a global living wage; wider ratification of the ILO Domestic Workers Convention; rights-based approach to migration, *with the recognition that our global economy thrives on the backs of unskilled laborers whose lives are worth more than the commodities they make*; immigration reform; and the decriminalization of prostitution. As I mentioned earlier, sex workers' rights projects should move toward more coalition building in terms of broader labor rights, in addition to defending the rights to (and in) sex work. Sex work industries are part of global service industries, which include nannies and construction workers, and should be understood as connected, in order to advance a collective vision in opposition to the different forms of exploitation that exist in those industries. Furthermore, the police and well-meaning advocates should not, by attempting to decriminalize prostitution, target only sex workers in their efforts to eliminate exploitation. There is still a place for a juridical response to forced sexual labor, but legal attention should not just be placed on prostitution.

If we can open and broaden the scope of how we understand the rights at stake with human trafficking—as embedded in economies of violence—then some of the difficulties regarding identifying victims of trafficking will diminish. It may also be helpful to envision ways that the human and labor rights of trafficking victims can be collectively secured. For example, projects that empower people to collectively challenge exploitation will embed antitrafficking efforts more firmly in local conditions of precarity. Rather than focusing on educating vulnerable populations so that the horrors of trafficking do not befall individuals, we should support communities' responses to their own precarity. This might be an issue of advocating for affordable housing, or greater protections for labor migrants, or better social services. There is much discussion about the lack of resources for victims of trafficking, such as temporary housing. While this must be addressed, prevention should focus on the collective issue of housing, health care, and child care, for example. The reduction in individual harm does not take away from the systemic dynamics of vulnerability. In other words, antitrafficking projects should devise ways to address the problem as a collective, community, and transnational endeavor. Current attention to prosecution and protection could be reframed within this larger concept of rights. The state and its agencies, as well as advocacy organizations, could then broaden the scope of their agendas and align the ethos of their work with the primary concern of labor and human rights.

RESEARCH

Human trafficking is situated in practices and geographies that require further research. The people invested in antitrafficking should not make quick assumptions about what we are fighting against; we should invest in ongoing thinking and research into what the problem is and why it happens. Importantly, I think new economic analyses of trafficking as a dimension of precarious labor are sorely needed. In particular, I see the need for further research on the patterns of international migration as they are tied to global political economy and national migration policies; on the gendered and racial formations of deindustrialization and peripheralization; on national and international racial, class, and gender hierarchies and how they are (re)constituted in markets; and on the experiences of precarity in different industries. This research and the knowledge produced by advocates working with vulnerable communities should be allowed to trickle up into policy-making. I do not suggest that there is a simple economic solution to trafficking. Poverty alone does not explain exploitation, nor is there a causal relationship. Yet there *are* economic dimensions to trafficking that are underexplored and are essential to any long-term vision for transforming the lives of victims or addressing the systemic causes of exploitation.

The testimonies gathered by advocacy groups and researchers should be used to generate specific prevention programs that speak to the communities and survival circuits these actors came from. In this way, the universalizing antitrafficking paradigm must be broken down to accommodate the specificity of economies of violence. Furthermore, it will be important to generate new modes of evaluation for gauging how states are responding to human trafficking. Prosecution rates feed the violence of carceral states; can we not imagine metrics of justice that are not solely centered on the prosecution of traffickers?

RESPONSIBILITY

Possibly the most important suggestion of this book is that a reprioritization within the antitrafficking industry needs to take place. With so much focus on a carceral response, little room is left for other concerns. I understand the power and importance of criminalizing trafficking—I am not naïve toward that. But with so much confusion, as well as secondary victimization, that can go with prosecuting trafficking, it is not naïve but ethical to think beyond a juridical response. This reprioritization should privilege the responsibility societies have to the peoples and the environments that make them up. As a start, we should alter the global ranking system generated by the annual U.S. TIP report so that it no longer privileges a juridical metric of antitrafficking in ranking countries in the tier system. The presence of antitrafficking laws or the rates of prosecution alone do not constitute ethical standards for assessing progress. Such measures are a practical necessity, but they are currently stifling new ways to address (and conceive of) the problem. The focus on these measures also obscures the responsibility citizens and governments have to carry the burden of economies of violence. What other metrics can we use to measure the ethical progress toward eliminating trafficking? What about the funding levels committed to organizations providing services to victims of trafficking? What about a measure for the degree to which human rights concerns are mainstreamed within police, immigration, medical, and other institutions that deal with trafficking and precarious labor? What about the number of community-led responses to exploitative labor that are supported? And, finally, there is the obvious measure of poverty reduction—not as a panacea but as the looming elephant in the antitrafficking room. In this area, prevention programs aimed primarily at entrepreneurship are insufficient for addressing deeper dynamics.

A focus on responsibility in a newly fashioned antitrafficking paradigm might also invite fresh imaginings of translocal community and resistance. If the millions who have been mobilized to fight human trafficking as modern-day slavery can reach through to the other side of their compassion—to the side where the losers of globalization reside—then broader and bigger coalitions can be built. If at the local level we can connect modern-day slavery to histories of violent settlement and slavery, then our projects for prevention may be more deeply grounded. If governments and advocacy groups see anti-trafficking as part of the work of social provisioning and community empowerment, then states will be held more accountable for its role in trafficking. If making a life worth living is seen as part of our collective humanity and not just an individual choice, then possibly we will have less tolerance for economies of violence.

NOTES

Introduction

1 "Natasha" was the generic name given to describe victims of trafficking from the former Soviet Union and Eastern Bloc.

2 Sex trafficking is often recognized as a unique form of forced labor, as in the 2000 Optional Protocol to the UN Convention against Transnational Organized Crime: the Optional Protocol to Prevent, Suppress and Punish Trafficking in Persons, Especially Women and Children. This book focuses on sex trafficking because I analyze how the example of postsocialist sex trafficking in particular set the course for contemporary antitrafficking agendas. However, my position is that sex trafficking should not be treated as distinct from other forms of forced labor. Sexual violence and forced sex can occur in other labor situations, and sexual labor is labor. At times, I use the terms "human trafficking" and "sex trafficking" interchangeably, although I am aware that they legally are made distinct.

3 This photo is particularly relevant given the collapse of an eight-story building in 2013 in Savar, a subdistrict in the Dhaka District in Bangladesh.

4 I use the term "violence against women" throughout this book to stand for this composite category, which I introduce below; I use the phrase without quotation marks in the broader, ordinary sense.

5 U.S. Department of State, Office to Monitor and Combat Trafficking in Persons website. n.d. "Four 'Ps': Prevention, Protection, Prosecution, Partnerships," accessed December 31, 2014, www.state.gov/j/tip/4p/.

6   One prominent example is the work of Kevin Bales, a well-known antitrafficking advocate who has written several books and founded the NGO Free the Slaves. For an excellent analysis of this language see Hua (2011).

7   Barack Obama, Presidential Proclamation, December 31, 2012, accessed April 3, 2013, www.whitehouse.gov/the-press-office/2012/12/31/presidential-proclamation -national-slavery-and-human-trafficking-prevent.

8   There is growing acknowledgment of this lack of recognition. Jacqui True makes the claim that "official UN approaches make no linkages between the effects of financial crisis, macroeconomic policies, and trade liberalization and the prevalence of violence against women in particularly affected regions" (True 2012, 5).

9   It is important to note that countries considered part of the Eastern Bloc were not always aligned with the Soviet Union, including Albania and Yugoslavia.

10 Most of my fieldwork occurred in Russia, though there is a "deterritorialized" dimension as well (Merry 2006). The first trip was to St. Petersburg, Russia, in 2001 for nine months when I gathered data for my dissertation on the legal history of sex crimes. Much of that work is not directly represented here, but the conversations and thinking that I did during that stay informed my approach to postsocialist cultural studies. I have taken many subsequent trips to Moscow, Saratov, St. Petersburg, and Nizhniy Novgorod. Over the past decade I interviewed and talked with approximately ninety-five NGO representatives, researchers, librarians, journalists, and government officials. Interviews typically were unrecorded and conducted in Russian. I wrote down notes during and after conversations and followed up by e-mail when I could. Some conversations were strictly through e-mail. Other key interviews with advocacy groups in Europe and the United States were conducted via phone, e-mail, and in person in Holland.

11 Important exceptions exist. The Center for Women's Global Leadership, a key actor in the struggle to recognize "violence against women" and led by the indefatigable Charlotte Bunch, recently released a statement declaring the need to prioritize economic and social rights (Center for Women's Global Leadership 2011). Other organizations, such as the Association for Women's Rights in Development, center macroeconomics in their work. In partnership with feminist organizations such as Development Alternatives with Women for a New Era, Women in Development Europe, and the Association for Women's Rights in Development, the Center for Women's Global Leadership submitted a statement to the UN CSW advocating for the central role of critical feminist economic approaches to women's rights issues (see Charkiewicz 2009).

12 For other critiques of Fraser's work see Aslan and Gambetti 2011 and Funk 2012.

13 For an analysis of similar dynamics in Poland see Binnie 2013.

14 Thus, "while most accounts assume the diffusion of preexisting neoliberalism as ideology from the West to the Rest, in fact, neoliberalism developed within liminal spaces, in which the participants created new forms of social scientific, historical, and philosophical knowledge" (Bockman 2007, 346).

15 For example, the Cold War was not in fact cold for many countries in the global south who played the hot locations for East/West competition.

16 One example is the "Washington Consensus," which prevailed in Latin America (though, importantly, these principles were developed by those in Latin America as well). See Yergin and Stanislaw (1998) for an analysis of how the Washington Consensus was built.

17 The Cold War metageography also concealed the connections and tensions between the second and third worlds that were present prior to and during the Soviet period. There were also south-south relations and partnerships, but these too get overshadowed by the dominant metageography I am critiquing.

18 It should be noted that in the past ten years, there has been increased activism and critical discourse on "neoliberal postsocialism" throughout the region. The web platform CriticAtac (www.criticatac.ro) is an example of this activism, as well as the summer conferences organized by scholars and activists across the region on the subject.

19 Feminists have always been a part of antiglobalization movements but not always successful in having their perspectives heard. There is a vast literature on feminist organizing against globalization (Eschle and Maiguashca 2011; Hawkesworth 2006; Naples and Desai 2002).

20 Michael Burawoy uses the term "economic involution" to describe the economic primitivization of postsocialist societies (1996).

21 The presence of poverty is often cited as an important factor in the existence of human and sex trafficking. Yet in directing antitrafficking efforts, how precarity is structured has not yet been given much analysis (Danailova-Trainor and Laczko 2010; Friesendorf 2007).

22 Nor do I think that "precarious labor" is a common cause based on a political subject (Neilson and Rossiter 2008).

23 Academic discussions of precarity were predated by grassroots activism, as in the EuroMayDay demonstrations in Western Europe that began in 2001.

24 According to a World Bank study, "the shadow economy has reached remarkable proportions, with a weighted average value of 17.2 percent of official GDP over 162 countries between 1999 and 2006/2007" (Schneider, Buehn, and Montenegro 2007). According to journalist Robert Neuwirth, the annual profit of the global informal economy is $10 trillion (Neuwirth 2011).

Part I: Global

1 "Natasha" is a Slavic name, but the region of Eastern and Central Europe and the Former Soviet Union includes many non-Slavic ethnic and linguistic groups. The use of the name Natasha to cover all the new victims of trafficking from the region reveals ignorance as well as an overemphasis on Russia that is reminiscent of the Cold War.

Chapter 1: Sex Trafficking and the Making of a Feminist Subject of Analysis

1   A report of the workshop was published (Barry, Bunch, and Castley 1984).

2   Friedrich Engels wrote the definitive piece on women's emancipation in "The Origin of the Family, Private Property, and the State" (Tucker 1978). Alexandra Kollontai wrote many pieces on the family, sexual relations, and prostitution (Kollontai 1977).

3   At the time of the 1983 workshop, the language of "sex workers" was not in use. The terms "prostitutes" and "prostitute organizing" were used (Barry et al. 1984, 20). In the report from the workshop, it is noted that Margot St. James, the founder of the sex workers' rights organization COYOTE and activist with the National Task Force on Prostitution, spoke, but her talk is not included in the published compilation.

4   "As a young feminist in the early 1970s I had worked as a rape crisis counselor. Now I began to understand that what those women had endured as a one-time assault was the ongoing condition of women and girls in prostitution—a prolonged, numbing series of sexual violations carried out by multiple violators" (Leidholdt 2004).

5   Most notably, she distinguishes the work of CATW from the Global Alliance Against Trafficking in Women and COYOTE.

6   The concept of "trafficking" loses its specificity and comes to define any exchange in women's bodies. Again, in Leidholdt's recollection of the 1988 conference she states, "The conference organizers understood trafficking in women as a broad, umbrella concept that encompassed all practices of buying and selling women's and children's bodies. Trafficking as we understood it included American pornography, temple prostitution in India, military prostitution in the Philippines, street prostitution in Peru, sex tourism from Europe to Asia" (Leidholdt 2004).

7   The quote comes from an extensive report by the *Christian Science Monitor* after the final conference of the UN Decade for Women (1985). Importantly, the series title is "The Neglected Resource, Women in the Developing World" (Helmore 1985).

8   For example, Thailand earned more foreign currency from tourism in 1986, $1.5 billion, than from any other economic activity (Enloe 1990, 37). The government's development plan for 1978–1991 made tourism and exports a priority, indicating that foreign currency revenue would only increase as a proportion of total revenue.

9   Evidence of this is the report in which the South Korean minister for education stated that "the sincerity of girls who have contributed their cunts to their fatherland's economic development is indeed praiseworthy" (Ryan and Hall 2001, 141).

10   The WID group had commissioned an evaluation of UN and development agencies as part of the Nairobi preparatory process. The report showed that development assistance programs to developing countries were often worsening the economic, social, and political situation of women (Jain 2005, 95). This analysis was shared and supported the work of networks like DAWN (95).

11   However, it is important to note the first International Tribunal on Crimes Against Women in 1976, which took place in Brussels. The tribunal was orga-

nized by feminists across the globe and lasted five days (Russell and Van de Ven 1976).

12 A primary bureaucratic entity for women's rights at the UN is the CSW. It is a commission of the UN Economic and Social Council. "It is the principal global policy-making body dedicated exclusively to gender equality and advancement of women" (Commission on the Status of Women). The institutionalization of the CSW has an important history as well (Boutros-Ghali 1995; Pietilä 2007).

13 Resolution 7, "Prevention of the Exploitation of Women and Girls" (UN 1975). Evidently this resolution was adopted through negotiations at the 1980 conference and not originally in the World Plan of Action (Barry 1981, 49).

14 The International Day Against Violence Against Women was established at this first Latin American feminist *Encuentro* (Sternbach et al. 1992).

15 Recommendation 19 states: "Gender-based violence is a form of discrimination that seriously inhibits women's ability to enjoy rights and freedoms on a basis of equality with men" (Committee on the Elimination of Discrimination against Women 1992).

16 Telephone interview, January 26, 2011. Charlotte Bunch's current position on sex trafficking, and the prostitution debates that often take center stage in those discussions, is different from that of Kathleen Barry and contemporary bearers of the sexual slavery position (such as Donna Hughes and Susan Jeffreys).

17 The Global Tribunal on Violations of Women's Human Rights was held at the UN World Conference on Human Rights in 1993 in Vienna. The tribunals consisted of thirty-three testimonies on five themes: human rights abuse in the family, war crimes against women, violations of bodily integrity, socioeconomic rights, and political persecution and discrimination (Bunch and Reilly 1994). There is one testimony on sex trafficking that was provided by the story of a Polish woman trafficked into Dutch prostitution during the session on bodily integrity. Sex trafficking was briefly mentioned in, though not the central focus of, another testimony on women labor migrants during the session on social and economic rights (Bunch and Reilly 1994).

18 The timeline for women's rights at the UN represents time after the 1995 Beijing conference as Beijing plus number of years since 1995. There is no milestone yet to replace Beijing as the referent for the promotion of women's rights.

19 In the Beijing Platform for Action sex trafficking is mentioned in: section C on "women and health"; section D on "violence against women"; section H on "mechanisms for the advancement of women"; section I on "human rights of women"; and section L on the "girl child" (Beijing Platform for Action 1995). It is only in the short mentioning of sex trafficking in the section on women and health that it is not specifically positioned within the context of violence against women.

20 The language of agency is commonly used in campaigns against gender violence. For example, in 2009, the UN secretary general, Ban Ki-moon, launched UNiTE to End Violence Against Women, a campaign aimed at preventing and eliminating violence against women and girls around the world. The primary meme of

the campaign is "Say NO." A powerful verbal gesture, but the concept of saying no relies on a limited understanding of violence that supports an individual rather than structural response (United Nations UNITE to End Violence Against Women 2009).

Chapter 2: The Natasha Trade and the Post–Cold War Reframing of Precarity

1   Human rights lawyer and scholar Anne Gallagher writes: "I was amongst those who, in the late 1990s, decried the removal of trafficking from the sacred chambers of the international human rights system to the area of the United Nations that dealt with drugs and crime. When it became clear that the UN Crime Commission was going to develop a treaty on trafficking, we human rights lawyers and practitioners were, in the best tradition of our profession, righteously outraged" (Gallagher 2008).

2   The 1930 ILO Forced Labor Convention defines forced labor as "all work or service which is exacted from any person under menace of any penality and for which the said person has not offered himself voluntarily" (article 2). However, human trafficking was not framed by this convention on forced labor because of the political need to distinguish between trafficking (involuntary migration) and smuggling (voluntary migration). For a discussion see 2005a.

3   For example, the 1985 UN Declaration of Basic Principles of Justice for Victims of Crime and Abuse of Power put the spotlight on rape and "secondary victimization" by the criminal justice system.

4   The 2013 reauthorization document can be found on the government website, accessed January 6, 2015, www.govtrack.us/congress/bills/113/s47/text#.

5   Famously, Francis Fukuyama declared the end of history in his book suggesting that Soviet totalitarianism was the last ideological competitor to western democracy (Fukuyama 1992).

6   The tendency to present macroeconomics as a positive outcome of the prosecutorial state is an indication of the impossibility of getting outside of the logic of prosecution. For example, some suggested that postsocialist criminality would impede economic development (Shelley 1998). Another example is the tendency to see the relevance of economics in thinking about violence against women only in terms of the economic productivity of women (i.e., violence against women keeps them from being successful economic actors). There are economic outcomes to securing justice, but there is much less attention to the role of economics in generating injustice.

7   Preceding the 1949 Convention, agreements were drawn within the League of Nations that included the 1904 Suppression of White Slave Traffic agreement, the 1910 International Convention for the Suppression of the White Slave Traffic, and two additional revisions in 1921 and 1933. A special body of experts was appointed by the League of Nations in 1927 and 1932 to study white slavery. The issue was not touched during the war, but upon the creation of the UN the 1949 Convention was drafted based on the League of Nations agreements (Osmańczyk 2003).

8 In 1959, twenty-five states had ratified the Convention; in 1983, fifty-three states had ratified it, and by the time of the 2000 UN Convention, eighty states had ratified it.

9 Fernand-Laurent comments at the start of the report that his work was rushed due to the time frame presented to him. The rushed terms of his project were mirrored in his observation that at the Working Group meetings "very little time is devoted to such a tragic and complex problem" (Fernand-Laurent 1985, 25).

10 He lists the Centre for Social Development and Humanitarian Affairs; the Crime Prevention and Criminal Justice Branch; the Advancement of Women Branch (the secretariat for the CSW); the CSW; the Division of Narcotic Drugs; the regional commissions for Asia and the Pacific, Latin America and the Caribbean, Africa and Western Asia; UNICEF; the Office of the UN High Commissioner for Refugees; the ILO; UNESCO; WHO; and broadly the Economic and Social Council.

11 Roger Clark argues, "the Human Rights Centre in Geneva seems to have won a turf war here" (Clark 1994, 13).

12 Fernand-Laurent acknowledges that there are associated issues as well. "There are two associated issues that have not been considered here: the selling of young girls into domestic service and the international traffic in young children for adoption" (Fernand-Laurent 1985, 16).

13 In the early 1990s, only the Netherlands had a specific policy against sex trafficking in Europe (De Stoop 1994, 121). From roughly 1989 to 1992, there were twenty-one trials for sex trafficking. The advancement of antitrafficking litigation in the Netherlands is attributed to the advocacy work of the Foundation Against Trafficking in Women, a Dutch NGO started in 1987 (122). The organization is still operating but changed its name to CoMensha in 2007. The Foundation Against Trafficking in Women spearheaded the network LaStrada, the European Network Against Human Trafficking.

14 The wave metaphor illustrates the Eurocentrism of global antitrafficking discourse. This bias continues. For example, in a recent IOM survey of publications on trafficking, a majority of the more than 260 publications focus on Europe (44 percent) and Asia-Pacific (35 percent) (Laczko 2005).

15 Brussa says, "recognizing the structural causes of migratory prostitution will situate the problems and the policies within a socio-economic context. Recognizing the structural causes makes it possible to formulate a long-term plan of action" (1991, 35).

16 For example, in one of the first steps toward a common European policy on trafficking, the European Council of Justice and Home Affairs Ministers passed a resolution in 1989 on "the exploitation of prostitution and the traffic in human beings" (European Council of Justice and Home Affairs 1989). The resolution is premised on the recognition of several European and UN norms, such as the 1986 European Parliament Resolution on Violence Against Women, the 1949 UN Convention on the Suppression of the Traffic in Persons and of the Exploitation of the Prostitution of Others, the 1985 UN Forward Looking Strategies from the World Conference on Women (Forward Looking Strategies 1985), and a 1983 Report of the UN Economic and Social Council (Fernand-Laurent 1985).

17 The IOM is an intergovernmental organization established in 1951 and is influential in the field of international migration.

18 "This preliminary study appears to be the first attempt to examine systematically the ways in which, and the reasons why, a growing number of women from Central and Eastern Europe are trafficked to Western Europe" (IOM 1995, 3).

19 For example, the UN special rapporteur on violence against women relied on the circumscribed data of the 1995 IOM document (IOM 1995) in her 1996 report. The report claims "trafficking of Central and Eastern European women reached epidemic proportions in the beginning of the 1990s" (Coomeraswamy 1996, 44). It then explains that experts provided information about the different waves of sex trafficking to Europe and then directly references the data from the Foundation Against Trafficking in Women used in the 1995 IOM report.

20 Data on the prevalence of trafficking is dependent on how trafficking is defined and the willingness of people to claim a victim status. Both of these variables made numeric accounts of the rate of trafficking in the 1990s highly suspect because a clear definition of trafficking was not agreed on and many victims were identified as illegal immigrants.

21 As Frank Laczko points out, small-scale studies of trafficking depend on first-hand information from those who have been exploited. Yet, "the actual ratio of assisted survivors to the total number of victims is unknown, meaning that studies based only on assisted cases may not be representative of the total number of trafficked persons which remain undiscovered" (Laczko 2005, 8).

22 I address the ongoing link between magnitude and how trafficking is conceptualized in chapter 5.

23 This absence is notable given how little had been written on the issue of trafficking and the fact that standard protocol is to reference preceding research reports.

24 Mimi Chakarova uses the idea of missing girls in her documentary *The Price of Sex* (2011) as well. She invokes the idea collectively, including herself as a Bulgarian immigrant. She asks the antitrafficking NGO representative: what has become of us? There is a powerful dimension to this imagining of postsocialist trafficking victims, and it parallels the statement made by Amartya Sen regarding 100 million missing women in Asia (Sen 1990). Sen's provocative statement was an attempt to expose structural disadvantages against women. However, there is a troubling aspect to the idea of missing girls, it seems to me, because it tends to erase their agency. This is particularly the case with trafficking because women who migrate and search for labor are indeed agents for economic survival.

25 A decade earlier, Mikhail Stern's *Sex in the Soviet Union* (1980) fulfilled a similar fascination with the sexual lives of Soviet Russians for an American audience.

26 I place the word "Slavic" in scare quotes to denote the common slippage between Slavic, Russian, and Eastern European. Technically not all languages/cultures in Central and Eastern Europe and the former USSR root from a Slavonic language, including peoples and languages in Hungary, Romania, the Caucuses, and Central Eurasian Republics. Women from all of these regions were pulled into

trafficking, yet the image of the white Slavic woman was the centerpiece of the "Natasha" discourse.

27 Another example of this racialized language is the use of the name "Natasha" to refer to all prostitutes in Turkey. Valentine Moghadam alerted me to a case of a woman who was raped by a Turkish taxi driver. The driver claimed that he thought she was a "Natasha." For more on this see Uygun (2004).

28 Ann-Sofi Sidén's installation *Warte Mal!: Prostitution after the Velvet Revolution* is a provocative counterrepresentation to this image of the "Slavic" woman. This "walk-in documentary" is an installation combining her diary, interviews, and visual media made from prolonged trips to Dubí, Czech Republic (which is on the border with Germany). She documents the lives of sex workers, the traveling clients, and hotel/bar owners. It is a complicated picture with no single focus on *a* victim and highlights, in my evaluation, the core economic dimensions at play. The title *Warte Mal!* (Hey wait!) is a reference to the call shouted by women working along the E55 highway linking the Czech Republic and Germany. The picture Sidén portrays is bleak but also multidimensional; the women are not just victims of prostitution in this new tourist industry. On the other hand, from Kristen Ghodsee's ethnographic work in Bulgaria we learn that women's elevated educational status actually benefited many of them when the country opened up to western tourism markets (Ghodsee 2005).

29 As Francine Pickup laments, "those addressing trafficking in women are in an uncomfortable position of feeling compelled to produce ever more horrifying victims' stories, higher numbers, and younger girls" (Pickup 1998, 997).

30 For example, the IOM-sponsored antitrafficking campaign by Russian pop star and IOM ambassador Valeria. Her song "Back to Love" (2007) tells the story of an underage girl trafficked for forced prostitution. Mimi Chakarova's documentary *The Price of Sex* (2011) is a more nuanced representation of trafficking.

31 Eugen Berwald was sentenced to twenty-five years in prison after he was found in possession of the dead brothel owner's watch and passports.

32 Interestingly, Shevchenko argues that a discourse on a "crisis of socialism" was replaced by a "crisis of postsocialism"; thus a sense of crisis was actually a continuation of rather than a break from the past (Shevchenko 2009, 23).

33 From 1992 to 1994 the Yeltsin government introduced large-scale privatization by selling state-owned assets to private hands incredibly quickly and without a transparent bidding system. A part of that privatization was the distribution of vouchers to each citizen, thus allowing citizens to pool their resources together to buy assets or to sell them for cash. "Popularly considered the largest scam in Russian history, this privatization is often labeled 'grabitization' (*prikhvatizatsiia*), and many hold it responsible for the immense economic polarization of contemporary Russian society" (Oushakine 2009, 44–45).

34 Humphrey classifies the dispossessed to include: refugees going to Russia from the successor states of the CIS; the unemployed; economic migrants; demobilized soldiers, abandoned pensioners, invalids, and single-parent families; vagrants and

the homeless; and people living in various illegal ways, such as contract laborers without residence permits in large cities (Humphrey 2002, 21).

35 These depictions of Russian criminality were not isolated to the early 1990s. A recent History Channel program, *Organized Crime: The Russian Mafia* (2009), presented a fairly culturally stereotyped image of Russian crime.

36 This is not to say that criminal gangs or corruption do not exist. The point is that this dimension overshadowed other equally salient explanations for human trafficking. However, on the need to translate legal cultures as a way to understand the perceived lack of rule of law in the former East, see Kurkchiyan (2003).

37 The impact of the "Natasha" discourse also speaks to the disproportionate influence of an east-west perspective through the 1990s and as the new UN Optional Protocol on Trafficking was formulated. Examples of trafficking, and not just sex trafficking, abound across the globe. Yet a specifically European-centric view of the problem has tended to dominate discussion (Laczko 2005).

38 Kimberly Williams makes the same argument in her excellent essay (2011).

39 For example, Wellstone presented a map of trafficking routes as a visual during his speech that focused on routes from the Newly Independent States of the USSR to the rest of the world for forced prostitution. In addition, with the Resolution, Wellstone submitted excerpts from the Global Survival Network report "Crime and Servitude: An Expose of the Traffic in Women for Prostitution from the Newly Independent States" (Global Survival Network 1997). This was the only supplemental evidence provided.

40 For examples of publications where the "Russian mafia" is depicted see Sterling 1994; Vassalo 1996; and Webster 1997.

41 For example, Shelley states the following: "The heavy involvement of organized crime, and this has been mentioned before, but I would reiterate that there is a level of coercion not previously used against women that are being used by organized crime groups from the former Soviet Union" (*The Sex Trade* 1999).

42 Victims of Trafficking and Violence Protection Act of 2000 (reauthorized in 2003, 2006, and 2008) text available on government website, accessed January 6, 2015, www.state.gov/j/tip/laws/index.htm.

43 Scholars have argued that antitrafficking legislation relies on the idea of a "perfect victim" and thus makes it difficult to provide services to a variety of people who are in need of help but do not fit the prototype for trafficking victims. See Haynes (2007) and Uy (2011) in particular.

44 The Act reads: "The term 'severe forms of trafficking in persons' means—(A) sex trafficking in which a commercial sex act is induced by force, fraud, or coercion, or in which the person induced to perform such act has not attained 18 years of age; or (B) the recruitment, harboring, transportation, provision, or obtaining of a person for labor or services, through the use of force, fraud, or coercion for the purpose of subjection to involuntary servitude, peonage, debt bondage, or slavery." Victims of Trafficking and Violence Protection Act of 2000 (reauthorized in 2003, 2006, and 2008). Text available, accessed January 6, 2015, www.state.gov/j/tip/laws/index.htm.

45 With the 2008 reauthorization of the Act, the meaning of coercion was expanded to include "serious harm" to mean any harm, including psychological, financial, or reputational harm, that would compel a reasonable person to perform labor, services, or commercial sex acts to avoid that harm. In addition, the mens rea requirement for the crime of sex trafficking was expanded to include "reckless disregard" in addition to actual knowledge that force, fraud, or coercion caused a person to engage in a commercial sex act. Victims of Trafficking and Violence Protection Act of 2000 (reauthorized in 2003, 2006, and 2008). Text available, accessed January 6, 2015, www.state.gov/j/tip/laws/index.htm.

46 Anne Gallagher argues that human trafficking was concentrated in the human rights domain of the UN and that the move to a transnational crime domain meant that the issue was "snatched away from its traditional home" (Gallagher 2008, 790). Gallagher was part of the internal lobbying for revised antitrafficking norms in the UN as a representative of Mary Robinson, the UN High Commissioner for Human Rights at the time.

47 "It was felt that greater emphasis needed to be placed on violence against women in situations involving refugees and migrants and in acts and processes related to trafficking, labour and exploitation, prostitution, pornography, sex trade and the like, all of which fell within the scope and definition of 'violence against women', and that the measures being proposed were of concern for both women and the girl child" (UN 1997).

48 UN Trafficking Protocol, article 4. UN Smuggling Protocol, article 4.

49 But, as Anne Gallagher states, it is important to acknowledge that the victim protections "are geared toward making sure that criminal justice [is] given the best possible chance to secure prosecutions and convictions through the cooperation of victims" (Gallagher 2006, 182).

50 In a conversation with Melissa Hope Ditmore, she explained that, while there were voices present within the Human Rights Caucus who were concerned with economic issues and the uneven geopolitical weight of lobbying groups, the conversation at the table was confined to the narrow debate about agency/consent. Telephone interview with author, January 28, 2011.

Part II: Postsocialist

1 Francisca de Haan argues that the assumption that western feminist groups were politically neutral, and that communist feminist groups were politicized, was part of a Cold War bias. In fact, de Haan argues that the organizations such as the International Council of Women and the International Alliance of Women actively promoted a western worldview that supported colonialism (de Haan 2010, 552).

Chapter 3: Second World/Second Sex

1 For example, *Soviet Women's World, The United Nations Decade for Women 1976–1985* (Moscow: Novosti Press Agency Publishing House 1983) and *Women in the GDR, Notes on the Implementation for the World Plan of Action of the UN*

Decade for Women 1976–1985 (Berlin: Council of Ministers of the German Democratic Republic 1985).

2   De Haan makes the important argument that the Women's International Democratic Federation was not exclusively a "second world" organization. "The WIDF was a global organization which from the beginning included women from 'First-,' 'Second-,' and 'Third-World' countries, as well as prominent Communist and non-Communist women, on its board and among its various activities" (de Haan 2010, 564).

3   I see the need for additional archival research on this topic and do not want to oversimplify the closed political setting of state socialism. Kristen Ghodsee argues that Bulgarian feminists were able to use their state organizations to highlight shortcomings in their society. The rhetoric used to critique always drew on sanctioned socialist rhetoric, but it was a strategic use of that rhetoric (Ghodsee 2013). The specific point I am making is very germane to the politicization of violence against women and may not transfer to other issue areas. For crafting alternative histories see Bucur 2008; de Haan, Daskalova, and Loutfi 2008; Havelková and Oates-Indruchová 2014; and Loutfi 2008.

4   Of course, networks between the second and third worlds existed, but they were not emphasized (at least not outside of the threat of communism). For research on Soviet–third world ties see Kret (2013). There is also the issue of the "south" of the (former) second world that I am not addressing here (Engerman 2011; Philliou 2013).

5   I am aware of such projects in Russia, Czech Republic, and Poland (Graff 2003; Iukina 2003; Oates-Indruchová 2012; Pushkareva 2002).

6   According to Pietilä, "the single most important international legal instrument adopted by the UN is the Convention on the Elimination of All Forms of Discrimination Against Women" (2007, 27).

7   The Equal Rights Amendment never passed in the United States, and the Voting Rights Act did not pass until 1965.

8   Group of Seventy-Seven Website, accessed January 6, 2015, www.g77.org/doc.

9   The main objectives of the second Development Decade "were to promote sustained economic growth, particularly in the developing countries; ensure a higher standard of living, and facilitate the process of narrowing the gap between developed and developing countries" (Osmańczyk 2003).

10   Kristen Ghodsee is completing a book on the activities of the Bulgarian state socialist women's organization and its work training African feminists on political organizing at the UN and socialist solutions to women's issues.

11   A counter-example is provided by Ghodsee (2013).

12   Graff explains that "most backlash products marketed in Poland are, however, nothing more than translations and borrowings: self-help books and women's magazines telling their readers how to win back the men feminism so recklessly scared away; pop versions of evolutionary psychology, which prove beyond doubt that men and women are an entirely different species, or indeed, that they come from different planets; familiar images of man-hating hairy-legged feminists.

The Catholic Church and ultra-conservative parties serve as our version of the New Right, and in fact maintain close links with their American counterparts. Polish media delight in 'statistics' showing that ordinary people have had it with women's lib. One magazine announced that an average Pole would prefer living next door to a former communist agent than to a feminist" (Graff 2003, 106).

13 There was some momentum behind the idea of holding a Fifth World Conference on Women in 2015, in honor of the 20th anniversary of the first world conference. However, the idea failed to pass muster inside the UN.

14 Nongovernmental organizations from Eastern and Central Europe and the CIS submitted a document at the New York preparatory meeting, which was the thirty-ninth session of the CSW, titled "Zhenshchiny stran s ekonomikoi perekhodnogo perioda" [Women from countries in the economic transition period].

15 This experience of second world women's groups at the Beijing conference spurred the creation of the KARAT Coalition—a network of women's organizations throughout the former second world, including Central Eastern Europe and the CIS. They state on their website that "KARAT Coalition was established as a response to the invisibility of women from Central and Eastern Europe and the Commonwealth of Independent States (CEE/CIS) and their concerns and needs in the international area. It was related closely to the Beijing Conference on Women in 1995," accessed January 6, 2015, www.karat.org.

16 According to one account, of the 362-plus articles of the Beijing Platform for Action only three mentioned the specific interests of the postsocialist region (Information Center of the Independent Forum n.d.).

17 A compounding factor in the sense of being left out was the fact that the Russian language was not a working language at the forum, despite the fact that it is one of the UN official languages (Information Center of the Independent Forum n.d.).

18 What I mean by "neutral" is that the transition did not include a cultural translation. It was assumed that the only difference between east/west was a political ideology that could easily be discarded.

19 Of course, for those westerners whose work focused on the former Socialist bloc, the problem of translation and the pitfalls of feminist thinking and networking across the east/west divide were recognized (Funk and Mueller 1993; Holmgren 1995). A growing literature and feminist collaboration continues across the east/west divide, even as some tensions linger (Funk 2004; 2007).

20 This was conveyed to me in an interview with Nadezhda Azhgikhina, a prominent feminist journalist in Russia who participated in the Beijing conference. Interview with author, Moscow, July 5, 2010. Other funding sources included Open Society (Soros) and Women East/West.

21 The meaning of gender and equality on a personal or psychological level are not addressed here. Of course individual women may not have viewed such burdens as burdens. For example, Russian author Natalia Baranskaya has resisted a feminist interpretation of her short story *A Week Like Any Other*. The story depicts one grueling week of a Soviet woman's life balancing work and family commitments. On the other hand, Larisa Shepitko's film *Krylya* (Wings; 1966) depicts the deep

psychological crisis of an "emancipated" Soviet woman fighter pilot after World War II.

22 Russian as well as foreign historical research clearly shows that a plethora of feminists and feminist thinking has always existed in Russia and that feminism is not a "foreign" import. See Iukina 2003; Ruthchild 2010.

23 The summary document states that there were around two hundred participants from across the USSR and forty-eight organizations, as well as twenty-six foreign "guests" from the United States, Canada, Britain, India, Sweden, Austria, Germany, and France (Dubna 1991).

24 Richter's research on foreign assistance reveals that some Russian women's organizations had hoped for funding that would give a "push to the grassroots" rather than support for proposal-making at the UN level (Richter 2002).

25 More than five hundred representatives from women's organizations and initiatives from Russia, Belarus, Ukraine, Estonia, Latvia, Kazakhstan, and Uzbekistan and more than eighty representatives from Finland, the United Kingdom, Sweden, Switzerland, Belgium, Poland, Czech Republic, France, Italy, Austria, Germany, Holland, Bulgaria, India, and the United States were present.

26 The Women's Information Network (Zhenset) was established in the wake of the Forum.

Chapter 4: Lost in Transition

1 Three crucial policies were implemented in many of the transition schemes: a reliance on a powerful state and/or elites to execute so-called privatization; a reaffirmation of the hierarchal control of managers and owners; and a disempowerment of workers/citizens for the sake of "the market" (Bockman 2011).

2 See Judith Butler (2006) on violence and intelligibility.

3 I do not mean to overstate this point. Certainly during glasnost there was already growing criticism of Soviet society. For example, Susan Buck-Morss discusses the east/west dialogue that she took part in in the late 1980s. She refers to that time as a moment of open discussion about the similarities between the Soviet and American "mass utopia" projects (Buck-Morss 2002). Some of the critical thinkers associated with that dialogue could not relate to leftist intellectual concerns in the west after the end of state socialism. More recently, there is growing leftist critique throughout the former second world, both inside and outside the EU. This criticism has intensified since 2005 and is in response to the success of right-leaning nationalist parties as well as to economic austerity (Horvat and Stiks 2012; Vassilev 2011). Social networking groups such as CriticAtac and LeftEast are online platforms for critical commentary from the region (see the website of CriticAtac, accessed January 5, 2015, www.criticatac.ro/lefteast/).

4 The quotation from David Ellerman in the epigraph to this section is quoted in Appel (2004, 5).

5 Joachim Zweynert has provided a close analysis of ideological beliefs in the evolution of Russian economic thinking (Zweynert 2006; 2007).

6   Transition policies and their relative success differed across Central and Eastern Europe and the former Soviet Union. Some of the worst effects of shock therapy were felt early on in Poland and the Czech Republic, but those economies (and populations) seemed to recover more quickly than Russia, for example, which began with shock therapy and moved toward a more gradualist approach. The accession of some states to the EU as well as membership to the World Trade Organization played a role in the long-term outcomes of transition.

7   See also Gordon and Temkina (1993).

8   Olga Shevchenko makes the important point that the options for disavowing the past were different in Eastern Europe and in Russia. "While the former socialist countries of Eastern Europe could frame the time after 1989 as the period of national liberation from oppression, such an option was closed to Russia, in which the seventy-odd years of Communist rule were not imposed from abroad, but rather fueled by an internal political dynamic" (Shevchenko 2009, 23).

9   Accessed January 6, 2015, www.karat.org/.

10 Skype interview with author, December 11, 2012.

11 Szabunko said that she and other NGOs are critical of such an approach. Rather, she explained that KARAT tries to convey the Polish failures in gender policy-making to NGOs in developing countries—not a triumphalist success story. Consequently, she agreed that the Polish government's approach was based on an American model of capacity building. Interview with author (Skype), December 11, 2012.

12 KARAT Coalition.

13 Another important example to consider is the web-based journalism and commentary site Transitions Online (accessed January 6, 2015, www.tol.org/). The project began in 1994 as a print publication called the *Transitions Magazine*. In 1999 it transformed into a digital only project but continued to support professionalism and freedom of journalism in the region. Begun as a Radio Free Europe/Radio Liberty and Open Society Institute initiative, the project reflects an open-ended meaning of "transition." But this example is rare in comparison to the neoliberal uses of the term "transition," as explained by Joanna Szabunko as well.

14 The explanation for the name change is provided on the publication's website: "In December 2004 the *Newsletter* changed its title to *Beyond Transition* to reflect increasingly different circumstances in which the transition countries find themselves and the broadening of the Newsletter's geographic scope" (accessed January 6, 2015, http://web.worldbank.org/WBSITE/EXTERNAL/NEWSLETTERS/EXTTRANSITION/EXTDECBEYTRANEWLET/0,,contentMDK:20612067~menuPK:1542379~pagePK:64168445~piPK:64168309~theSitePK:1542353,00.html).

15 From the journal's website, accessed January 6, 2015, http://link.springer.com/journal/11300. In an editor's piece on the expansion of the journal's content, Furio Honsell states, "The transformation of the former socialist countries started in 1989 was only the original meaning of 'transition.' In effect, that transformation had a far greater impact, it actually triggered the present transition era. The

transition perspective appears to be the only viable epistemic principle we can apply to make sense of the most peculiar trait of or [*sic*] present societies: innovation" (Honsell 2004, 2).

16   The Human Development Index is a composite measurement including health, income, and education levels. According to the website of the United Nations Development Programme in Russia: "Human Development is the most credible and most known intellectual concept of UNDP. UNDP's activities in human development contain the following programme elements in Russia: Human Development per se, including National Human Development Reports, Regional Human Development Reports and human development education; sustainable social and economic recovery in selected Russian regions; and contribution to the reduction of HIV/AIDS incidences in the Russian Federation combined with the mitigation of the impact of the epidemic on the population" (accessed January 6, 2015, www .undp.ru/index.php?iso=RU&lid=1&pid=302).

17   Website of the United Nations Development Programme, accessed January 6, 2015, www.undp.ru/index.php?iso=RU&lid=1&pid=302).

18   Unemployment statistics tend to vary depending on the agency calculating the numbers. In the past, the ILO publicized an unemployment rate that was higher than that of the Russian Federation Work and Employment Service [Federal'naia Sluzhba po Trudu i Zanyatosti]. There are also a variety of social factors that contribute to the inaccuracy of any unemployment statistics, including the percentage of individuals working in the informal economy and the percentage of workers who are not receiving wages but working (Füllsack 2001).

19   Women's rate of employment was high in the early 1990s (over 90 percent in 1993) (Glass 2008, 771). By 2000, 66 percent of working-aged women were employed, compared to 91 percent of men (772).

20   See the website of the Brooklyn Museum, accessed January 6, 2015, www .brooklynmuseum.org/eascfa/feminist_art_base/gallery/tanja_ostojic.php?i=1360.

21   This sexualization of women's labor is humorously if perversely represented in the popular Russian NTV series *Prokliatnyi Rai* [Accursed paradise] of 2007. The drama takes place in an elite brothel in Moscow and centers on the brothel owner, a single mother balancing work and motherhood. The young sex workers at the brothel are trafficked there but mostly come to revel in the glamorous makeovers made available to them. In contrast to this, see the documentary *Ukraine Is Not a Brothel* (2013), which depicts the activism of the Ukrainian feminist group Femen.

22   Boris and Salazar Parreñas explain that intimate labor exists on a continuum of service and caring labor, including caring, sexual, and domestic work (Boris and Salazar Parreñas 2010, 3).

23   Susanne Cohen's work explores counter-discourses to this view of secretarial work in secretarial training centers in St. Petersburg, Russia (Cohen 2013). She suggests that a discourse on *imidzh* [image] is a practice for gaining control of one's self and one's career rather than just feeding into the individualistic and sexualized views of women's labor in Russia.

24 There is some evidence that this moral register for harassment existed through-out Russian history (Fitzpatrick and Slezkine 2000; Glickman 1984).

25 The problem of sexism is not popularly legitimated, as a recent interview with Russian culture icon Ksenia Sobchak revealed. Sobchak interviewed Pussy Riot defendant Yekaterina Samutsevich in *Snob* magazine (October 2012). She expressed surprise that the young girls [*devushki*] of Pussy Riot had gotten together to talk about sexism. "I am trying to understand how young, pretty girls could get together and talk about sexism!" (accessed January 6, 2015, www.snob.ru/selected /entry/53946).

26 Interview with author, St. Petersburg, October 8, 2002.

27 United Russia [Edinaia Rossiia], the most powerful political party in Russia, is putting forward plans to amend the Administrative Code of Law to address ha-rassment ("Deputaty zashchitiat zhenshchin ot seksual'nykh domogatel'stv" 2012; "Deputaty zanialis' seksual'nymi domogatel'stvami" 2012).

28 The International Federation of Business and Professional Women is an organi-zation with networks across Russia. According to Khiltova, the central purpose of the organization is to help women prepare themselves for the current workplace. They provide training in how to prepare a resume, in interviewing skills, and in how to negotiate contracts. Khiltova believes that women need to be educated about how to navigate the work world and in our conversation was adamant that women should go through employment agencies, such as Kelly Girl or Man-power, rather than through want ads to find a job. She also discussed the fact that sexual harassment is an issue of not only gender but also age. Women over the age of thirty-five and especially forty have had a difficult time finding work in the private sphere. Women who are older than thirty-five are often forced to work in the government sector, which is not as competitive and typically poorly paid. The irony here, as she explained it, is that Soviet women are demographically a highly trained and educated population. To shut these women out of private sector jobs does not work to the advantage of economic development. Interview with author, St. Petersburg, February 7, 2003.

29 At the same time, Khiltova believes sexual harassment will become less of a prob-lem when firms realize that it can jeopardize their economic vitality. Interview with author, St. Petersburg, February 7, 2003.

30 An obvious cause for why sex trafficking has received more attention is because it is more egregious; it is a violation of human rights and often women's sexual inviolabil-ity, while sexual harassment is a form of nonviolent discrimination. This is un-deniably true. Yet in terms of total potential victims, sex trafficking likely impacts far fewer women in Russia. Using estimates of population and labor force rates for women, currently there are 54 million women in the Russian labor force. Compara-tively, according to Russian estimates, between 35,000 and 57,750 women are traf-ficked out of Russia every year (Tiuriukanova 2006b). These numbers may be high, but they also do not include the influx of trafficking from the CIS (Tiuriukanova 2006b). Even if these are general estimates, it is reasonable to suggest that more women are likely to experience workplace discrimination than being trafficked.

31   Julie Hemment's ethnographic work with women's groups as they were emerg-
     ing in the post-Soviet Russian context illustrates these dynamics. She states: "In
     Russia, campaigns against domestic violence and sexual violence are prioritized
     by foundations which support women's non-governmental activity (the U.S.
     Congress alone recently allocated $1 million to support programs combating
     violence against women in Russia). This attention has been rewarded by the
     development of a network of crisis centers in Russia, extending from Irkutsk
     to Moscow" (Hemment 1999, 35). She also claims that "the problem of violence
     against women was discursively created in the early 1990s by the meeting of west-
     ern feminists and Russian women's organizations and now assumes a distinctly
     'fashionable' prominence" (36).

32   One of the reasons there were so few laws addressing prostitution or domestic
     violence, for example, is that Marxist doctrine claims that such problems are
     eliminated in a classless society. The mechanism for exploitation is absent
     when women are employed in waged labor and freed from the patriarchal
     domestic economy. Feminists have long critiqued the limitations of this orthodox
     Marxist view.

33   I am referring to how advocacy organizations approach "violence against
     women." This categorization is not reflected in Russian law per se.

34   No dates are given for the poll.

35   To my knowledge, the first post-Soviet Russian case of sexual harassment that
     received press coverage occurred in the city of Barnaul when Tatyana Smyshlayeva
     advanced a case against her employer in 1994. The judge dismissed the case, stating
     that there was no precedent for criminally prosecuting sexual harassment.

36   Dr. Zoya Khotkina provided information on cases.

37   In Russia's most recent CEDAW report in 2010, there is no mention of sexual
     harassment. In general, Russia has not been compliant with CEDAW guidelines.
     In their shadow report for the Russian 2010 CEDAW report, the Consortium of
     Women's Non-Governmental Associations claims that Russia lacks a definition
     of discrimination against women and that there is no national machinery to
     address such issues (Consortium of Women's Non-Governmental Associations
     2010).

38   In interviews with legal professionals in St. Petersburg, they reported a uniform
     experience with the difficulty of successfully prosecuting sexual violence despite
     clear signs of physical violence on women's bodies.

39   In 1999, a similar conference took place in the city of Tula with the help of Diane
     Post (affiliated with the American Bar Association's Central European and Eur-
     asian Law Initiative).

40   However, Liudmila Iakhontova, a Russian lawyer who specializes in gender
     issues, stated that in cases of sexual harassment women seek legal advice only
     when they are unsure how to fix their situation. If women are able to leave their
     jobs or arrange some other way out of their unwelcome circumstances at work,
     then they are not likely to seek out help from support groups or legal advocates.
     Unlike cases of domestic violence or rape, the victims of sexual harassment want

to exit their work situations and not place a legal complaint against their perpetrators. Interview with author, St. Petersburg, January 28, 2003.

41 Janet Johnson argues that when the democracy assistance funding disappeared, women's crisis centers drew on antitrafficking grants (Johnson 2009, 61). Organizations established in the 1990s as part of the crisis center movement were joined by new organizations focused exclusively on trafficking, such as the Angel Coalition. While the opportunities for funding (especially through USAID) were much needed, the thematic narrowing of assistance to antitrafficking was detrimental to the anti–gender violence movement that had been nurtured through democracy assistance (Johnson 2009).

42 Interview with author, Moscow, July 7, 2010.

43 To my knowledge, the Angel Coalition ceased operation as of 2012. No one responded to my in-person queries in Moscow (2010) nor responded to subsequent e-mail. Their website has not been updated since 2012 and no annual reports have been issued since 2009 (Johnson 2013).

44 Interview with author, Utrecht, June 25, 2012.

45 Skype interview with author, September 7, 2012.

46 Baerbel Heide Uhl, a Czech Republic member of LaStrada, has echoed many of these views as well in e-mail correspondence with me. She has gone on to do her own research on EU antitrafficking legislation and is critical of the frameworks that developed at the end of the Cold War (Uhl 2010).

47 Interview with author, Amsterdam, June 18, 2012.

48 According to a timeline created by Elena Tiuriukanova, one of the most prominent researchers on human trafficking and migration in Russia, the 1997 conference was the first major event on trafficking in Russia. Although the issue was raised before on a smaller scale, this is an important first in terms of coordinated Russian official, NGO, and international governmental and nongovernmental representatives. In terms of the evolution of discourse, this is an important moment when the parameters of sex trafficking are expressed.

49 Transcripts from the conference only provide a summary of Zavadskaya's remarks. In that summary she is noted as saying that a "major impediment to combating trafficking is that only a portion of the crime occurs in Russian territory, and even then it is not easy or even possible to detect all related criminal activities. The majority of the criminal activity occurs once a woman crosses the border and arrives in the transit or receiving country" ("Trafficking of NIS Women Abroad" 1997).

50 On a similar analysis of the Eastern European context, see Rutvica Andrijasevic (2010).

51 Sadly, she unexpectedly passed away in 2012.

52 Although migrants from the CIS typically do not need a visa, work permits and registration are required upon entry. This part of the process is where migrants face difficulty and labor abuse.

53 Denise Brennan makes a similar argument in the context of the United States. I agree with her claim that labor trafficking is not pursued in the same ways that

sex trafficking is by law enforcement or antitrafficking organizations (Brennan 2008).

54 Donna Hughes wrote a scathing piece in the *National Review* claiming that U.S. antitrafficking activities in Russia would support prostitution there (Hughes 2002). This piece likely influenced President George W. Bush. During his administration, USAID antitrafficking funds could only go to organizations that had a clear antiprostitution agenda.

55 The historical roots of the current Russian legal statutes also have kept certain gendered understandings of human trafficking in play. In Soviet criminal law, it was punishable to compel someone [*prinuzhdenie*] to practice prostitution. And while practicing prostitution was not a criminal offense (though it was added as an administrative offense in 1987), it was illegal to run a brothel and to involve children in prostitution. The criminal statutes on prostitution were included in the section on sex crimes (i.e., rape). These statutes on prostitution-related sex crimes were transferred to the first post-Soviet criminal code.

56 Website of Eurasia Net, accessed January 6, 2015, www.eurasianet.org/taxonomy /term/2801?page=2.

57 The Moscow-based organization Migration and Law works to publicize these violations and advocate on behalf of labor migrants (accessed January 6, 2015, http:// migrocenter.org). Evidently there are North Korean labor camps in Siberia, where Russian firms contract with North Korea for labor migrants in a tightly sealed work camp. For an unorthodox reporting of this, see the *Vice.com* North Korean Labor Camps report (accessed January 6, 2015, www.vice.com/vice-news/north-korean -labor-camps-full-length). I thank Ana Kabakova for sharing this source with me.

58 Natalia Khodyreva, director of the St. Petersburg Women's Crisis Center, is an important exception. Her organization does not work with sex workers per se, but she has written on the topic (Khodyreva 2006). Central and Eastern European organizations have been a part of sex worker rights networks for some time, including the European Network for HIV/STI Prevention and Health Promotion among Migrant Sex Workers, the Global Network of Sex Work Projects, and Sex Worker Advocacy Network. Ukraine is part of the the European Network for HIV/STI Prevention and Health Promotion among Migrant Sex Workers as well. Two Russian organizations, Siberian Initiative and Humanitarian Action, are now part of the Sex Worker Advocacy Network. Alexei Starostenko of the Siberian Initiative explained that the organization was first a government-sponsored AIDS program. Over time, the group shifted focus to work with sex workers (correspondence with author, July 6, 2010).

59 This dynamic was detailed to me by one of the first activists in the Angel Coalition, Marianna Tsepelva. The Angel Coalition did not begin with an abolitionist focus but over time took that position. Tsepelva said that this was due to the influence of partnering with the Swedish International Development Cooperation and the influence of U.S. feminists Donna Hughes and Janice Rammond. Interview with author, Moscow, July 4, 2010.

1   The estimate is based on the 2012 ILO estimate of 20.9 million people in forced labor per year. From that larger data, the estimate of profits was drawn from 18.7 million victims of forced labor in the specific areas of forced labor in domestic work, forced domestic labor, and forced sexual exploitation (but does not include pornography) (ILO 2014).

2   This method was refined for the report on global estimates of forced labor (ILO 2012).

3   The ILO is cautious about operating under the broader concern for forced labor but does distinguish between populations in forced versus trafficked labor. Trafficked labor is also divided into sexual and nonsexual labor.

4   Using this date range, the forced labor incidences are gathered from news sources, government sources, and NGO publications. This estimate was used for the 2005 ILO estimate of profits. The new population estimates provided by the ILO in 2012 were used for the 2014 ILO profit estimate.

5   Specifically, the 2012 estimate uses country surveys from Armenia, Georgia, Moldova, Nepal, Niger, Bangladesh, Bolivia, Côte d'Ivoire, Guatemala, and Mali. The surveys were used to estimate the ratio of reported/nonreported cases of forced labor (ILO 2012).

6   The first step of the equation is to calculate an annual salary per forced laborer. The calculation of forced sexual work is done separately from other forms of forced labor. The annual salary is calculated by subtracting VA (value added) from W (wages). The number of forced laborers is then multiplied by the annual salary total. Forced laborers work in various industries. The VA figure is drawn from the agricultural industry (ILO 2005).

7   A key recommendation from the 2014 ILO report is to further empower police interventions to find labor violations. However, these strategies can lead to more violence and precarity.

8   For a reading of this through neoliberalism and race, see Shannon Winnubst's *Way Too Cool*, 2015.

9   All numbers taken from the website Companies and Markets, accessed January 6, 2015, www.companiesandmarkets.com.

10 Interestingly, the conclusion of the 2014 ILO report (2014, 47) includes the following statement: "The need to address the socio-economic root causes of this hugely profitable illegal practice is urgent. Comprehensive measures are required that involve governments, workers, employers and other stakeholders working together to end forced labour." This kind of statement is not uncommon, but it is rare to have studies start from this premise. The report does provide important information about socioeconomic vulnerabilities (such as lack of social provisioning, education, and migration policies). It is vital to move these observations to the forefront of advocacy, including critical economic analysis at the country and regional levels.

11 For excellent analyses of labor practices that are contextualized see Molland 2010; Keough 2003; and Salazar Parreñas 2011.

12 Kara is also an advisor to the ILO projects analyzed in the previous section.

13 Carol Leigh coined the term "sex worker" in 1978 (Leigh 2004). Terms such as "sex worker," "sex work," and "sex industry" are used in lieu of "prostitute" and "prostitution" to recast paid sex as legitimate labor.

14 See Rhacel Salazar Parreñas's work on Filipina labor migrants in Japan for an excellent analysis of how neither neoabolitionist nor sex workers' rights perspectives accurately addresses the autonomy and vulnerability that these women experience. She explains: "Filipina hostesses' labor migration inhabits a middle zone between human trafficking and labor migration, which I describe as a process of indentured mobility" (Salazar Parreñas 2011, 10).

15 For example, the Global Network of Sex Work Projects briefing paper "Sex Work Is Not Trafficking" (2011) states that the member organizations are "united in their conviction that no person should be trafficked or forced to do work that they have not chosen. The conflation of trafficking and migration with sex work, in law, policies and practice, presents a serious challenge to NSWP [Global Network of Sex Work Projects] as it negatively impacts on sex workers' work and lives."

16 It is important to note the work of the Global Alliance Against the Traffick in Women for strategically connecting the rights of sex workers with antitrafficking.

17 One video from their campaign declares that real men do laundry, real men don't buy girls; Real Men Do Their Own Laundry with Ashton Kutcher YouTube video, posted by Thorn Digital Defenders of Children, accessed January 6, 2015, http://youtu.be/2n5jazoLQrM.

18 Elizabeth Bernstein's ethnographic work on commercial sex industries in San Francisco, Holland, and Sweden reveals an important similarity between contexts despite clear political differences of approach to regulating sex work. "In San Francisco, Stockholm, and Amsterdam, three quite disparate versions of policy reform in the late 1990s resulted in a common series of alterations to the social geography of sexual commerce: the removal of economically disenfranchised and racially marginalized streetwalkers and their customers from gentrifying city centers; the de facto tolerance of a small tier of predominantly white and relatively privileged indoor clients and workers; and the driving of illegal migrant sex workers further underground" (Bernstein 2007, 146).

19 The image is no longer on the Salvation Army's website but can be viewed elsewhere (accessed January 6, 2015, http://eniojergovic.files.wordpress.com/2013/01/Human_trafficking21.jpg).

20 Slavoj Žižek has a critique of this false sense of ethical consumerism, available in a video: Royal Society for the encouragement of Arts, Manufactures and Commerce, First as Tragedy, Then as Farce, YouTube video, posted by Royal Society for the encouragement of Arts, Manufactures and Commerce, accessed January 6, 2015, www.youtube.com/watch?v=hpAMbpQ8J7g.

21 Not For Sale is also the name of the book and organization created by David Batstone, who in 2007 realized that his favorite restaurant in San Francisco was operated with trafficked labor (see the Not For Sale website, accessed January 6, 2015, www.notforsalecampaign.org).

22 Total compiled by adding annual reported U.S. expenditures on antitrafficking as reported by the Office to Monitor and Combat Trafficking in Persons. I thank Andrea Breau for her research assistance on this work.

23 In recent years, there has been more attention to what is called domestic trafficking, which refers to the trafficking of U.S. citizens within the borders of the United States. I do not have the space to address this here; it is the focus of other research I am conducting.

24 This has shifted in the past decade with the turn to recognizing domestic victims of trafficking.

25 See the U.S. Health and Human Services website, accessed January 6, 2015, www .acf.hhs.gov/program-topics/human-trafficking.

26 MTV Exit, It Could Happen to Any of Us, 2013, Vimeo video, 1.02, posted by MTV Exit, accessed January 6, 2015, http://vimeo.com/mtvexit/indopsa.

27 *The Price of Sex*, 2004, available at the website of Mimi Chakarova, accessed January 6, 2015, www.mclight.com/gallery/113.html.

REFERENCES

Abalkin, Leonid. 1990. "The Market in a Socialist Economy." *Problems of Economic Transition* 32 (10): 6–19.

Abubikirova, Svetlana, S. Klimenkova, E. Kochkina, and M. Regentova. 1998. "Zhenskoe organizatsii v Rossii sevodnia" [Women's organizations in Russia today]. In *Spravochnik Zhenskie Nepravitel'stvenniie organizatsii Rossii i SNG* [Guidebook of women's independent organizations in Russia and the FSU]. Compiled by M. Eslan. Accessed January 6, 2015. www.a-z.ru/women/texts/wom_org_Today.htm.

Agathangelou, Anna M. 2004. *The Global Political Economy of Sex: Desire, Violence, and Insecurity in Mediterranean Nation States.* New York: Palgrave.

Agustín, Laura. 2007. *Sex at the Margins: Migration, Labour Markets and the Rescue Industry.* London: Zed Books.

Aivazova, Svetlana. 1998. *Russkie zhenshchiny v labirinte ravopraviia* [Russian women in the labyrinth of equality]. Moscow: Rik Rusanova.

Alchuk, Anna. 2006. "The Tactics and Strategy of Resisting Masculine Culture: A Long-term Artistic Project." In *Gender Check: A Reader Art and Theory in Eastern Europe*, ed. Bojana Pejić, 225–32. Cologne: Verlag der Buchhandlung.

Alexseev, Mikhail. 2010. "Majority and Minority Xenophobia in Russia: The Importance of Being Titulars." *Post-Soviet Affairs* 26 (2): 89–120.

Altman, Dennis. 2001. *Global Sex.* Chicago: University of Chicago Press.

American Bar Association Central European and Eurasian Law Intiative. 2006. *CEDAW Assessment Tool Report for the Russian Federation.* Moscow: ABA/CEELI.

Anderson, Benedict. 1991. *Imagined Communities: Reflections on the Origins and Spread of Nationalism*. New York: Verso Press.

Andrijasevic, Rutvica. 2007. "Beautiful Dead Bodies: Gender, Migration and Representation in Anti-trafficking Campaigns." *Feminist Review* 86:24–44.

Andrijasevic, Rutvica. 2010. *Migration, Agency and Citizenship in Sex Trafficking*. New York: Palgrave.

Anker, Christien van den, and Jeroen Doomernik, eds. 2006. *Trafficking and Women's Rights*. New York: Palgrave Macmillan.

Appel, Hilary. 2004. *A New Capitalist Order: Privatization and Ideology in Russia and Eastern Europe*. Pittsburgh: University of Pittsburgh Press.

Aslan, Özlem, and Zeynep Gambetti. 2011. "Provincializing Frasers' History: Feminism and Neoliberalism Revisited." *History of the Present* 1 (1): 130–47.

Attwood, Lynn. 1997. "She Was Asking for It: Rape and Domestic Violence against Women." In *Post-Soviet Women: From the Baltic to Central Asia*, ed. Mary Buckley, 99–118. Cambridge: Cambridge University Press.

Azhgikhina, Nadezhda. 1995. "Women as Presented by the Russian Media." A Report for the United Nations Department of Economic and Social Affairs. Accessed January 6, 2015. http://un.org/documents/ecosoc/cn6/1996/media/rmediaen.htm.

Azhgikhina, Nadezhda. 1998. "Democracy Minus Women Is Not Democracy." *Current Digest of the Soviet Press*, April 8.

Azhgikhina, Nadezhda. 2000. "Empowering Russia's Women: Will Their Potential Be Tapped?" In *Russia's Fate through Russian Eyes: Voices of the New Generation*, ed. Heyward Isham, 212–34. Boulder, CO: Westview Press.

Babenko, Mikhail. 2009. "Understanding Russia's Demographic Challenge." *Development and Transition* 14:30–31.

Bakker, Isabella, and Stephen Gill. 2003. *Power, Production, and Social Reproduction: Human In/Security in the Global Political Economy*. Hampshire, UK: Palgrave Macmillan.

Bales, Kevin. 1999. *Disposable People: New Slavery in the Global Economy*. Berkeley: University of California Press.

Barker, Joanne. 2008. "Gender, Sovereignty, Rights: Native Women's Activism against Social Inequality and Violence in Canada." *American Quarterly* 60 (2): 259–66.

Barry, Kathleen. 1979. *Female Sexual Slavery*. Englewood Cliffs, NJ: Prentice-Hall.

Barry, Kathleen. 1981. "International Feminism: Sexual Politics and the World Conference on Women in Copenhagen." *Feminist Issues* 1 (2): 37–50.

Barry, Kathleen, Charlotte Bunch, and Shirley Castley. 1984. *International Feminism: Networking against Female Sexual Slavery: Report of the Global Feminist Workshop to Organize against Traffic in Women, Rotterdam, the Netherlands, April 6–15, 1983*. New York: International Women's Tribune Centre.

Basu, Amrita. 2000. "Globalization of the Local/Localization of the Global: Mapping Transnational Women's Movements." *Meridians: Feminism, Race, Transnationalism* 1 (1): 68–84.

Belyakova, A. M., Z. S. Bekiayeva, N. N. Sheptulina, and V. N. Tokunova, eds. 1978. *Soviet Legislation on Women's Rights*. Moscow: Progress.

Benería, Lourdes. 2003. *Gender, Development, and Globalization: Economics as If All People Mattered*. New York: Routledge.

Benería, Lourdes, and Gita Sen. 1981. "Accumulation, Reproduction, and 'Women's Role in Economic Development': Boserup Revisited." *Signs* 7 (2): 279–98.

Berman, Jacqueline. 2010. "Biopolitical Management, Economic Calculation and 'Trafficked Women.'" *International Migration* 48 (4): 84–113.

Bernstein, Elizabeth. 2007. *Temporarily Yours: Intimacy, Authenticity, and the Commerce of Sex*. Chicago: University of Chicago Press.

Bernstein, Elizabeth. 2012. "Carceral Politics as Gender Justice? The 'Traffic in Women' and Neoliberal Circuits of Crime, Sex, and Rights." *Theory and Society* 41 (3): 233–59.

Bernstein, Laurie. 1995. *Sonia's Daughters: Prostitutes and Their Regulation in Imperial Russia*. Berkeley: University of California Press.

Bevacqua, Maria. 2000. *Rape on the Public Agenda: Feminism and the Politics of Sexual Assault*. Boston: Northeastern University Press.

Bhattacharjee, Anannya. 1997. "The Public/Private Mirage: Mapping Homes and Undomesticating Violence Work in the South Asian Immigrant Community." In *Feminist Genealogies, Colonial Legacies, Democratic Futures*, ed. M. Jacqui Alexander and Chandra Mohanty, 308–29. New York: Routledge.

Binnie, Jon. 2013. "Neoliberalism, Class, Gender and Lesbian, Gay, Bisexual, Transgender and Queer Politics in Poland." *International Journal of Politics, Culture and Society* 27 (2): 241–57.

"Biznes Zhenshchinam k Litsy" [Business ladies up close]. 1996. *Ekonomika i Zhizn* [Economics and life], March 9.

Bloch, Alexia. 2013. "Citizenship, Belonging, and Moldovan Migrants in Post-Soviet Russia." *Ethnos: Journal of Ethnography* 79 (4): 1–28.

Blomfield, Adrian. 2008. "Sexual Harassment Okay as It Ensures Human Breed, Russian Judge Rules." *Telegraph*, July 29.

Bockman, Johanna. 2007. "The Origins of Neoliberalism between Soviet Socialism and Western Capitalism: 'A Galaxy without Borders.'" *Theory and Society* 36 (4): 343–71.

Bockman, Johanna. 2011. *Markets in the Name of Socialism: The Left-Wing Origins of Neoliberalism*. Stanford, CA: Stanford University Press.

Bockman, Johanna, and Gil Eyal. 2002. "Eastern Europe as a Laboratory for Economic Knowledge: The Transnational Roots of Neoliberalism." *American Journal of Sociology* 108 (2): 310–52.

Borenstein, Eliot. 2008. *Overkill: Sex and Violence in Contemporary Russian Popular Culture*. Ithaca, NY: Cornell University Press.

Boris, Eileen, and Jennifer Klein. 2012. *Caring for America: Home Health Workers in the Shadow of the Welfare State*. Oxford: Oxford University Press.

Boris, Eileen, and Rhacel Salazar Parreñas, eds. 2010. *Intimate Labors: Cultures, Technologies, and the Politics of Care*. Stanford, CA: Stanford University Press.

Boserup, Ester. 1970. *Woman's Role in Economic Development*. London: Earthscan.

Bought and Sold. 1997. Directed by Gillian Caldwell and Anne Gartlan, produced by the Global Survival Network.

Boutros-Ghali, Boutros. 1995. "Overview." In *The United Nations and The Advancement of Women 1945–1995*, 1–9. New York: United Nations.

Boyer, Dominic, and Alexei Yurchak. 2010. "American Stiob: Or, What Late-Socialist Aesthetics of Parody Reveal about Contemporary Political Culture in the West." *Cultural Anthropology* 25 (2): 179–221.

Bradshaw, Michael, and Alison Stenning, eds. 2004. *East Central Europe and the Former Soviet Union: The Post-socialist States*. Harlow, UK: Pearson.

Brainerd, Elizabeth. 2010. "Human Development in Eastern Europe and the CIS since 1990." Geneva: UNDP. Accessed January 6, 2015. http://hdr.undp.org/en/content/human-development-eastern-europe-and-cis-1990.

Brennan, Denise. 2004. *What's Love Got to Do with It? Transnational Desires and Sex Tourism in the Dominican Republic*. Durham, NC: Duke University Press.

Brennan, Denise. 2008. "Competing Claims of Victimhood?: Foreign and Domestic 'Victims' of Trafficking in the United States." *Sexuality Research and Social Policy* 5 (4): 45–61.

Bristow, Edward J. 1983. *Prostitution and Prejudice: The Jewish Fight against White Slavery, 1870–1939*. Oxford: Clarendon Press.

Browning, Genia. 1987. *Women and Politics in the USSR*. New York: St. Martin's Press.

Brussa, Licia. 1991. *Survey on Prostitution, Migration and Traffic in Women: History and Current Situation*. Strasbourg: Council of Europe.

Buck-Morss, Susan. 2002. *Dreamworld and Catastrophe: The Passing of Mass Utopia in East and West*. Cambridge, MA: MIT Press.

Bucur, Maria. 2008. "An Archipelago of Stories: Gender History in Eastern Europe." *American Historical Review* 113 (5): 1375–89.

Bumiller, Kristin. 2008. *In an Abusive State: How Neoliberalism Appropriated the Feminist Movement against Sexual Violence*. Durham, NC: Duke University Press.

Bunch, Charlotte, and Roxanna Carillo. 1991. *Gender Violence: A Development and Human Rights Issue*. New York: Garland.

Bunch, Charlotte, and Niamh Reilly, eds. 1994. *Demanding Accountability: The Global Campaign and Vienna Tribunal for Women's Human Rights*. New Brunswick, NJ: Rutgers University, Center for Women's Global Leadership.

Burawoy, Michael. 1996. "The State and Economic Involution: Russia through a Chinese Lens." *World Development* 24 (6): 1105–17.

Burawoy, Michael. 2002. "Transition without Transformation: Russia's Involuntary Road to Capitalism." *East European Politics and Societies* 15 (2): 269–90.

Burawoy, Michael, and Pavel Krotov. 1993. "The Economic Basis of Russia's Political Crisis." *New Left Review* 198 (March–April): 49–69.

Burawoy, Michael, and Katherine Verdery. 1999. *Uncertain Transition: Ethnographies of Change in the Postsocialist World*. Lanham, MD: Rowman and Littlefield.

Burdeau, C. 2001. "Russian Women Find Success in Workplace." *Russia Journal*, December 14.

"Business Ladies Increasing in Russia." 2004. RIA *Novosti*, November 29.

Butler, Judith. 2006. *Precarious Life: The Powers of Mourning and Loss.* London: Verso Press.

Buvinic, Mayra. 1976. "A Critical Review of Some Research Concepts and Concerns." In *Women and World Development, an Annotated Bibliography*, ed. Mayra Buvinic, 1–20. Washington, DC: Overseas Development Office.

Byrd, Jodi. 2011. *The Transit of Empire: Indigenous Critiques of Colonialism.* Minneapolis: University of Minnesota Press.

Cabezas, Amalia L. 2009. *Economies of Desire: Sex and Tourism in Cuba and the Dominican Republic.* Philadelphia: Temple University Press.

Caldwell, Melissa. 2004. *Not by Bread Alone.* Berkeley: University of California Press.

Castellas, Manuel. 2000. *End of Millennium.* Vol. 3. 2nd ed. Oxford: Blackwell.

Center for Women's Global Leadership. 2011. "Making Macroeconomics Work for Us: A Feminist Perspective." New Brunswick, NJ: Rutgers University, Center for Women's Global Leadership. Accessed January 6, 2015. www.cwgl.rutgers.edu /docman/economic-and-social-rights-publications/nexus/384-nexus-brief1/file.

Chapkis, Wendy. 1997. *Live Sex Acts: Women Performing Erotic Labor.* New York: Routledge.

Charkiewicz, Ewa. 2009. "The Impact of the Crisis on Women in Central and Eastern Europe." Association for Women's Rights in Development Brief 8. Accessed January 6, 2015. www.awid.org/About-AWID/AWID-News/Briefs-The-Impact-of-the-crisis -on-Women.

Chaterjee, Partha. 2005. "The Nation in Heterogeneous Time." *Futures* 37:925–42.

Chen, Martha Alter. 1995. "Engendering World Conferences: The International Women's Movement and the United Nations." *Third World Quarterly* 16 (3): 477–93.

Chew, Lin. 2005. "Reflections by an Anti-trafficking Activist." In *Trafficking and Prostitution Reconsidered: New Perspectives on Migration, Sex Work, and Human Rights*, ed. Kamala Kempadoo, 65–80. Boulder, CO: Paradigm.

Chirkova, Alla. 2002. "Zhenskoe predprinimatl'stvo v Rossii" [Female entrepreneurship in Russia]. In *Gender i Ekonomika: Mirovoi opyt i ekspertiza Rossiiskoi praktiki*, ed. Elena Mezentseva, 234–429. Moscow: Russkaia Panorama.

Chow, Rey. 2006. *The Age of the World Target: Self-Referentiality in War, Theory, and Comparative Work.* Durham, NC: Duke University Press.

Chuang, J. 2006. "Beyond a Snapshot: Preventing Human Trafficking in the Global Economy." *Indiana Journal of Global Legal Studies* 13 (1): 137–63.

Clark, Roger. 1994. *The United Nations Crime Prevention and Criminal Justice Program: Formulation of Standards and Efforts at Their Implementation.* Philadelphia: University of Pennsylvania Press.

Clinton, William Jefferson. 1996. "Remarks by the President at Human Rights Day Event, December 10, 1996." Accessed January 6, 2015. www.state.gov/1997–2001 -NOPDFS/picw/trafficking/96pres.htm.

Clinton, William Jefferson. 1998. "Memorandum on Steps to Combat Violence Against Women and Trafficking in Women and Girls, March 11, 1998." Accessed January 9, 2015. www.gpo.gov/fdsys/pkg/WCPD-1998–03–16/pdf/WCPD-1998–03–16 -Pg412.pdf.

Cohen, Susanne. 2013. "Image of a Secretary: A Metapragmatic Morality for Post-Soviet Capitalism." *Anthropological Quarterly* 86 (3): 725–58.

Commission on the Status of Women. n.d. Accessed January 9, 2015. www.un.org/women watch/daw/csw/index.html#about.

Committee on the Elimination of Discrimination against Women. 1992. "General Recommendation No. 19." Accessed January 9, 2015. www2.ohchr.org/english/bodies /cedaw/comments.htm.

Consortium of Women's Non-Governmental Associations. 2010. "Implementation by the Russian Federation of UN Convention on Elimination of All Forms of Discrimination Against Women." Accessed January 6, 2015. www2.ohchr.org/english/bodies /cedaw/docs/ngos/CWNGOSA_RussianFederation_cedaw46.pdf.

Coomeraswamy, Radhika. 1996. *Report of the Special Rapporteur on Violence Against Women, Its Causes and Consequences*. Geneva: United Nations.

Crawshaw, Steve. 1994. "Gangland Feud Suspected as Six Die in Frankfurt Brothel." *Independent*, August 17.

Crenshaw, Kimberle. 1991. "Mapping the Margins: Intersectionality, Identity Politics, and Violence against Women of Color." *Stanford Law Review* 43 (6): 1241–99.

Danailova-Trainor, Gergana, and Frank Laczko. 2010. "Trafficking in Persons and Development: Towards Greater Policy Coherence." *International Migration* 48 (4): 38–83.

Davidson, Julia O'Connell. 2006. "Will the Real Sex Slave Please Stand Up?" *Feminist Review* 83: 4–22.

Davis, Angela. 2000. "The Color of Violence against Women." *Colorlines: The Newsmagazine on Race and Politics* 10. Accessed January 6, 2015. www.colorlines.com.

"Deputaty zanialis' seksual'nymi domogatel'stvami" [Deputies consider sexual harassment]. 2012. Newsru.com, September 24. Accessed January 6, 2015. www.newsru .com/russia/24sep2012/harassment.html.

"Deputaty zashchitiat zhenshchin ot seksual'nykh domogatel'stv" [Deputies protect women from sexual harassment]. 2012. *Izvestia*, September 24.

DAWN (Development Alternatives with Women for a New Era). 1987. *Development, Crises, and Alternative Visions: Third World Perspectives*. New York: Monthly Review Press.

de Haan, Francisca. 2010. "Continuing Cold War Paradigms in the Western Historiography of Transnational Women's Organizations: The Case of the Women's International Democratic Federation (WIDF)." *Women's History Review* 19 (4): 547–673.

de Haan, Francisca, Krassimira Daskalova, and Anna Loutfi, eds. 2008. *A Biographical Dictionary of Women's Movements and Feminisms: Central, Eastern, and South Eastern Europe, Nineteenth and Twentieth Centuries*. Budapest: Central European University Press.

Desai, Padma. 1997. *Going Global: Transition from Plan to Market in the World Economy*. Cambridge, MA: MIT Press.

DeStefano, Anthony. 2008. *The War on Human Trafficking: U.S. Policy Assessed*. New Brunswick, NJ: Rutgers University Press.

De Stoop, Chris. 1994. *They Are So Sweet, Sir: The Cruel World of Traffickers in Filipinas and Other Women*. Leuven, Belgium: Limitless Asia.

Ditmore, Melissa. 2005. "Trafficking in Lives: How Ideology Shapes Policy." In *Trafficking and Prostitution Reconsidered*, ed. Kamala Kempadoo, 107–26. Boulder, CO: Paradigm.

Djankov, Simeon, Edward Glaeser, Rafael La Porta, Florencio Lopez-de-Silanes, and Andrei Shleifer. 2003. "The New Comparative Politics." *Journal of Comparative Economics* 31:595–619.

Doezma, Jo. 2010. *Sex Slaves and Discourse Masters: The Construction of Trafficking*. London: Zed Books.

Eastern Promises. Directed by David Cronenberg. 1997. New York: Focus Features.

Einhorn, Barbara. 1991. "Where Have All the Women Gone? Women and the Women's Movement in East Central Europe. *Feminist Review* 39:16–36.

Einhorn, Barbara. 2006. *Citizenship in an Enlarging Europe: From Dream to Awakening*. London: Palgrave.

Ellerman, David. 2003. "On the Russian Privatization Debate." *Challenge* 46 (3): 6–28.

Engerman, David. 2011. "The Second World's Third World." *Kritika* 12 (1): 183–211.

Enloe, Cynthia. 1990. *Bananas, Beaches and Bases: Making Feminist Sense of International Politics*. London: Pandora.

Eschle, Catherine, and Bice Maiguashca. 2011. *Making Feminist Sense of the Global Justice Movement*. Lanham, MD: Roman and Littlefield.

Escobar, Arturo. 1992. "Imagining a Postdevelopment Era? Critical Thought, Development, and Social Movements." *Social Text* 31/32:20–56.

Escobar, Arturo. 1995. *Encountering Development: The Making and Unmaking of the Third World*. Princeton, NJ: Princeton University Press.

Etkind, Alexander. 2013. "Post-Soviet Hauntology: Cultural Memory of the Soviet Terror." *Constellations* 16 (1): 182–200.

European Council of Justice and Home Affairs Ministers. 1989. Resolution on the Exploitation of Prostitution and the Traffic in Human Beings. European Parliament Doc. A2–52/89.

Eyal, Gil. 2000. "Anti-politics and the Spirit of Capitalism: Dissidents, Monetarists, and the Czech Transition to Capitalism." *Theory and Society* 29 (1): 49–92.

Fábián, Katalin. 2010. *Domestic Violence in Postcommunist States: Local Activism, National Policies, and Global Forces*. Bloomington: Indiana University Press.

Fábián, Katalin. 2014. "Disciplining the 'Second World': The Relationship between Transnational and Local Forces in Contemporary Hungarian Women's Social Movements." *East European Politics* 30 (1): 1–20.

Fernand-Laurent, Jean. 1985. *Activities for the Advancement of Women: Equality, Development, and Peace: Report of Jean Fernand-Laurent, Special Rapporteur on the Suppression of the Traffic in Persons and the Exploitation of the Prostitution of Others*. New York: United Nations.

Fieldon, Sandra, and Marilyn J. Davidson, eds. 2010. *Handbook on Successful Women Entrepreneurs*. Northamptom, MA: Edward Elgar.

Finckenauer, James. 2001. "Russian Transnational Organized Crime and Human Trafficking." In *Global Human Smuggling: Comparative Perspectives*, ed. David Kyle and Rey Koslowski, 166–86. Baltimore: Johns Hopkins University Press.

Fitzpatrick, Sheila, and Yuri Slezkine. 2000. *In the Shadow of Revolution: Life Stories of Russian Women from 1917 to the Second World War*. Princeton, NJ: Princeton University Press.

Fleming, Michael. 2012. "The Regime of Violence in Socialist and Postsocialist Poland." *Annals of the Association of American Geographers* 102 (2): 482–89.

Fodor, Éva. 1997. "Gender in Transition: Unemployment in Hungary, Poland, and Slovakia." *East European Politics and Societies* 11 (3): 470–500.

Fodor, Éva. 2004. "The State Socialist Emancipation Project: Gender Inequality in Workplace Authority in Hungary and Austria." *Signs* 29 (3): 782–813.

Foucault, Michel. 1972. *The Archeology of Knowledge and the Discourse on Language*. New York: Pantheon.

Fraser, Arvonne. 1987. *The U.N. Decade for Women Documents and Dialogue*. Boulder, CO: Westview Press.

Fraser, Nancy. 1997. *Justice Interruptus: Critical Reflections on the "Postsocialist" Condition*. New York: Routledge.

Fraser, Nancy. 2009. "Feminism, Capitalism and the Cunning of History." *New Left Review* 56: 97–117.

Fraser, Nancy, and Linda Gordon. 1994. "A Genealogy of Dependency: Tracing a Keyword of the U.S. Welfare State." *Signs* 19 (2): 309–36.

Fregoso, Rosa-Linda, and Cynthia Bejarano, eds. 2010. *Terrorizing Women: Feminicide in the Américas*. Durham, NC: Duke University Press.

Friedman, Robert. 2002. *Red Mafiya: How the Russian Mob Has Invaded America*. Boston: Berkley.

Friesendorf, Cornelius. 2007. "Pathologies of Security Governance: Efforts against Human Trafficking in Europe." *Security Dialogue* 38 (3): 379–402.

Fudge, Judy, and Rosemary Owens. 2006. *Precarious Work, Women and the New Economy: The Challenge to Legal Norms*. Oxford: Hart.

Fukuyama, Francis. 1992. *The End of History and the Last Man*. Ann Arbor, MI: Free Press.

Füllsack, Manfred. 2001. "Official Figures and Unofficial Realities: Employment Rates and Their Significance in Russia." *Europe-Asia Studies* 53 (4): 613–25.

Funk, Nanette. 2004. "Feminist Critiques of Liberalism: Can They Travel East? Their Relevance in Eastern and Central Europe and the Former Soviet Union." *Signs* 29 (3): 695–726.

Funk, Nanette. 2007. "Fifteen Years of the East-West Women's Dialogue." In *Living Gender after Communism*, ed. Janet Elise Johnson and Jean C. Robinson, 203–26. Bloomington: Indiana University Press.

Funk, Nanette. 2012. "Contra Fraser on Feminism and Neoliberalism." *Hypatia* 28 (1): 179–96.

Funk, Nanette, and Magda Mueller, eds. 1993. *Gender Politics and Post-Communism*. New York: Routledge.

Gaidar, Egor. 2003. *State and Evolution: Russia's Search for a Free Market*. Seattle: University of Washington Press.

Gal, Susan, and Gail Kligman. 2000. *The Politics of Gender and Socialism: A Comparative-Historical Essay*. Princeton, NJ: Princeton University Press.

Gallagher, Anne. 2001. "Human Rights and the New UN Protocols on Trafficking and Migrant Smuggling: A Preliminary Analysis." *Human Rights Quarterly* 23 (4): 975–1004.

Gallagher, Anne. 2006. "Recent Legal Developments in the Field of Human Trafficking: A Critical Review of the 2005 European Convention and Related Instruments." *European Journal of Migration and Law* 8:163–89.

Gallagher, Anne. 2009. "Human Rights and Human Trafficking: Quagmire or Firm Ground? A Response to James Hathaway." *Virginia Journal of International Law* 49 (4): 789–848.

Gallagher, Anne, and Elaine Pearson. 2010. "The High Cost of Freedom: A Legal and Policy Analysis of Shelter Detention for Victims of Trafficking." *Human Rights Quarterly* 32 (1): 73–114.

Gerber, Theodore, and Olga Mayorova. 2006. "Dynamic Gender Differences in a Postsocialist Labour Market: Russia, 1991–1997." *Social Forces* 84 (4): 2047–75.

Ghodsee, Kristen. 2003. "And If the Shoe Doesn't Fit? (Wear It Anyway?): Economic Transformation and Western Paradigm of 'Women in Development' in Postcommunist Central and Eastern Europe." *Gender and Women's Studies Quarterly* 31 (3/4): 19–36.

Ghodsee, Kristen. 2005. *The Red Riviera: Gender, Tourism, and Postsocialism on the Black Sea*. Durham, NC: Duke University Press.

Ghodsee, Kristen. 2010. "Revisiting the United Nations Decade for Women: Brief Reflections on Feminism, Capitalism and Cold War Politics in the Early Years of the International Women's Movement." *Women's Studies International Forum* 33:3–12.

Ghodsee, Kristen. 2012. "Rethinking State Socialist Mass Women's Organizations: The Committee of the Bulgarian Women's Movement and the United Nations Decade for Women, 1975–1985." *Journal of Women's History* 24 (4): 49–73.

Ghodsee, Kristen. 2013. "Transnational State Feminisms: Bulgarian, African and South Asian Women's Movements during the Cold War." Lecture presented at Ohio State University, Sawyer Seminar, October 14.

Gibson-Graham, J. K. 1996. *The End of Capitalism (As We Knew It): A Feminist Critique of Political Economy*. Oxford: Blackwell.

Gille, Zsuzsa. 2010. "Is There a Global Postsocialist Condition?" *Global Society* 24 (1): 9–30.

Glajar, Valentina, and Domnica Radulescu, eds. 2004. *Vampirettes, Wretches, and Amazons: Western Representations of East European Women*. New York: East European Monographs.

Glass, Christy. 2008. "Gender and Work during Transition." *East European Politics and Societies* 22 (4): 757–83.

Glickman, Rose L. 1984. *Russian Factory Women: Workplace and Society, 1880–1914*. Berkeley: University of California Press.

Glinski, Dmitri, and Peter Reddaway. 1999. "The Ravages of Market Bolshevism." *Journal of Democracy* 10 (2): 19–34.

Global Alliance Against Traffic in Women. 2007. *Collateral Damage: The Impact of Anti-trafficking Measures on Human Trafficking*. Bangkok: Global Alliance Against Traffic in Women.

"Global Mafia." 1993. *Newsweek*, December 12.

Global Network of Sex Work Projects (NSWP). 2011. "Sex Work Is Not Trafficking: Briefing Paper No. 3." Accessed January 13, 2015. www.nswp.org/resource/sex-work-not-trafficking.

Global Survival Network. 1997. "Crime and Servitude: An Epose of the Traffic in Women for Prostitution from the Newly Independent States." Presented at the International Conference, "The Trafficking of NIS Women Abroad," Moscow, November 3–5.

Global Tribunal on Violations of Women's Human Rights. 1994. *Testimonies of the Global Tribunal on Violations of Women's Human Rights at the United Nations World Conference on Human Rights, Vienna, June 1993*. New Brunswick, NJ: Rutgers University, Center for Women's Global Leadership.

Goodey, Jo. 2004. "Sex Trafficking in Women from Central and East European Countries: Promoting a 'Victim-Centered' and 'Woman-Centered' Approach to Criminal Justice Intervention." *Feminist Review* 76:26–45.

Goodman, Walter. 1990. "Koppel on 'Sex in the Soviet Union.'" *New York Times*, December 19.

Gorbachev, Mikhail. 1987. *Perestroika: New Thinking for Our Country and the World*. New York: Harper and Row.

Gordon, Leonid, and Anna Temkina. 1993. "Rabochee dvizhenie v postsotsialisticheskoi Rossii" [The labor movement in postsocialist Russia]. *Obshchestvenye Nauki i Sovremenost* 3:31–44.

Goscilo, Helena. 1996. *Dehexing Sex: Russian Womanhood during and after Glasnost*. Ann Arbor: University of Michigan Press.

Gowan, Peter. 1995. "Neo-liberal Theory and Practice for Eastern Europe." *New Left Review* 213:3–60.

Graff, Agnieszka. 2003. "Lost between the Waves? The Paradoxes of Feminist Chronology and Activism in Contemporary Poland." *Journal of International Women's Studies* 4 (2): 100–116.

Greskovits, Béla. 1998. *The Political Economy of Protest and Patience: East European and Latin American Transformations Compared*. New York: Central European University Press.

Grewal, Inderpal, and Caren Kaplan. 2004. *Scattered Hegemonies: Postmodernity and Transnational Feminist Practices*. Minneapolis: University of Minnesota Press.

Grinberg, Ruslan. 2004. "To the Readers of 'The World of Transformations.'" *Mir Peremen* [World of transformations] vol. 1 (January). Accessed January 13, 2015. www.imepi-eurasia.ru/eng/mir.php.

Grjebine, Lois, ed. 1986. "Reporting on Prostitution: The Media, Women and Prostitution in India, Malaysia and the Philippines." UNESCO report. New Delhi: UNESCO.

Guenther, Katja. 2011. "The Possibilities and Pitfalls of NGO Feminism: Insights from Postsocialist Eastern Europe." *Signs* 36 (4): 863–87.

Gunning, Isabelle R. 1998. "Cutting through the Obfuscation: Female Genital Surgeries in Neoimperial Culture." In *Talking Visions: Multicultural Feminism in a Transnational Age*, ed. Ella Shohat, 203–24. New York: MIT Press.

Hall, Lisa Kahaleole. 2008. "Strategies of Erasure: U.S. Colonialism and Native Hawaiian Feminism." *American Quarterly* 60 (2): 273–80.

Hamilton, Denise. 1991. "Changing Lifestyles—Prostitution Rising as Tough Times Wear on Soviet People." *Los Angeles Times*, November 12.

Harrington, Carol. 2011. "Resolution 1325 and Post–Cold War Feminist Politics." *International Feminist Journal of Politics* 13 (4): 557–75.

Harvey, David. 2005. *A Brief History of Neoliberalism*. Oxford: Oxford University Press.

Hašková, Hana. 2005. "Czech Women's Civic Organizing under the State Socialist Regime, Socio-economic Transformation and the EU Accession Period." *Czech Sociological Review* 41 (6): 1077–110.

Havelková, Hana, and Libora Oates-Indruchová, eds. 2014. *The Politics of Gender under State Socialism: An Expropriated Voice*. New York: Routledge.

Hawkesworth, Mary. 2006. *Globalization and Feminist Activism*. Lanham, MD: Rowan and Littlefield.

Haynes, Dina Francesca. 2007. "(Not) Found Chained to a Bed in a Brothel: Conceptual, Legal, and Procedural Failures to Fulfill the Promise of the Trafficking Victims Protection Act." *Georgetown Immigration Law Journal* 21 (3): 337–81.

Heise, L., and J. R. Chapman. 1992. "Reflections on a Movement: The U.S. Battle against Women Abuse." In *Freedom from Violence: Women's Strategies from around the World*, ed. Margaret Schuler, 257–96. Washington, DC: OEF International.

Helmore, K. 1985. "The Neglected Resource: Women in the Developing World." *Christian Science Monitor*, December 19.

Hemment, Julie. 1999. "Gender Violence in Crisis: Russian NGOs Help Themselves to Liberal Feminist Discourse." *Anthropology of East Europe Review* 17 (1): 35–38.

Hemment, Julie. 2004. "Global Civil Society and the Local Costs of Belonging: Defining Violence against Women in Russia." *Signs* 29 (31): 815–40.

Hemment, Julie. 2007. *Empowering Women in Russia: Activism, Aid and NGOs*. Bloomington: Indiana University Press.

Hewitt, Nancy, ed. 2010. *No Permanent Waves: Recasting Histories of U.S. Feminism*. New Brunswick, NJ: Rutgers University Press.

Holmgren, Beth. 1995. "Bug Inspectors and Beauty Queens: The Problems of Translating Feminism into Russian." In *Genders 22: Postcommunism and the Body Politic*, ed. Ellen Barry, 15–31. New York: NYU Press.

Holmgren, Beth. 2013. "Toward an Understanding of Gendered Agency in Contemporary Russia." *Signs* 38 (3): 535–42.

Honsell, Furio. 2004. "'The Times They Are A-Changin': Research Networks for Understanding and Disseminating Transition and Innovation." *Transition Studies Review* 11 (3): 1–3.

Horvat, Srećko, and Igor Štiks. 2012. "Welcome to the Desert of Transition!: Postsocialism, the European Union, and a New Left in the Balkans." *Monthly Review* 63 (10): 38–48.

Hrycak, Alexandra. 2010. "Transnational Advocacy Campaigns and Domestic Violence Prevention in Ukraine." In *Domestic Violence in Postcommunist States: Local Activism, National Policies and Global Forces*, ed. Katalin Fábián, 45–77. Bloomington: Indiana University Press.

Hrycak, Alexandra. 2012. "Theorizing the Response of the Ukrainian State to Transnational Campaigns to Combat Violence against Women." Paper presented at the Forty-Fourth Annual Convention of the Association for Slavic, East European and Eurasian Studies. New Orleans, November 15.

Hua, Julietta. 2011. *Trafficking Women's Human Rights*. Minneapolis: University of Minnesota Press.

Hughes, Donna. 2000. "The 'Natasha' Trade: The Transnational Shadow Market of Trafficking in Women." *Journal of International Affairs* 53 (2): 625–51.

Hughes, Donna. 2002. "Prostitution in Russia, Does the U.S. State Department Back the Legalization of Prostitution?" *National Review*, November 21.

Hughes, Donna, and Tatyana Denisova. 2002. *Trafficking in Women from Ukraine*. Report funded by the U.S. Department of Justice. Washington, DC: U.S. Department of Justice.

Human Rights Watch. 1995. *Neither Jobs nor Justice: State Discrimination against Women in Russia*. Accessed January 13, 2015. www.hrw.org/reports/1995/03/01 /neither-jobs-nor-justice.

Humphrey, Caroline. 2002. *The Unmaking of Soviet Life: Everyday Economies after Socialism*. Ithaca, NY: Cornell University Press.

Hunt, Swanee. 1997. "For East Bloc Women, A Dearth of Democracy." *International Herald Tribune*, July 10.

Huntington, Samuel P. 1991. *The Third Wave: Democratization in the Late Twentieth Century*. Norman: University of Oklahoma Press.

Huston, Patricia. 1979. *Third World Women Speak Out*. New York: Praeger.

Ibroscheva, Elza. 2013. *Advertising, Sex, and Post-Socialism: Women, Media, and Femininity in the Balkans*. Lanham, MD: Lexington Books.

Incite! Women of Color Against Violence. 2006. *Color of Violence: The Incite! Anthology*. Cambridge, MA: South End Press.

Informatsionnii Tsentr Nezavisimogo Forum [Information center of the independent forum]. n.d. "Polozhenie zhenshchin i Natsional'nyi mekhamizm" [Position of women in national mechanisms]. Accessed January 13, 2015. www.a-z.ru /women/.

International Labour Organization. 2005a. "A Global Alliance Against Forced Labour." Geneva: International Labour Office.

International Labour Organization. 2005b. "Forced Labour and Human Trafficking: Estimating the Profits." Geneva: International Labour Office.

International Labour Organization. 2009. "The Cost of Coercion." Geneva: International Labour Office.

International Labour Organization. 2012. "ILO Global Estimate of Forced Labour." Geneva: International Labour Office.

International Labour Organization. 2014. "Profits and Poverty: The Economics of Forced Labour." Geneva: International Labour Office.

International Meeting of Experts on Sexual Exploitation, Violence, and Prostitution. 1992. Penn State Report. Pennsylvania State University, UNESCO and Coalition Against Trafficking in Women.

IOM (International Organization for Migration). 1995. "Trafficking and Prostitution: The Growing Exploitation of Migrant Women from Central and Eastern Europe." Brussels: Migration Information Programme.

IOM. "It Could Happen to Any of Us." 2013. Anti-trafficking Public Service Announcement. MTV. Accessed January 13, 2015. http://vimeo.com/48386246.

Iukina, Irina. 2003. "Zhenskoe Dvizhenie Rossii, Tsenz Pola i Sufrazhizm" [The women's movement in Russia, sex restrictions and suffrage]. In *Gendernaia Rekonstruktsiia Politicheskikh Sistem* [A gendered reconstruction of the political system], ed. M. M. Kirichenko, E. V. Kochkina, and N. M. Stepanova, 279–99. St. Petersburg, Russia: ISPG.

Ivanova, Tamara. 1998. "Women Complain about Discrimination at Work, Low Wages." ITAR-TASS News Agency, March 7.

Jain, Devaki. 2005. *Women, Development, and the UN: A Sixty-Year Quest for Equality and Justice.* 2005. Bloomington: Indiana University Press.

Jegelevicius, Linas. "Transitions Online." *Transitions Online.* Accessed December 11, 2012. http://www.tol.org.

Johnson, Erika. 2007. *Dreaming of a Mail-Order Husband: Russian-American Internet Romance.* Durham, NC: Duke University Press.

Johnson, Janet Elise. 2001. "Privatizing Pain: The Problem of Woman Battery in Russia." *NWSA Journal* 13 (3): 153–68.

Johnson, Janet Elise. 2004. "Sisterhood versus the 'Moral' Russian State: The Postcommunist Politics of Rape." In *Post-Soviet Women Encountering Transition: National Building, Economic Survival, and Civic Activism*, ed. Kathleen Kuehnast and Carol Nechimas, 217–40. Baltimore: Johns Hopkins University Press.

Johnson, Janet Elise. 2009. *Gender Violence in Russia: The Politics of Feminist Intervention.* Bloomington: Indiana University Press.

Johnson, Janet Elise, and Jean C. Robinson, eds. 2007. *Living Gender after Communism.* Bloomington: Indiana University Press.

Kabeer, Naila. 1994. *Reversed Realities: Gender Hierarchies in Development Thought.* London: Verso.

Kalb, Don. 2009. "Conversations with a Polish Populist: Tracing Hidden Histories of Globalization, Class and Dispossession in Postsocialism (and Beyond)." *American Ethnologist* 36 (2): 207–23.

Kara, Siddharth. 2009. *Sex Trafficking: Inside the Business of Modern Slavery.* New York: Columbia University Press.

Karat Coalition. n.d. "Gender and Development." Accessed January 13, 2015. www.karat.org/programmes/gender—development.

Kaşka, Selemin. 2006. *The New International Migration and Migrant Women in Turkey: The Case of the Moldovan Domestic Workers*. MiReKoc Research Projects. Accessed January 13, 2015. http://portal.ku.edu.tr/~mirekoc/reports/2005_2006 _selmin_kaska.pdf.

Katz, Katarina. 2001. *Gender, Work, and Wages in the Soviet Union: A Legacy of Discrimination*. Hampshire, UK: Palgrave.

Kay, Rebecca. 2006. *Men in Contemporary Russia: The Fallen Heroes of Post-Soviet Change?* Aldershot, UK: Ashgate.

Keck, Margaret E., and Kathryn Sikkink. 1998. *Activists beyond Borders: Advocacy Networks in International Politics*. Ithaca, NY: Cornell University Press.

Kelly, Liz. 2005. " 'You Can Find Anything You Want': A Critical Reflection on Research on Trafficking in Persons within and into Europe." *International Migration* 43 (1/2): 235–65.

Kempadoo, Kamala, ed. 2005. *Trafficking and Prostitution Reconsidered: New Perspectives on Migration, Sex, Work, and Human Rights*. London: Pluto Press.

Keough, Leyla J. 2003. "Driven Women: Reconceptualizing the Traffic in Women in the Margins of Europe through the Case of Gagauz Mobile Domestics in Istanbul." *Anthropology of East Europe Review* 21 (2): 73–78.

Keough, Leyla J. 2006. "Globalizing Postsocialism: Mobile Mothers and Neoliberalism on the Margins of Europe." *Anthropological Quarterly* 79 (3): 431–61.

Khotkina, Zoya, ed. 1996. *Seksual'noe Domogatel'stvo na Rabote*. Moscow: RAN.

Khotkina, Zoya. 2001. "Female Unemployment and Informal Employment in Russia." *Problems of Economic Transition* 43 (9): 20–33.

Khodyreva, Natalia. 2004. "The Problem of Trafficking in Women at the Transnational and National Levels." In *Crossing Borders: Re-mapping Women's Movements at the Turn of the Twenty-First Century*, ed. H. Christensen, B. Halsaa, and A. Saarinen, 239–53. Odense: University Press of Southern Denmark.

Khodyreva, Natalia. 2006. *Sovremennye Debaty o Prostitutsii: Gendernyi podkhod* [Contemporary debates on prostitution: Gendered approaches]. St. Petersburg, Russia: Aleteiia.

Kletsin, Alexander. 1998. Sotsiologicheskii analiz seksual'nykh domogatel'stva na rabote [Sociological analysis of sexual harassment at work]. St. Petersburg, Russia: Institut Sotsiologii RAN.

Kochkina, Elena. 1997. "Co-operation between Eastern and Western Women's NGOs as Illustrated by the Preparations for the Beijing Conference." In *Feminist Theory and Practice: East-West: Papers Presented at International Conference, St. Petersburg, Russia, June 9–12, 1995*, ed. by D. Deppe, O. Lipovskaya, A. Klyotsina, M. Kominskaya, I. Kormanshaus, and J. Zhukova. St. Petersburg, Russia: Petersburg Center for Gender Issues.

Kofman, Eleonore, and Parvati Roghuram. 2012. "Women, Migration, and Care: Explorations of Diversity and Dynamism in the Global South." *Social Politics* 19 (3): 408–32.

Kollontai, Alexandra. 1977. *Selected Writings*. With an introduction by Alix Holt. New York: Norton.

Kołodko, Grzegorz W. 2000. *From Shock to Therapy: The Political Economy of Postsocialist Transformation*. Oxford: Oxford University Press.

Konstantinova, Svetlana. 1996. "Russia's Portrait in the Women's World Gallery." *SAIS Review* 16 (1): 179–85.

Kopp, Pierre. 2012. "Human Trafficking and International Financial Flows." In *Draining Development: Controlling Flows of Illicit Funds from Developing Countries*, ed. Peter Reuter, 171–202. Washington, DC: World Bank.

Kostera, Monica. 1995. "The Modern Crusade: The Missionaries of Management Come to Eastern Europe." *Management Learning* 26 (3): 331–52.

Kret, Abigail Judge. 2013. "'We Unite with Knowledge': The Peoples' Friendship University and Soviet Education for the Third World." *Comparative Studies of South Asia, Africa and the Middle East* 33 (2): 239–56.

Kubicek, Paul. 2004. *Organized Labor in Postcommunist States: From Solidarity to Infirmity*. Pittsburgh: University of Pittsburgh Press.

Kurkchiyan, Marina. 2003. "The Illegitimacy of Law in Post-Soviet Societies." In *Law and Informal Practices: The Post-communist Experience*, ed. Denis Galligan and Marina Kurkchiyan, 25–46. Oxford: Oxford University Press.

Kuvshchinova, Ol'ga. 2002. "Menedzher. Sexual Harassment. Novoe slovo na bukvu X" [Manager: Sexual harassment: A new word that starts with the letter H]. *Delovoy Peterburg*, February 4.

Laczko, Frank. 2005. "Introduction: Data and Research on Human Trafficking." *International Migration* 43 (1/2): 5–16.

Laczko, Frank, and Elżbieta M. Goździak. 2005. *Data and Research on Human Trafficking: A Global Survey*. Geneva: International Organization for Migration.

Lang, Sabine. 1997. "The NGOization of Feminism: Institutionalization and Institution Building within the German Women's Movements." In *Transitions, Environments, Translations: Feminisms in International Politics*, ed. Joan Scott, Cora Kaplan, and Debra Keates, 101–20. New York: Routledge.

Laszlo, Andor, and Summers Martin. 1998. *Market Failure: A Guide to the East European "Economic Miracle."* London: Pluto Press.

Latouche, Serge. 1993. *In the Wake of Affluent Society: An Exploration of Post-Development*. London: Zed Books.

Ledeneva, Alena V. 2006. *How Russia Really Works: The Informal Practices That Shaped Post-Soviet Politics and Business*. Ithaca, NY: Cornell University Press.

Leidholdt, Dorchen. 2004. "Demand and the Debate." Speech transcript. Accessed January 13, 2015. www.childtrafficking.com/Docs/coalition_against_trafficki.htm.

Leigh, Carol. 2004. *Unrepentant Whore: The Collected Writings of Scarlot Harlot*. San Francisco: Last Gasp of San Francisco.

Lewis, Martin, and Kären Wigen. 1997. *The Myth of Continents: A Critique of Metageography*. Berkeley: University of California Press.

Liborakina, Marina. 2002. "Zhenshchiny i Privatizatsiia: Rossiiskii Opyt" [Women and privatization: The Russian experience]. In *Gender i Ekonomika: mirovoi opyt i ekspertiza Rossiiskoi praktiki*, ed. Elena Mezentseva, 250–58. Moscow: Russkaia Panorama.

Lilya 4-Ever. 2002. Directed by Lukas Moodyson. Memfis Film.

Lippe, Tanja Van Der, and Eva Fodor. 1998. "Changes in Gender Inequality in Six Eastern European Countries." *Acta Sociologica* 41 (2): 131–49.

Lipton, David, Jeffrey Sachs, Stanley Fischer, and Janos Kornai. 1990. "Creating a Market Economy in Eastern Europe: The Case of Poland." *Brookings Papers on Economic Activity* 1:75–147.

Lobasz, Jennifer. 2009. "Beyond Border Security: Feminist Approaches to Human Trafficking." *Security Studies* 18 (2): 319–44.

Lovell, Stephen. 2006. *Destination in Doubt: Russia since 1989*. London: Zed Books.

Mackie, Vera. 2001. "The Language of Globalization, Transnationality and Feminism." *International Feminist Journal of Politics* 3 (2): 190–206.

Mader, Mary Beth. 2011. *Sleights of Reason: Norm, Bisexuality, Development*. Albany: SUNY Press.

Malarek, Victor. 2004. *The Natashas: Inside the New Global Sex Trade*. New York: Arcade.

Maltseva, Inna, and Sergei Roshchin. 2006. *Gendernaia segregatsiia i trudovaia mobili'nost' na rossiiskom rynke truda* [Gender segregation and labor mobility in the Russian labor market]. Moscow: SU-HSE Publishing House.

Mamonova, Tatyana, Sarah Matilsky, Rebecca Park, and Catherine Fitzpatrick, eds. 1984. *Women and Russia: Feminist Writings from the Soviet Union*. Boston: Beacon Press.

Marable, Manning. 1999. *How Capitalism Underdeveloped Black America: Problems in Race, Political Economy, and Society*. Cambridge, MA: South End Press.

Marciniak, Katarzyna. 2009. "Postsocialist Hybrids." In *Media Globalization and Post-socialist Identities*, special issue. *European Journal of Cultural Studies* 12 (2): 173–90.

Materialyi Vtorogo Nezavisimogo Zhenskogo Foruma [Material from the Second Independent Women's Forum]. 1992. Record of forum held in Dubna, Russia, November 27–29. Accessed January 13, 2015. www.a-z.ru/women/texts/forumr.htm.

Mazzarino, Andrea. 2013. "Entrepreneurial Women and the Business of Self-Development in Global Russia." *Signs* 38 (3): 623–45.

McGuire, Danielle. 2010. *At the Dark End of the Street: Black Women, Rape, and Resistance—A New History of the Civil Rights Movement from Rosa Parks to the Rise of Black Power*. New York: Vintage.

McRobbie, Angela. 2011. "Reflections on Feminism, Immaterial Labour and the Post-Fordist Regime." *New Formations* 70:60–76.

Merry, Sally Engle. 2006. *Human Rights and Gender Violence: Translating International Law into Local Justice*. Chicago: University of Chicago Press.

Meshcherkina, Elena. 2000. "New Russian Men: Masculinity Regained?" In *Gender, State and Society in Soviet and Post-Soviet Russia*, ed. Sarah Ashwin, 105–17. London: Routledge.

Mies, Maria. 1986. *Patriarchy and Accumulation on a World Scale*. London: Zed Books.

Miroiu, Mihaela. 2007. "Communism Was a State Patriarchy, not State Feminism." *Aspasia* 1 (1): 197–201.

Moghadam, Valentine. 2005. *Globalizing Women: Transnational Feminist Networks*. Baltimore: Johns Hopkins University Press.

Mohanty, Chandra. 1988. "Under Western Eyes: Feminist Scholarship and Colonial Discourses." *Feminist Review* 30:61–88.

Mohanty, Chandra. 1997. "Women Workers and Capitalist Scripts: Ideologies of Domination, Common Interests, and the Politics of Solidarity." In *Feminist Genealogies, Colonial Legacies, Democratic Futures*, ed. M. Jacqui Alexander and Chandra Mohanty, 3–29. New York: Routledge.

Molland, Sverre. 2010. "'The Perfect Business': Human Trafficking and Lao-Thai Cross-border Migration." *Development and Change* 41 (5): 831–55.

Morokvasic, Mirjana. 2004. "'Settled in Mobility': Engendering Post-Wall Migration Europe." *Feminist Review* 77:7–25.

Nadezhdina, Nadezhda. 2000. "Ne chastoe delo po dolgu sluzhby, no s otvrashcheniem. Vse bol'she zhenshchin v nashei podvergaiutsia seksual'nym domogatel'svam na rabote" [Not a frequent issue at the workplace, but a disgusting one. More and more women are subject to sexual harassment in our workplaces]. *Trud*, June 22.

Nagle, Jill. 1997. *Whores and Other Feminists*. New York: Routledge.

Naples, Nancy, and Manisha Desai, eds. 2002. *Women's Activism and Globalization: Linking Local Struggles and Global Politics*. New York: Taylor and Francis.

Neilson, Brett, and Ned Rossiter. 2008. "Precarity as a Political Concept, or, Fordism as Exception." *Theory, Culture and Society* 25 (7–8): 51–72.

Neuwirth, Robert. 2011. *Stealth of Nations: The Global Rise of the Informal Economy*. New York: Random House.

"New UN Crime Commission Meets in Vienna." 1992. *United Nations Chronicle* 29 (3): 73.

Nikolić-Ristanović, Vesna. 2002. *Social Change, Gender, and Violence: Post-communist and War Affected Societies*. Dordrecht: Kluwer Academic.

Nordhaus, William. 1990. "Soviet Economic Reform: The Longest Road." *Brookings Papers on Economic Activity* 1:287–318.

Novikova, Irina. 2006. "Gender Equality in Latvia: Achievements and Challenges." In *Women and Citizenship in Central and Eastern Europe*, ed. Jasmina Lukić, Joanna Regulska, and Darja Zaviršek, 101–20. Bennington, VT: Ashgate.

Nowicka, Wanda. 1995. "Statement from a Non-Region." Statement presented at the Fourth World Conference on Women, Beijing, September 13. Accessed January 13, 2015. http://pdf.usaid.gov/pdf_docs/Pdabp563.pdf.

Oates-Indruchová, Libora. 2012. "Continuities and Discontinuities from State Socialism in Czech Feminist Research." Unpublished manuscript.

Ong, Aihwa. 1985. "Industrialization and Prostitution in S.E. Asia." In *Female Sexual Slavery and Economic Exploitation: Making Local and Global Connections*, Report of a Consultation Organized by the Non-governmental Liaison Service, 11–24. San Francisco: UN Nongovernmental Liaison Service.

Ong, Aihwa. 2006. *Neoliberalism as Exception: Mutations in Citizenship and Sovereignty*. Durham, NC: Duke University Press.

Osipovich, Tatiana. 2004. "Russian Mail-Order Brides in U.S. Public Discourse: Sex, Crime, and Cultural Stereotypes." In *Sexuality and Gender in Postcommunist Eastern Europe and Russia*, ed. Aleksander Stulhofer and Theo Sandfort, 263–96. New York: Haworth Press.

Osmańczyk, Edmund. 2003. *Encyclopedia of the United Nations and International Agreements.* Vol. 2. *G to M.* New York: Routledge.

Ost, David. 2005. *The Defeat of Solidarity: Anger and Politics in Postcommunist Europe.* Ithaca, NY: Cornell University Press.

Oushakine, Sergei. 2009. *The Patriotism of Despair: Nation, War, and Loss in Russia.* Ithaca, NY: Cornell University Press.

Parreñas, Rhacel Salazar. 2011. *Illicit Flirtations: Labor, Migration and Sex Trafficking in Tokyo.* Stanford, CA: Stanford University Press.

Parvulescu, Anca. 2014. *The Traffic in Women's Work: East European Migration and the Making of Europe.* Chicago: University of Chicago Press.

Patton, Cindy. 2002. *Globalizing AIDS.* Minneapolis: University of Minnesota Press.

Penn, Shana. 2006. *Solidarity's Secret: The Women Who Defeated Communism in Poland.* Ann Arbor: University of Michigan Press.

Penttinen, Elina. 2008. *Globalization, Prostitution and Sex-Trafficking: Corporeal Politics.* London: Routledge.

Perpiñan, Soledad. 1986. "The Philippines: Prostitution and Sexual Exploitation." In *Empowerment and the Law: Strategies of Third World Women,* ed. Margaret Schuler, 155–65. Washington, DC: OEF International.

Pervogo Nezavisimogo Zhenskogo Foruma [First independent women's forum]. 1991. Record of forum held in Dubna, Russia, March 29–31. Accessed January 13, 2015. www.a-z.ru/women/rubrikator/p3.htm#7.

Peterson, V. Spike. 2003. *A Critical Rewriting of Global Political Economy: Integrating Reproductive, Productive, and Virtual Economies.* New York: Routledge.

Pheterson, Gail. 1989. *A Vindication of the Rights of Whores.* Seattle: Seal Press.

Philliou, Christine. 2013. "Introduction USSR South: Postcolonial Worlds in the Soviet Imaginary." *Comparative Studies of South Asia, Africa and the Middle East* 33 (2): 197–200.

Phongpaichit, Pasuk. 1982. *From Peasant Girls to Bangkok Masseuses.* Geneva: International Labour Office.

Pickles, John, and Adrian Smith. 1998. *Theorizing Transition: The Political Economy of Post-Communist Transformations.* London: Routledge.

Pickup, Francine. 1998. "Deconstructing Trafficking in Women: The Example of Russia." *Millennium: Journal of International Studies* 27 (4): 995–1021.

Pickup, Francine, Suzanne Williams, and Caroline Sweetman. 2001. *Ending Violence against Women: A Challenge for Development and Humanitarian Work.* Oxford: Oxfam.

Pietilä, Hilkka. 2007. *The Unfinished Story of Women and the United Nations.* New York: United Nations.

Pietilä, Hilkka, and Jeanne Vickers. 1994. *Making Women Matter: The Role of the United Nations.* London: Zed Books.

Pitcher, Anne, and Kelly Askew. 2006. "African Socialisms and Postsocialisms." *Africa* 76 (1): 1–14.

Ponarina, Larisa. 2000. "Seksual'nye domogatel'stva n rabote: sluzhebnyi roman ili torzhestvo muzhskogo bezpredela?" [Sexual harassment at work: Work romance or unleashed male uncontrolled behavior?] In *Nasilie i Sotsial'nye Izmeneniia*, ed. ANNA (Assotsiatsiia Net Nasiliiu), 63–76. Moscow: Tsentrp.

Popa, Raluca Maria. 2003. "The Socialist Project for Gender (In)Equality: A Critical Discussion." *Journal for the Study of Religions and Ideologies* 6 (4) (winter): 49–72.

Popa, Raluca Maria. 2009. "Translating Equality between Women and Men across the Cold War Divides: Women Activists from Hungary and Romania and the Creation of International Women's Year." In *Gender Politics and Everyday Life in State Socialist Eastern and Central Europe*, ed. Shana Penn and Jill Massino, 59–74. New York: Palgrave Macmillan.

Posadskaya, Anastasia. 1993. "Changes in Gender Discourses and Policies in the Former Soviet Union." In *Democratic Reform and the Position of Women in Transitional Economies*, ed. Valentine Moghadam, 162–79. New York: Oxford University Press.

Posadskaya, Anastasia. 1994. Introduction to *Women in Russia: A New Era in Russian Feminism*, ed. Anastasia Posadskaya and Moscow Gender Center, 1–7. London: Verso.

Posadskaya-Vanderbeck, Anastasia. 1996. "Voice from the Non-Region: How the Statement from a Non-region Found Its Way to the Plenary Session of the IV World Conference on Women on September 13, 1995." Warsaw: ASTRA Network.

Posadskaya-Vanderbeck, Anastasia. 1997. "On the Threshold of the Classroom: Dilemmas for Post-Soviet Russian Feminism." In *Transitions, Environment and Translations: Feminism in International Politics*, ed. Joan Scott, Caren Kaplan, and Debra Keates, 373–82. New York: Routledge.

Post, Dianne. 2000. "Domestic Violence in Russia." *Journal of Gender Studies* 9:81–84.

The Price of Sex. 2011. Directed by Mimi Chakarova. Accessed January 13, 2015. http://priceofsex.org.

Pushkareva, Natal'ia. 2002. *Russkaia Zhenshchina: Istoriia i sovremennost'* [Russian women: History and the present]. Moscow: Ladomir.

Racioppi, Linda, and Katherine O'Sullivan. 1995. "Organizing Women before and after the Fall: Women's Politics in the Soviet Union and Post-Soviet Russia." *Signs* 20 (4): 818–50.

Radulescu, Domnica. 2004. "Amazons, Wretches and Vampirettes: Essentialism and beyond in the Representation of East Europe." In *Vampirettes, Wretches, and Amazons: Western Representations of East European Women*, ed. Valentina Glaja and Domnica Radulescu, 23–59. Boulder, CO: East European Monographs.

Rawley, James. 2009. *The Transatlantic Slave Trade: A History*. Rev. ed. Lincoln: University of Nebraska Press.

Raymond, Janice G. 1998. "Prostitution as Violence against Women: NGO Stonewalling in Beijing and Elsewhere." *Women's Studies International Forum* 21 (1): 1.

Regulska, Joanna, and Magdalena Grabowska. 2012. "Post-1989 Women's Activism in Poland." In *Women and Gender in Postwar Europe: From Cold War to European Union*, ed. Joanna Regulska and Bonnie Smith, 212–30. New York: Routledge.

Reis, Nancy. 2002. "'Honest Bandits' and 'Warped People': Russian Narratives about Money, Corruption, and Moral Decay." In *Ethnography in Unstable Places: Everyday Lives in Contexts of Dramatic Political Change*, ed. Carol Greenhouse, Elizabeth Merz, and Kay Warren, 276–315. Durham, NC: Duke University Press.

Richter, James. 2002. "Evaluating Western Assistance to Russian Women's Organizations." In *The Power and Limit of NGOs*, ed. Sarah Mendelson and John Glenn, 54–90. New York: Columbia University Press.

Riley, Denise. 1988. *"Am I That Name?" Feminism and the Category of "Women" in History*. London: Macmillan.

Rogers, Douglas. 2010. "Postsocialisms Unbound: Connections, Critiques, Comparisons." *Slavic Review* 69 (1): 1–15.

Roman, Denise. 2006. "Missing in Action: On Eastern European Women and Transnational Feminism." *CSW Update*, November 5–8.

Ross, Andrew. 2009. *Nice Work If You Can Get It: Life and Labor in Precarious Times*. New York: NYU Press.

Roth, Benita. 2003. "Second Wave Black Feminism in the African Diaspora: News from New Scholarship." *Agenda: Empowering Women for Gender Equity* 58:46–58.

Roth, Silke. 2007. "Sisterhood and Solidarity? Women's Organizations in the Expanded European Union." *Social Politics* 14 (4): 460–87.

Ruffin, M. Holt, Joan McCarter, and Richard Upjohn. 1996. *The Post-Soviet Handbook: A Guide to Grassroots Organizations and Internet Resources in the Newly Independent States*. Seattle: Center for Civil Society International.

Rupp, Leila. 1998. *Worlds of Women: The Making of the International Women's Movement*. Princeton, NJ: Princeton University Press.

Ruthchild, Rochelle. 2010. *Equality and Revolution: Women's Rights in the Russian Empire, 1905–1917*. Pittsburgh: University of Pittsburgh Press.

Ruthchild, Rochelle. 2012. "From West to East: International Women's Day, the First Decade." *Aspasia* 6:1–24.

Rutland, Peter. 2014. "Neoliberalism and the Russian Transition." *Review of International Political Economy* 20 (2): 332–62.

Rutland, Peter, and Natasha Kogan. 1998. "The Russian Mafia: Between the Hype and Reality." *Transitions* 5 (3): 24–34.

Ryan, Chris, and Colin Michael Hall. 2001. *Sex Tourism: Marginal People and Liminalities*. London: Routledge.

Sakwa, Richard. 1999. *Postcommunism*. Oxford: Oxford University Press.

Salazar Parreñas, Rhacel. 2000. "Migrant Filipina Domestic Workers and the International Division of Reproductive Labor." *Gender and Society* 14 (4): 560–80.

Salmenniemi, Suvi. 2008. *Democratization and Gender in Contemporary Russia*. London: Routledge.

Salmenniemi, Suvi, Päivi Karhunen, and Riitta Kosonen. 2011. "Between Business and *Byt*: Experiences of Women Entrepreneurs in Contemporary Russia." *Europe-Asia Studies* 63 (1): 77–98.

Sancho-Liao, N. 1993. "'Clutching a Knifeblade': Human Rights and Development from Asian Women's Perspective." *Focus on Gender* 1 (2): 31–37.

Sandul, I. 2002. "Trying to Break through the Glass Ceiling." *Russia Journal*, March 22.

Sassen, Saskia. 2000. "Women's Burdens: Counter Geographies of Globalization and the Feminization of Survival." *Journal of International Affairs* 53 (12): 503–24.

Sassen, Saskia. 2003. "Global Cities and Survival Circuits." In *Global Woman: Nannies, Maids, and Sex Workers in the New Economy*, ed. Barbara Ehrenreich and Arlie Russell Hochschild, 254–74. New York: Henry Holt.

Sassen, Saskia. 2006. *Territory, Authority, Rights: From Medieval to Global Assemblages*. Princeton, NJ: Princeton University Press.

Schneider, Friedrich, Andreas Buehn, and Claudio E. Montenegro. 2010. "Shadow Economies All over the World: New Estimates for 162 Countries from 1999 to 2007." Policy Research Working Paper 5356, World Bank. Accessed January 13, 2015. www-wds.worldbank.org/external/default/WDSContentServer/IW3P/IB/2010/10/14/000158349_20101014160704/Rendered/PDF/WPS5356.pdf.

School for Johns. n.d. "School for Johns." Accessed January 13, 2015. www.schoolforjohns.com/.

Schuler, Margaret. 1992. *Freedom from Violence: Women's Strategies from around the World*. New York: UNIFEM.

Seabright, Paul, ed. 2000. *The Vanishing Rouble: Barter Networks and Non-Monetary Transactions in Post-Soviet Societies*. Cambridge: Cambridge University Press.

Sen, Amartya. 1999. *Development as Freedom*. Oxford: Oxford University Press.

Serio, Joseph. 2008. *Investigating the Russian Mafia: An Introduction for Students, Law Enforcement, and International Business*. Durham, NC: Carolina Academic Press.

Shapkina, Nadezhda. 2006. "Sex, Gender, and Migration: Analyzing Campaigns against Sex Trafficking in Russia and Ukraine." Paper presented at the National Convention of the American Association for the Advancement of Slavic Studies, Washington, DC, November 17.

Shelkovnikova, Elena. 1999. "Sluzhebny roman is sexual harassment: Distantsiia ogromnogo razmera." [Work romance is sexual harassment: A major difference]. *Argumenty i Fakty*, September 16.

Shelley, Louise. 1998. "Organized Crime and Corruption in Ukraine: Impediments to the Development of a Free Market." *Demokratizatsiya* 6 (4): 648–63.

Shevchenko, Olga. 2009. *Crisis and the Everyday in Postsocialist Moscow*. Bloomington: Indiana University Press.

Shohat, Ella. 1992. "Notes on the 'Post-Colonial.'" *Social Text* 31/32:99–113.

Sirotkin, Vladlen. 2006. *Anatolii Chubais: Velikii inkvizitor* [Anatoly Chubais: The Great inquisitor]. Moscow: Algoritm.

"Skrytnaia kamera zapechatlela khishchnykh muzhchin" [Hidden camera reveals predatory men]. 2012. *Ekho Moskvy*, October 2.

Slavova, Kornelia. 2006. "Looking at Western Feminisms through the Double Lens of Eastern Europe and the Third World." In *Women and Citizenship in Central and Eastern Europe*, ed. Jasmina Lukić, Joanna Regulska, and Darja Zaviršek, 245–63. Aldershot, UK: Ashgate.

Sloat, Amanda. 2005. "The Growth of Women's NGOs in Central and Eastern Europe." *European Journal of Women's Studies* 12 (4): 437–52.

Smith, Adrian. 2002. "Culture/economy and Spaces of Economic Practice: Positioning Households in Post-Communism." *Transactions of the Institute of British Geographers* 27 (2): 232–50.

Smith, Adrian, and Alison Stenning. 2006. "Beyond Household Economies: Articulations and Spaces of Economic Practice in Postsocialism." *Progress in Human Geography* 30 (2): 190–213.

Smith, Andrea. 2005. *Conquest: Sexual Violence and American Indian Genocide.* Cambridge, MA: South End Press.

Smith, Andrea. 2008. "American Studies without America: Native Feminisms and the Nation-State." *American Quarterly* 60 (2): 309–15.

Smith, Andrea. 2011. "Against the Law: Indigenous Feminism and the Nation-State." *Affinities: A Journal of Radical Theory, Culture, and Action* 5 (1): 56–69.

Soderlund, Gretchen. 2005. "Running from the Rescuers: New U.S. Crusades against Trafficking and the Rhetoric of Abolition." *Feminist Formation* 17 (3): 64–87.

Sokolova, Mariia. 2012. "Otvedite zhenshchine lichnoe prostranstvo" [Women must claim their personal space]. *Parlamentskaia Gazeta*, October 5.

Sperling, Valerie. 1998. "Foreign Funding of Social Movements in Russia." Policy Memo 26. Program on New Approaches to Russian Security (PONARS). Accessed January 13, 2015. www.ponarseurasia.org/sites/default/files/policy-memos-pdf/pm_0026.pdf.

Sperling, Valerie. 1999. *Organizing Women in Contemporary Russia: Engendering Transition.* Cambridge: Cambridge University Press.

Springer, Kimberly. 2001. "The Interstitial Politics of Black Feminist Organizations." *Meridians* 4 (1): 155–91.

Springer, Kimberly. 2005. *Living for the Revolution: Black Feminist Organizations, 1968–1980.* Durham, NC: Duke University Press.

Standing, Guy. 2011. *The Precariat: The New Dangerous Class.* London: Bloomsbury Academic.

Stenning, Alison. 2005. "Post-socialism and the Changing Geographies of the Everyday in Poland." *Transactions of the Institute of British Geographers* 30 (1): 113–27.

Stenning, Alison, and Kathrin Hörschelmann. 2008. "History, Geeography and Difference in the Post-socialist World: Or, Do We Still Need Post-Socialism?" *Antipode* 40 (2): 312–35.

Stenning, Alison, Adrian Smith, Alena Rochovská, and Dariusz Świątek. 2010. *Domesticating Neo-Liberalism: Spaces of Economic Practice and Social Reproduction in Post-socialist Cities.* Oxford: Wiley-Blackwell.

Sterling, Claire. 1994. "Redfellas: Inside the New Russian Mafia." *New Republic* 210 (15): 19–22.

Sternbach, Nancy, Marysa Navarro-Aranguren, Patricia Chuchryk, and Sonia Alvarez. 1992. "Feminisms in Latin America: From Bogotá to San Bernardo." *Signs* 17 (2): 393–434.

Stiglitz, Joseph E. 2002. *Globalization and Its Discontents.* New York: W. W. Norton.

Stoecker, Sally. 2000. "The Rise in Human Trafficking and the Role of Organized Crime." *Demokratizatsiya* 8 (1): 129–44.

Strokan, Sergei. 1995. "Russia: NGOs Condemn Sexual Discrimination in the Moscow Workplace." Inter Press News Agency (Moscow), November 3.

Suchland, Jennifer. 2008. "Contextualizing Discrimination: The Problem with Sexual Harassment in Russia." *Journal of Women, Politics and Policy* 29 (3): 335–63.

Suchland, Jennifer. 2011. "Is Postsocialism Transnational?" *Signs* 36 (4): 837–62.

Suchland, Jennifer. 2013. "Double Framing in *Lilya 4-Ever*: Sex Trafficking and Postso-cialist Abjection." *European Journal of Cultural Studies* 16 (3): 362–76.

Sudburry, Julia. 2006. "Rethinking Antiviolence Strategies: Lessons from the Black Women's Movement in Britain." In *Color of Violence: The Incite! Anthology*, ed. Incite! Women of Color Against Violence, 13–24. Cambridge, MA: South End Press.

Sukhov, Oleg. 2012. "Intim ne predlagat'" [Unsolicited intimacy]. *Chastnyi Korrespon-dent*, November 21.

Sullivan, Barbara. 2003. "Trafficking in Women: Feminism and New International Law." *International Feminist Journal of Politics* 5 (1): 67–91.

Sullivan, Mary Lucille. 2007. *Making Sex Work: A Failed Experiment with Legalized Prostitution*. Melbourne: Spinifex Press.

Sundstrum, Lisa. 2002. "Women's NGOs in Russia: Struggling from the Margins." *Demokratizatsiya* 19 (2): 207–29.

Sweet, James. 1997. "The Iberian Roots of American Racist Thought." *William and Mary Quarterly* 54 (1): 143–66.

Taraban, Svitlana. 2007. "Birthday Girls, Russian Dolls, and Others: Internet Brides as the Emerging Global Identity of Post-Soviet Women." In *Living Gender after Communism*, ed. Janet Elise Johnson and Jean C. Robinson, 105–27. Bloomington: Indiana University Press.

Thompson, Becky. 2002. "Multiracial Feminism: Recasting the Chronology of Second Wave Feminism." *Feminist Studies* 28 (2): 337–60.

Tiefenbrun, S. W. 2006. "Updating the Domestic and International Impact of the U.S. Victims of Trafficking Protection Act of 2000: Does Law Deter Crime?" *Case West-ern Reserve Journal of International Law* 38 (2): 249–80.

Tiers, K. 2002. "Gender Prejudice Still Strong in Russia." *Russia Journal*, September 20.

Tinker, Irene, ed. 1990. *Persistent Inequalities: Women and World Development*. New York: Oxford University Press.

Tinker, Irene. 1976. "The Adverse Impact of Development on Women." In *Women and World Development*, ed. Irene Tinker and Michéle Bramsen, 22–34. New York: Praeger.

Tiuriukanova, Elena. 2006a. *Forced Labour in the Russian Federation Today: Irregular Migration and Trafficking in Human Beings*. Geneva: International Labour Office.

Tiuriukanova, Elena. 2006b. *Human Trafficking in the Russian Federation: Inventory and Analyses of the Current Situation and Responses*. Moscow: UN/IOM Working Group.

Tiuriukanova, Elena. 2008. "Illegal, Trafficked, Enslaved? Irregular Migration and Trafficking in Persons in Russia." *NATO Science for Peace and Security Series E: Human and Societal Dynamics* 46:104–30.

Tlostanova, Madina. 2006. "The Imagined Freedom: Post-Soviet Intellectuals between the Hegemony of the State and the Hegemony of the Market." *South Atlantic Quar-terly* 105 (3): 637–59.

Todorova, Maria, and Zsuzsa Gille, eds. 2010. *Post-Communist Nostalgia*. New York: Berghahn.

Tracy, Jen. 1999. "Wanted: A Girl Who'll Work for Less." *Moscow Times*, November 17.

"Trafficking of NIS Women Abroad: An International Conference in Moscow." 1997. November 3–5. Conference report prepared by Global Survival Network.

True, Jacqui. 2003. *Gender, Globalization, and Postsocialism: The Czech Republic after Communism*. New York: Columbia University Press.

True, Jacqui. 2012. *The Political Economy of Violence against Women*. Oxford: Oxford University Press.

Truong, Thanh-Dam. 1990. *Sex, Money and Morality: Prostitution and Tourism in Southeast Asia*. London: Zed Books.

Tucker, Robert. 1978. *The Marx-Engels Reader*. 2nd ed. New York: W. W. Norton.

Tyldum, Guri, and Anette Brunovskis. 2005. "Describing the Unobserved: Methodological Challenges in Empirical Studies on Human Trafficking." *International Migration* 43 (1/2): 17–34.

Uhl, Bärbel Heide. 2010. "Lost in Implementation? Human Rights Rhetoric and Violations—A Critical Review of Current European Anti-trafficking Policies." *Security and Human Rights* 2:119–26.

Ukraine Is Not a Brothel. 2013. Directed by Kitty Green. Noise and Light Productions.

United Nations UNiTE to End Violence Against Women. 2009. Website. Accessed January 9, 2015. www.unwomen.org/en/what-we-do/ending-violence-against -women/take-action/say-no.

Uvin, Peter. 1998. *Aiding Violence: The Development Enterprise in Rwanda*. West Hartford, CT: Kumarian Press.

Uy, Robert. 2011. "Blinded by Red Lights: Why Trafficking Discourse Should Shift away from Sex and the 'Perfect Victim' Paradigm." *Berkeley Journal of Gender, Law and Justice* 26 (1): 204–19.

Uygun, Banu Nilgün. 2004. "Post-socialist Scapes of Economy and Desire: The Case of Turkey." *Focaal—European Journal of Anthropology* 43:27–45.

Vassalo, Peter V. 1996. "The New Ivan the Terrible: Problems in International Criminal Enforcement and the Specter of the Russian Mafia." *Case Western Reserve Journal of International Law* 28 (1): 173–96.

Vassilev, Rossen. 2011. "The Tragic Failure of 'Post-Communism' in Eastern Europe." *Global Research* (March). Accessed January 13, 2015. www.globalresearch.ca/the -tragic-failure-of-post-communism-in-eastern-europe.

Velikonja, Mitja. 2009. "Lost in Transition: Nostalgia for Socialism in Post-socialist Countries." *East European Politics and Societies* 23 (4): 535–51.

Verdery, Katherine. 1996. *What Was Socialism, and What Comes Next?* Princeton, NJ: Princeton University Press.

Volkov, Vadim. 2002. *Violent Entrepreneurs: The Use of Force in the Making of Russian Capitalism*. Ithaca, NY: Cornell University Press.

Volpp, Leti. 2003. "Feminism and Multiculturalism." In *Critical Race Feminism*, ed. Adrien Katherine Wing, 395–405. New York: NYU Press.

Voronina, Olga. 1993. "Soviet Patriarchy: Past and Present." *Hypatia* 8 (4): 97–112.

Voronina, Olga. 1994. "The Mythology of Women's Emancipation in the USSR as the Foundation for a Policy of Discrimination." In *Women in Russia: A New Era in*

Russian Feminism, ed. Anastasia Posadskaya and Moscow Gender Center, 37–56. London: Verso.

Warren, Kay B. 2012. "The 2000 UN Human Trafficking Protocol: Rights, Enforcement, Vulnerabilities." In *The Practice of Human Rights: Tracking Law between the Global and the Local*, ed. Mark Goodale and Sally Engle Merry, 242–62. Cambridge: Cambridge University Press.

Watson, Peggy. 1993. "The Rise of Masculinism in Eastern Europe." *New Left Review* 198:71–82.

Webster, William. 1997. *Russian Organized Crime*. Washington, DC: Center for Strategic and International Studies.

Wedel, Janine. 2001. *Collision and Collusion: The Strange Case of Western Aid to Eastern Europe*. New York: Palgrave Macmillan.

Weiner, Elaine. 2007. *Market Dreams: Gender, Class, and Capitalism in the Czech Republic*. Ann Arbor: University of Michigan Press.

Weldon, S. Laurel. 2002. *Protest, Policy, and the Problem of Violence against Women: A Cross-national Comparison*. Pittsburgh: University of Pittsburgh Press.

Welter, Friederike, David Smallbone, and Nina Isakova, eds. 2006. *Enterprising Women in Transition Economies*. Aldershot, UK: Ashgate.

Willetts, Peter. 1978. *The Non-aligned Movement: The Origins of Third World Alliance*. Ann Arbor: University of Michigan Press.

Williams, Colin. 2005. "Market delusions: rethinking the trajectories of post-socialist societies." *foresight* 7 (3): 48–60.

Williams, Colin, and John Round. 2007a. "Evaluating the Penetration of Capitalism in Post-socialist Ukraine." *Journal of Economic Studies* 34 (5): 415–29.

Williams, Colin, and John Round. 2007b. "Re-thinking the Nature of the Informal Economy: Some Lessons from Ukraine." *International Journal of Urban and Regional Research* 31 (2): 425–41.

Williams, Colin, John Round, and Peter Rodgers. 2013. *The Role of Informal Economies in the Post-Soviet World: The End of Transition?* London: Routledge.

Williams, Kimberly. 2011. "Crime, Corruption and Chaos: Sex Trafficking and the 'Failure' of US Russia Policy." *International Feminist Journal of Politics* 13 (1): 1–24.

Williams, Kimberly. 2012. *Imagining Russia: Making Feminist Sense of American Nationalism in U.S.-Russian Relations*. Albany: SUNY Press.

Winnubst, Shannon. 2015. *Way Too Cool*. New York: Columbia University Press.

Wood, Elizabeth. 1997. *The Baba and the Comrade: Gender and Politics in Revolutionary Russia*. Bloomington: Indiana University Press.

World Bank. *Beyond Transition Newsletter*. Accessed January 9, 2015. http://go .worldbank.org/Y406GSE090.

World Bank. 2002. *Gender in Transition*. Washington, DC: World Bank.

World Bank. 2003. *Project Performance Assessment Report: Russian Federation*. Report No. 25478. Washington, DC: World Bank.

Yergin, Daniel, and Joseph Stanislaw. 1998. *The Commanding Heights: The Battle for the World Economy*. New York: Simon and Schuster.

Yurchak, Alexei. 2003. "Russian Neoliberal: The Entrepreneurial Ethic and the Spirit of 'True Careerism.'" *Russian Review* 62 (1): 72–90.

Zabadykina, Elena. 2000. "Pomoshch zhertvam domashchnego nasiliia v sovremennoi Rossii" [Help to victims of domestic violence in contemporary Russia]. In *Nasilie i Sotsial'nyie Ismeneniia* [Violence and social change], ed. Tsentr ANNA (Assotsiatsiia Net Nasiliiu), 113–42. Moscow: TACIS i CARITAS.

Zabelina, Tat'iana. 1996. "Sexual Violence towards Women." In *Gender, Generation and Identity in Contemporary Russia*, ed. Hilary Pilkington, 169–86. London: Routledge.

Zabelina, Tat'iana, ed. 2002. *Rossiia: Nasilie v sem'e—nasilie v obshchestve.* [Russia: Violence in the family, violence in society]. Moscow: UNIFEM.

Zavyalova, Elena K., and Sofia V. Kosheleva. 2010. "Gender Stereotyping and Its Impact on Human Capital Development in Contemporary Russia." *Human Resource Development International* 13 (3): 341–49.

Zdravomyslova, Elena, and Anna Temkina. 1996. "Vvedenie: Sotsial'naia konstruktsiia gendera i gendernaia sistema v Rossii" [Introduction: Social construction of gender and gender system in Russia]. In *Gendernoe Izmerenie Sotsial'noe i Politicheskoi Aktivnosti v Perekhodnyi Period* [Gender transformation of social and political activism in the transition period], ed. Elena Zdravomyslova and Anna Temkina, 5–13. St. Petersburg, Russia: TsNSI.

Zdravomyslova, Elena, and Anna Temkina. 1999. "Sotsial'noe Konstruirovanie Gendera kak Feministskaia Teoriia" [Social construction of gender as feminist theory]. In *Zhenshchina, Gender, Kul'tura* [Women, gender, culture], ed. Zoya Khotkina, Nataliia Pushkareva, and Elena Troffimova, 46–65. Moscow: RLShchGI.

Zdravomyslova, Elena, and Anna Temkina. 2002. "Institutsionalizatsiia Gendernykh Issledovanii v Rossii" [Institutionalization of gender research in Russia]. In *Gendernyi Kaleidoskop* [Gender kaleidoscope], ed. M. Malysheva, 33–51. Moscow: Academia.

Zdravomyslova, Elena, and Anna Temkina. 2003. "Gender Studies in Post-Soviet Society: Western Frames and Cultural Differences." *Studies in East European Thought* 55:51–61.

Zheng, Tiantian. 2009. *Red Lights: The Lives of Sex Workers in Postsocialist China.* Minneapolis: University of Minnesota Press.

Zhurzhenko, Tat'iana. 1999. "Analiz polozheniia zhenshchin v perekhodnoi ekonomike: V poiskakh feministkoi epistemologii." In *Zhenshchina, Gender, Kul'tura* [Women, gender, culture], ed. Zoya Khotkina, Nataliia Pushkareva, and Elena Trofimova, 160–70. Moscow: RLShGI.

Zimmerman, Susan. 2010. "Gender Regime and Gender Struggle in Hungarian State Socialism." *Aspasia* 4:1–24.

Žižek, Slavoj. 2005. "Lenin Shot at Finland Station." *London Review of Books* 27 (16): 23.

Žižek, Slavoj. 2008. *Violence: Six Sideways Reflections.* New York: Picador.

Zubarevich, Natalia. 2003. "Russia: Case Study on Human Development Progress towards the MDGs at the Sub-national Level." Geneva: United Nations Development Programme.

Zweynert, Joachim. 2006. "Economic Ideas and Institutional Change: Evidence from Soviet Economic Debates, 1987–1991." *Europe-Asia Studies* 58 (2): 169–92.

Zweynert, Joachim. 2007. "Conflicting Patterns of Thought in the Russian Debate on Transition: 1992–2002." *Europe-Asia Studies* 59 (1): 47–69.

Government Documents

Council of Justice. 1989. "The Exploitation of Prostitution and the Traffic in Human Beings." Resolution. *Official Journal of the European Communities* 32 (May 16).

International Trafficking in Women and Children, Hearings before the Subcommittee on Near Eastern and South Asian Affairs of the Committee on Foreign Relations, United States Senate. 2000. 106th Congress, second sess., February 22 and April 4. Washington, DC: Government Printing Office.

The Sex Trade: Trafficking of Women and Children in Europe and the United States, Hearing before the Commission on Security and Cooperation in Europe. 1999. 106th Congress, first sess., June 28. Washington, DC: Government Printing Office.

UN. 1949. *The Suppression of the Traffic in Persons and of the Exploitation of the Prostitution of Others.* Lake Success, NY, March 21.

UN. 1959. Department of Economic and Social Affairs. *"Study on Traffic in Persons and Prostitution, Suppression of the traffic in persons and the exploitation of the prostitution of others."* UN Doc ST/SOA/SD/8, United Nations Publication Sales no. 59.IV.5, 27.

UN. 1975. *World Plan for Action.* Report of the World Conference of the International Women's Year. Mexico City, June 19–July 2.

UN. 1985. *Forward Looking Strategies.* Report of the World Conference to Review and Appraise the Achievements of the United Nations Decade for Women: Equality, Development and Peace. Nairobi, July 26.

UN. 1995. *Beijing Platform for Action.* Report of the Fourth World Conference on Women.

UN. 1997. "Sixth Session (Vienna, 28 April–9 May, 1997) of the Commission on Crime Prevention and Criminal Justice." United Nations Office on Drugs and Crime. Accessed January 13, 2015. www.unodc.org/unodc/en/commissions/CCPCJ/session/06 _Session_1997/CCPCJ_06.html.

UN. 1998. "Seventh Session (Vienna, 21–30 April, 1998) of the Commission on Crime Prevention and Criminal Justice." United Nations Economic and Social Council. UN DocE/CN.15/1998/5.

UN Development Fund for Women. 1985. *Development Co-operation with Women: The Experience and Future Directions of the Fund.* New York: United Nations.

UNESCO. 1976. *UNESCO's Contribution to the Improvement of the Status of Women: Report of the Director-General.* New York: UNESCO.

UNESCO. 2004. "Data Comparison Sheet: Worldwide Trafficking Estimates by Organizations." UNESCO Trafficking Project. Accessed January 13, 2015. www.unescobkk .org/fileadmin/user_upload/culture/Trafficking/statdatabase/Copy_of_Graph _Worldwide__2_.pdf.

U.S. Agency for International Aid (USAID). 2004. *United States Assessment Report on Anti-trafficking in Eurasia.* Washington, DC: Government Printing Office.

U.S. Department of State. 2002. *Trafficking in Persons Report.* Washington, DC: Government Printing Office.

U.S. Department of State. 2003. *Trafficking in Persons Report.* Washington, DC: Government Printing Office.

U.S. Department of State. 2005. *Trafficking in Persons Report.* Washington, DC: Government Printing Office.

U.S. Department of State. 2006. *Trafficking in Persons Report.* Washington, DC: Government Printing Office.

U.S. Department of State. 2011. *Trafficking in Persons Report.* Washington, DC: Government Printing Office.

U.S. Department of State. "U.S. Government Anti-trafficking in Persons Program Funding 2002–2008." Accessed January 9, 2015. http://2001–2009.state.gov/g/tip/c12606.htm.

U.S. Department of State. Office to Monitor and Combat Trafficking in Persons. "Four 'Ps': Prevention, Protection, Prosecution, Partnerships." Accessed January 13, 2015. www.state.gov/j/tip/4p/.

INDEX

Page numbers followed by *f* indicate figures; page numbers followed by *t* indicate tables.

Bales, Kevin, 170, 174, 196n6
Bangalore, India, conference (1984), 99–100
Ban Ki-moon, 199n20
Baranskaya, Natalia, 207n21
Barry, Kathleen, 30–34, 43, 48, 58, 60, 173
Batstone, David, 216n21
Beijing Conference and NGO Forum (1995),
  42t; American reaction to, 54; Inter-
  agency Council on Women (U.S.), 54;
  KARAT Coalition, 132, 207n15, 209n11; new
  organizations and states at, 104–5; NGO
  Forum (Huairou), 92, 104; second world
  representation at, 87, 88, 118–19; significance of, 94, 104–5; state socialist feminist
  organizations in, 91
Beijing Declaration and Platform for Action
  (1995): antitrafficking advocacy, 151; Declaration on the Elimination of Violence
  Against Women (1993), 42t, 45, 47, 49, 53,
  71, 79, 199n18; Eastern Bloc women represented in, 106, 207nn14,15, 207n17; significance of, 92; state socialist governments'
  sense of exclusion, at Beijing conference,
  106–8, 207nn14,15, 207n17; trafficking as
  "violence against women," 79–80. See also
  Convention on the Suppression of the
  Traffic in Persons and the Exploitation of
  the Prostitution of Others (UN, 1949)
Beijing Platform for Action, 34, 45, 49, 53,
  105–6, 151, 199nn18,19, 207n14
Bernstein, Elizabeth, 16, 20, 216n18
Berwald, Eugen, 203n31
bez komplekov [secretaries "without inhibi-
  tions"], 141, 210n23
blat [favors], 13, 68
Bockman, Johanna, 11, 125–26, 128, 129
Boltneva, Ol'ga, 143
Boris, Eileen, 141, 210n22
Boserup, Esther, 34, 39, 98, 108
Botti, Anita, 71, 73, 74, 75
Bought and Sold (documentary film), 67,
  151, 153
Boyer, Dominic, 11
Brennan, Denise, 213n52
Bristow, Anthony, 57
brothels, 57, 67–68, 171, 181, 203n31, 210n21
Browning, Genia, 114
Brussa, Licia, 60–62, 64, 150

Buchowska, Stana, 151
Buck-Morss, Susan, 13, 208n3
Bulgarian state socialist feminist organiza-
  tion, 89–90, 206n3, 206n10
Bumiller, Kristin, 10, 16
Bunch, Charlotte, 30, 48, 196n11, 199n16
Burawoy, Michael, 197n20
Bush, George W., 213n53
business sector, 140, 141, 143–44, 160, 169–72,
  210n23, 211n28
Buvinic, Mayra, 109

Cabeza, Amelia, 19, 20
Cadena case, 72
Caldwell, Gillian, 153
Call Off Your Old Tired Ethics (COYOTE),
  43, 198nn3,4
Canadian International Development Fund,
  155
capture-recapture method of data collection,
  165–66
Castley, Shirley, 30, 48
CATW. See Coalition Against Trafficking in
  Women
CCPCJ. See Commission on Crime
  Prevention and Criminal Justice
CEDAW. See Convention on the Elimination
  of All Forms of Discrimination Against
  Women
Center against Transnational Crime, 151, 152
Center for Gender Studies (Moscow), 113
Center for the Study of Transnational Crime
  and Corruption, 73
Center for Women's Global Leadership, 46,
  48, 118, 196n11
Centre for Human Rights, 59, 201nn9,10
Chakarova, Mimi, 185–86, 202n24, 203n30,
  217n27
Charter of Economic Rights and Duties in
  States (1974), 98
Chatterjee, Partha, 95
children, 64–65, 77, 111, 153, 179, 202n24
Clinton, Bill, 54, 71–72, 78, 151
Coalition Against Trafficking in Women
  (CATW), 32–33, 34, 198n4
Cohen, Susanne, 210n23
Cold War, 5, 8, 11, 13, 70, 86, 99, 127
colonialism, 14, 31, 96, 97, 135, 188

data collection: (*continued*)
    labor statistics, 109, 210n18; on macroeco-
    nomic policies, 99–100; methods of, 96,
    99, 146–47, 163, 165–70, 189–90, 196n10,
    215n3, 215nn5,6; migrant labor in Russia,
    156–57; on sexual harassment, 146–47; on
    trafficking, 62, 63–64, 73, 160, 163–64, 166,
    202nn19,20,21, 214n1
DAWN. *See* Developmental Alternatives with
    Women for a New Era
de Beauvoir, Simone, 101
Decade for Women (UN), 42t; Convention on
    the Elimination of All Forms of Discrimi-
    nation Against Women (CEDAW), 96, 100,
    206n6; Cold War three worlds division, 50;
    Developmental Alternatives with Women
    for a New Era (DAWN), 37–38, 40, 99–100,
    198n10; economic development discussions
    during, 34, 35; "Equality, Development
    and Peace," 41, 47; gender critique absent
    from, 102; International Women's Year, 89;
    Nairobi conference (NGO Forum in Nai-
    robi), 37, 42t, 43–44, 99, 105, 198n10; Soviet
    approach to gender equality, 100–102;
    Soviet position of "Peace," 94; state social-
    ism representation during, 89–90, 100,
    206n3; U.S. participation in, 93; "violence
    against women" agenda, 48–49; World Plan
    of Action (1975), 41, 99, 104, 199n13
Decade for Women conference (Copenha-
    gen, UN, 1980), 42t, 58–59
Declaration of Basic Principles of Justice for
    Victims of Crime and Abuse of Power
    (UN, 1985), 200n3
Declaration of Mexico, 41, 43
Declaration on a New International Eco-
    nomic Order (NIEO), 98, 104
Declaration on the Elimination of All Forms
    of Discrimination Against Women (1967),
    40–41
Declaration on the Elimination of Discrimi-
    nation Against Women (1967), 96
Declaration on the Elimination of Violence
    Against Women (1993), 42t, 45, 47, 49, 53,
    71, 79, 199n18
de Haan, Francisca, 205n1, 206n2
deindustrialization, 12, 13, 17–20, 36–37,
    68–69, 137, 139

demand reduction strategies, 160–61, 171,
    176–80, 182
democracy, 90, 112, 115–17
Department for International Economic and
    Political Studies, 133–34
Desai, Padma, 129
De Stoop, Chris, 60
"Development, Crises, and Alternative Vi-
    sions," 99–100
Development Alternatives with Women for
    a New Era (DAWN), 37–38, 40, 99–100,
    196n11, 198n10
Development Decade (UN, 1960–70), 97, 98
Development Fund for Women (UN), 39, 63,
    64, 100, 104
development programs, 132t; culture in,
    108–9; "Development, Crises, and
    Alternative Visions," 99–100; Develop-
    ment Alternatives with Women for a New
    Era (DAWN), 37–38, 40, 99–100, 198n10;
    East-West divide in, 62–63, 87, 97, 109–10,
    206n7, 207n19; "Equality, Development
    and Peace," 41, 47; former socialist states
    on, 109–10, 207n19; in Latin America, 11,
    46, 197n16, 199n14; tourism policy and,
    35–36; Western stereotypes in, 108–9;
    Women in Development (WID), 34, 37, 39,
    51, 98, 108–9, 198n10; women's economic
    development, 34–39, 51–52, 97–100, 116,
    132, 196n11, 198n9. *See also* transition
DIANA, 143–44
Ditmore, Melissa Hope, 205n50
Djankov, Simeon, 125, 131
documentary films, 66, 67, 138, 151, 153, 185f,
    189, 202n24, 203n30
domestic labor, 34, 111, 134–35, 139, 190
domestic violence, 16, 31, 45, 47, 49, 91,
    145–46, 188
Dworkin, Andrea, 173

Eastern European women: international-
    ization of prostitution, 60–61, 202n19;
    Moldovan women, 20, 184–86, 189; NGOs
    for, 106, 110–12, 115–19, 124, 207nn14,15,
    207n17, 207n20, 208n24, 212n31; stereo-
    types of, 86; in the West, 65–66, 202n26,
    207n27. *See also* Natasha trade; Russian
    women

media: (*continued*)
  sexual harassment in, 143, 147; sexualiza-
    tion of women's labor in, 141, 142*f*, 144,
    210n21, 210n23; transition and transi-
    tion programs in, 133–34, 209nn13,14,15;
    Zhenshchina i Rossii Al'manakh (Soviet
    feminist publication), 103
metageography, 14, 21, 50, 85–86, 90, 107, 111,
  119, 197n17
Mexican women, mass killing of, 188
Mexico City International Women's Year
  conference (1975), 41, 43
Mies, Maria, 38
migrant labor, 55, 64, 141, 155, 181
migration: East-West trafficking, 62–63,
  156; economic dimensions of, 81–82; IOM
  (International Organization for Migration), 6, 62, 63, 64, 73, 155; labor migration,
  55, 64, 141, 155–57, 181, 214n56, 216n14;
  patterns of, 155–56, 190–91; and the rise of
  sex trafficking, 1, 61, 64, 205n47; tourism
  industry, 19–20, 31, 33–36, 39, 44; trafficked women differentiated from illegal
  immigrants, 73, 74–75; wave metaphor of,
  60, 62, 65, 201n14; of women into European prostitution markets, 60–61, 202n19
Migration and Law (Moscow-based organization), 214n56
military prostitution, 31, 34, 198n6
missing girls, 64–65, 77, 202n24
Moldovan women, 20, 184–86, 189
Moore, Demi, 177
Moscow Center for Gender Studies, 147
Moscow Conference on Trafficking (1997),
  71, 151–55, 213n48
motherhood, 101, 102
MTV public service announcements in
  Indonesia, 184

Nairobi conference (NGO Forum in Nairobi),
  37, 42*t*, 43–44, 99, 105, 198n10
Naples Political Declaration and Global
  Action Plan Against Transnational Organized Crime (1994), 79
The Natashas (Malarek), 66
Natasha trade: *Bought and Sold* (documentary film), 67, 151, 153; emergence of, 26;
  fourth wave of trafficking, 10, 13, 14, 60,

70, 87, 121, 123, 201n14; governments'
  responses to, 56–57, 156, 213n53; racialized
  language to describe, 65, 66, 73, 76, 78,
  203n27; stereotypes of, 64–65, 66, 72–73,
  202n25; survival strategies of, 68–69; trafficking of, 64–65, 202n24; transnational
  organized crime, 13, 26, 53–54, 73, 78,
  79–81, 123, 151–52, 205n46; use of term,
  195n1, 197n1, 204n37
National Task Force on Prostitution, 198n3
neoabolitionism, 23, 169, 170, 174, 196n6
neoliberalism: approach to privatization, 128;
  depoliticization of the economic dimensions of sexual harassment, 91; development of, 11–12, 196n14; the individual, 23,
  159–60, 163–64, 179; informalization, 12,
  13, 17–20, 36–37, 68–69, 137, 139; neoliberal
  economism, 22, 161, 178, 186; peripheralization, 134, 191; privatization, 12, 68–69,
  127–29, 136, 203n33, 210n18; *stiob* (irony),
  11–12; Washington Consensus, 11, 197n16;
  and the welfare state, 15–16, 19. *See also*
  human trafficking; transition
Netherlands, 60, 63, 150, 201n13, 202n19
Neuwirth, Robert, 197n24
Nezavisimogo Zhenskogo Foruma (1992),
  118–19
NeZhDi (Don't Wait), 116
NGOs, 106, 110–12, 115–19, 124, 143–44,
  207nn14,15, 207n17, 207n20, 208n24, 212n31
NIEO (Declaration on a New International
  Economic Order), 98, 104
"No More Violence Against Women" march
  (Puerto Rico, 1982), 46
Non-Aligned Movement, 97, 98, 100
"nonregion," 87, 88, 106–7, 132
NSWP. *See* Global Network of Sex Work
  Projects

Olesa (trafficking victim), 186
Ong, Aihwa, 36–37
Open Society, 207n20, 209n13
Optional Protocol to Prevent, Suppress and
  Punish Trafficking in Persons, Especially
  Women and Children (2000), 6, 53, 70–71,
  73–74, 77–81, 83–84, 175, 204n37, 204n44,
  205n45
Ostojíc, Tanja, 138

rape, 45, 145, 147, 148, 200n3
rational economic actor model, 169, 172, 173, 175, 176, 177
"Real Men Don't Buy Girls" campaign, 177, 178, 216n17
Redmon, David, 138
Reis, Nancy, 69
Resolution 7 ("Prevention of the Exploitation of Women and Girls"), 199n13
Resolution 40/36 (UN, 1985), 45, 47
Richter, James, 208n24
Robinson, Jean, 138–39
Robinson, Mary, 205n46
"Role of Women in Development" (1985), 100
Romania, antitrafficking projects in, 186
Rosnakhal, 143
Roth, Silke, 110
Russia: antitrafficking advocacy in, 124; concept of independence in, 117; crisis centers in, 148, 149–50, 154, 212n31, 213n41; disavowing the past in, 209n8; gendered division of public and private spheres, 141–43; gender equality in, 109–10; Human Development Index Score, 136, 210n16; jobless rate in, 136–37, 210n18; migrant-based development in, 155–56, 214n56; perestroika period, 102, 110–12, 113, 115–16; post-Soviet economic transformations in, 137; privatization in, 128, 129; reification of patriarchal values, 112–13; sexual harassment in, 91, 124, 141, 143–44, 147–49, 210n23, 212n32, 212n35; shock therapy in, 136, 209n6
Russian Federation Work and Employment Service, 210n18
Russian Independent Women's Forum (1991), 106
Russian law on sexual harassment, 141, 143–44, 147–49, 212n32, 212n35, 212n38
Russian women: as business owners, 140–41; educational status of, 65, 66, 76, 78; in informal economy, 137; as mail-order brides, 66; political activism of, 113–14, 116, 117–18; positive images of, 66; secretaries "without inhibitions" [bez komplekov], 141, 210n23; sexual harassment of, 141, 143–44, 147–49, 210n23, 212n32, 212n35;

unemployment, 137; in the West, 65–66, 202n26, 203n30, 207n27
Russian women's NGOs: bottom-up approach to collectivization, 116; changes in organization of, 114–15; "Democracy without women is not democracy," 116, 117; empowerment of, 106, 116–19; funding for, 110, 124, 207n20, 208n24, 212n31; global women's rights language used by, 118–19; grassroots organizing of, 115–16, 117, 208n24; independent structure of, 111, 113, 115–19; network (set') of, 115; preparation for Beijing conference, 106, 110–11; "Statement from a Non-Region," 106

Sabin, Ashley, 138
Sachs, Jeffrey, 127
Salazar Parreñas, Rhacel, 141, 210n22, 216n14
Salvation Army World Service, 179
Samarina, Olga, 152–53
Samutsevich, Yekaterina, 211n25
Sancho-Liao, Nelia, 38
San Francisco, 20, 177
School for Johns (San Francisco), 177
second world: cultural and political differences in women's advocacy, 93, 108, 115–17; in discourse on development, 108–10, 207n19; economic characteristics of, 135–36; treatment as nonregion, 87, 88, 106–8, 207nn14,15, 207n17
secretaries "without inhibitions" [bez komplekov], 141, 210n23
Sen, Amartya, 202n24
settler colonialism, 6, 14, 188
sex positive feminists, 173, 175
sex tourism, 19–20, 31, 33–36, 39, 44, 77
"The Sex Trade: Trafficking of Women and Children in Europe and the United States" (U.S. Congressional hearing), 72–76, 204n39
sex trafficking: as business, 31, 33, 160, 163–64, 169–72; carceral responses to, 16, 21, 26, 53–56, 166, 205n47, 205n49, 215n7; data on, 42t, 62, 63–64, 202nn19,20,21; documentaries on, 67, 202n24, 203n30; economics of, 13, 32, 43, 44, 60–61, 68–72, 77, 91, 171, 174, 195n1, 203n33; girls in, 64–65, 77, 199n13, 199n20, 202n24,

203n30; governments' responses to, 72–76, 204n39; politicization of, 30–33, 123, 152–53, 170; sensationalized images of, 65, 66, 67, 203n29; as slavery, 6, 30–31, 44, 57–58, 60–61, 169–73; studies of, 59–62, 201nn9,10, 201n13; transnational organized crime, 26, 42t, 53–54, 73, 78–81, 123, 151–52, 205nn46,47; United States initiatives on, 72–76, 123, 204n39; use of term, 74–75, 175, 198n6; visibility of, 123, 145, 146, 211n30; wave metaphor of, 60, 62, 65, 201n14; "women and children" as category of, 42t, 74, 75, 77–78. *See also* media; Natasha trade; prostitution; relevant United Nations conferences and protocols (e.g., Beijing Declaration and Platform for Action); sexual harassment; "violence against women"

Sex Trafficking: Inside the Business of Modern Slavery (Kara), 169–73

sexual harassment: ageism, 211n28; as economic discrimination, 91, 144; failure as feminist advocacy issue, 91–92, 212n32, 212n40; language of, 124, 148–49; legal responses to, 141, 143–44, 147–49, 212n32, 212n35, 212n38; opinion polls on, 146–47; rape associated with, 148, 198n4; *seksual'noe domogatel'stvo*, 141, 148; as understood as "sexual violence at work," 124, 149; valorization of the sexualization of women, 142–43; visibility of, 146, 147; women seeking legal advice, 212n40; in the workplace, 124, 140–41, 143–44, 147–49, 210n23

Sexual Health and Rights Project, 177

sex work: as choice, 32, 36, 57, 84, 152–53, 173–76; demand reduction strategies, 160–61, 171, 176–80, 182; in tourism industry, 19–20, 31, 33–37, 39, 44, 47–48, 77, 216n14

sex workers' advocacy: antiprostitution perspective and, 32, 57, 173–74, 175; antitrafficking advocacy, 157, 174, 176, 214n57, 216n16; COYOTE (sex workers' rights organization), 43, 198nn3,4; demand reduction strategies in, 160–61, 171, 176–80, 182; economics of, 152–53, 173–76; Global Network of Sex Work Projects (NSWP), 174,

176, 216n15; opposition to Convention on the Traffic in Persons and the Exploitation of the Prostitution of Others (1949), 33, 34; on rational actor model, 173, 175, 176; School for Johns (San Francisco), 177

Sex Workers Outreach Project, 177

Shelley, Louise, 73, 76, 204n41

Shevchenko, Olga, 68, 203n32, 209n8

shock therapy, 125–26, 128, 129–30, 136, 209n6

Sidén, Ann-Sofi, 203n28

16 Days Campaign (Center for Women's Global Leadership), 46

slavery, 6, 30–32, 43–44, 57–58, 60–61, 74–75, 169–73, 200n7

"Slavic" woman imagery, 65–66, 138–39, 202n26

Smith, Christopher, 73, 74–75

smuggling, 72, 74, 75, 80, 81, 165, 166

Smyshlyaeva, Tatyana, 212n35

Sobchak, Ksenia, 211n25

social movement organizing, 110, 207n20

Southeast Asia, 6, 34–38, 77, 198n8

South Korea, 198n9

Soviet–third world ties, 206n4

Soviet Union: academic feminism, 113–14; cooperative ownership, 127; feminist activism in, 101–2, 103; history of women's groups in, 114; laws on entrepreneurship, 126–27; patriarchy in, 30–33, 112–13, 137, 171; perestroika period, 102, 110–12, 113, 115–16; political and legal equality in, 97; rainbow economy, 136; sexual lives of Soviet Russians in the media, 65, 202n25; women's status in, 102–3, 111–13; *Zhenshchina i Rossii Al'manakh* (Soviet feminist publication), 103

Soyuz Zhenshchiny Dona (Union of Women of the Don), 115

Stalin, Joseph, 114

Starostenko, Alexei, 214n57

"Statement from a Non-Region," 106, 111

state socialism: burden of equality, 111; culture, 97; disavowed reality of, 131, 209n8; dismantling of, 125–26; economics of, 58–59, 68–69, 105, 109–10, 127, 202n19; emergence of women's rights, 87; gender inequality, 102–3; language of equality and